MEI Structured Mathematics

Mathematics is not only a beautiful and exciting subject in its own right but also one that underpins many other branches of learning. It is consequently fundamental to the success of a modern economy.

MEI Structured Mathematics is designed to increase substantially the number of people taking the subject post-GCSE, by making it accessible, interesting and relevant to a wide range of students.

It is a credit accumulation scheme based on 45 hour units which may be taken individually or aggregated to give Advanced Subsidiary (AS) and Advanced GCE (A Level) qualifications in Mathematics and Further Mathematics. The units may also be used to obtain credit towards other types of qualification.

The course is examined by OCR (previously the Oxford and Cambridge Schools Examination Board) with examinations held in January and June each year.

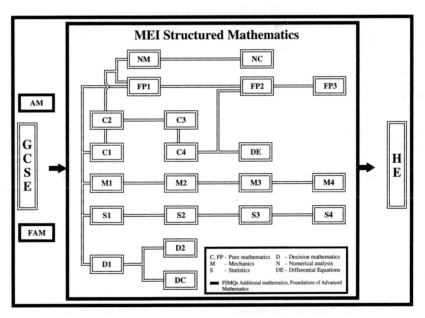

This is one of the series of books written to support the course. Its position within the whole scheme can be seen in the diagram above.

Mathematics in Education and Industry (MEI) is an independent curriculum development body which aims to promote links between education and industry in mathematics. MEI produce relevant examination specifications at GCSE, AS and A Level (including Further Mathematics) and for Free Standing Mathematics Qualifications (FSMQs); these are examined by OCR.

In partnership with Hodder Murray, MEI are responsible for three major series of textbooks: Formula One Maths for Key Stage 3, Hodder Mathematics for GCSE and the MEI Structured Mathematics series, including this book, for AS and A Level.

As well as textbooks, MEI take a leading role in the development of on-line resources to support mathematics. The books in this series are complemented by a major MEI website providing full solutions to the exercises, extra questions including on-line multiple choice tests, interactive demonstrations of the mathematics, schemes of work, and much more.

In recent years MEI have worked hard to promote Further Mathematics and, in conjunction with the DfES, they are now establishing the national network of Further Mathematics Centres.

MEI are committed to supporting the professional development of teachers. In addition to a programme of Continual Professional Development, MEI, in partnership with several universities, co-ordinate the Teaching Advanced Mathematics programme, a course designed to give teachers the skills and confidence to teach A Level mathematics successfully.

Much of the work of MEI is supported by the Gatsby Charitable Foundation.

MEI is a registered charity and a charitable company.

MEI's website and email addresses are www.mei.org.uk and office@mei.org.uk.

Introduction

This is the third of four Statistics books supporting the units in MEI Structured Mathematics. Together the first two cover the requirements of someone taking an A level in pure mathematics and statistics so the work in this book forms part of Further Mathematics. Together, these books are suitable for use on a variety of courses at this level.

In all strands of MEI Structured Mathematics the emphasis is on understanding, interpretation and modelling. This book begins with a chapter covering the techniques for continuous models, and this is followed by expectation algebra. The rest of the book is about inference. Chapter 3 is on sampling and then the final four chapters deal with the interpretation of sample data using the Normal and t distributions, and non-parametric and χ^2 tests.

As in the two earlier books in the series, several examples are taken from the pages of a fictional local newspaper, *The Avonford Star*. Much of the information that you receive from the media is of a broadly statistical nature. In these books you are encouraged to recognise this and are shown how to evaluate what you are told.

In a number of the contexts we have chosen to use the everyday English word 'weight' in preference to the more formal 'mass'.

This is the third edition of this series. The material in the various MEI statistics units has been rearranged and so this book is substantially different from the earlier editions. The original authors would like to thank the many people who helped in the preparation of the text, and particularly Ray Dunnett who compiled this edition, writing additional material where necessary. They would also like to thank the various awarding bodies for permission for their past questions to be included in the exercises.

Readers who are interested in a possible career in Mathematics may wish to visit *www.mathscareers.org.uk*.

Readers who are interested in a possible career involving statistics may wish to consult the Royal Statistical Society's careers website, *www.rss.org.uk/careers* for further information.

Roger Porkess
Series Editor

Key to symbols in this book

? This symbol means that you may want to discuss a point with your teacher. If you are working on your own there are answers in the back of the book. It is important, however, that you have a go at answering the questions before looking up the answers if you are to understand the mathematics fully.

⚠ This is a warning sign. It is used where a common mistake, misunderstanding or tricky point is being described.

▢ This is the ICT icon. It indicates where you should use a graphic calculator or a computer.

e This symbol and a dotted line down the right-hand side of the page indicates material which is beyond the criteria for the unit but which is included for completeness.

☆☆ Harder questions are indicated with stars. Many of these go beyond the usual examination standard.

Contents

Continuous random variables

A theory is a good theory if it satisfies two requirements: It must accurately describe a large class of observations on the basis of a model that contains only a few arbitrary elements, and it must make definite predictions about the results of future observations.

Stephen Hawking
A Brief History of Time

1

THE AVONFORD STAR

Lucky escape for local fisherman

Local fisherman George Sutherland stared death in the face yesterday as he was plucked from the deck of his 56 ft boat, the *Belle Star*, by a freak wave. Only the quick thinking of his brother James, who grabbed hold of his legs, saved George from a watery grave.

'It was a bad day and suddenly this lump of water came down on us,' said George. 'It was a wave in a million, higher than the mast of the boat, and it caught me off guard'.

Hero James is a man of few words. 'All in the day's work' was his only comment.

The Sutherland brothers contemplate the 'wave in a million' which almost caused a tragedy

Freak waves do occur and they can have serious consequences in terms of damage to shipping, oil rigs and coastal defences, sometimes resulting in loss of life. It is important to estimate how often they will occur, and how high they will be. Was George Sutherland's one in a million estimate for a wave higher than the mast of the boat (11 metres) at all accurate?

Before you can answer this question, you need to know the *probability density* of the heights of waves at that time of the year in the area where the *Belle Star* was fishing. The graph in figure 1.1 shows this sort of information; it was collected in the same season of the year as the Sutherland accident by the Offshore Weather Ship *Juliet* in the North Atlantic.

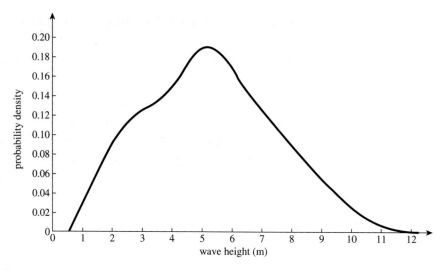

Figure 1.1

To obtain figure 1.1 a very large amount of wave data had to be collected. This allowed the class interval widths of the wave heights to be sufficiently small for the outline of the curve to acquire this shape. It also ensured that the sample data were truly representative of the population of waves at that time of the year.

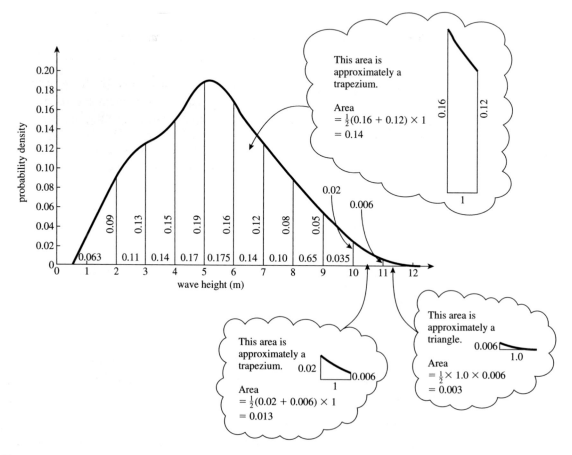

Figure 1.2

In a graph such as figure 1.1 the vertical scale is a measure of probability density. Probabilities are found by estimating the area under the curve. The total area is 1.0, meaning that effectively all waves at this place have heights between 0.6 and 12.0 m, see figure 1.2.

If this had been the place where the *Belle Star* was situated, the probability of encountering a wave at least 11 m high would have been 0.003, about 1 in 300. Clearly George's description of it as 'a wave in a million' was not justified purely by its height. The fact that he called it a 'lump of water' suggests that perhaps it may have been more remarkable for its steep sides than its height.

Probability density function

In the wave height example the curve was determined experimentally, using equipment on board the Offshore Weather Ship *Juliet*. The curve is continuous because the random variable, the wave height, is continuous and not discrete. The possible heights of waves are not restricted to particular steps (say every $\frac{1}{2}$ metre), but may take any value within a range.

 Is it reasonable to describe the height of a wave as *random*?

A function represented by a curve of this type is called a *probability density function*, often abbreviated to p.d.f. The probability density function of a continuous random variable, X, is usually denoted by $f(x)$. If $f(x)$ is a p.d.f. it follows that:

- $f(x) \geq 0$ for all x You cannot have negative probabilities.
- $\int_{\text{All values of } x} f(x)\,dx = 1$ The total area under the curve is 1.

For a continuous random variable with probability density function $f(x)$, the probability that X lies in the interval $[a, b]$ is given by

$$P(a \leq X \leq b) = \int_a^b f(x)\,dx.$$

You will see that in this case the probability density function has quite a complicated curve and so it is not possible to find a simple algebraic expression with which to model it.

Most of the techniques in this chapter assume that you do in fact have a convenient algebraic expression with which to work. However, the methods are still valid if this is not the case, but you would need to use numerical, rather than algebraic, techniques for integration and differentiation. In the high-wave incident mentioned on page 1, the areas corresponding to wave heights of less than 2 m and of at least 11 m were estimated by treating the shape as a triangle: other areas were approximated by trapezia.

Note: Class boundaries

If you were to ask the question *'What is the probability of a randomly selected wave being exactly 2 m high?'* the answer would be zero. If you measured a likely looking wave to enough decimal places (assuming you could do so), you would eventually come to a figure which was not zero. The wave height might be 2.01... m or 2.000 003... m but the probability of it being exactly 2 m is infinitesimally small. Consequently in theory it makes no difference whether you describe the class interval from 2 to 2.5 m as $2 < h < 2.5$ or as $2 \leqslant h \leqslant 2.5$.

However, in practice, measurements are always rounded to some extent. The reality of measuring a wave's height means that you would probably be quite happy to record it to the nearest 0.1 m and get on with the next wave. So, in practice, measurements of 2.0 m and 2.5 m probably will be recorded, and intervals have to be defined so that it is clear which class they belong to. You would normally expect $<$ at one end of the interval and $\leqslant$ at the other: either $2 \leqslant h < 2.5$ or $2 < h \leqslant 2.5$. In either case the probability of the wave being within the interval would be given by

$$\int_2^{2.5} f(x)\,dx.$$

THE AVONFORD STAR
Rufus foils council office break-in

Somewhere an empty-pocketed thief is nursing a sore leg and regretting the loss of a pair of trousers. Council porter Fred Lamming, and Rufus, a wiry-haired Jack Russell, were doing a late-night check round the council head office when they came upon the intruder on the ground floor.

'I didn't need to say anything,' Fred told me; 'Rufus went straight for him and grabbed him by the leg.' After a tussle the man's trousers tore, leaving Rufus with a mouthful of material while the man made good his escape out of a window.

Following the incident, Avonford Council are looking at an electronic security system. 'Rufus won't live for ever,' explained Council leader Sandra Martin.

EXAMPLE 1.1

Avonford District Council are thinking of fitting an electronic security system inside head office. They have been told by manufacturers that the lifetime, X years, of the system they have in mind has the p.d.f.:

$$f(x) = \frac{3x(20 - x)}{4000} \quad \text{for } 0 \leqslant x \leqslant 20,$$

and $\qquad f(x) = 0 \qquad\qquad$ otherwise.

(i) Show that the manufacturers' statement is consistent with $f(x)$ being a probability density function.

(ii) Find the probability that:

   (a) it fails in the first year

   (b) it lasts 10 years but then fails in the next year.

SOLUTION

(i) The condition $f(x) \geqslant 0$ for all values of x between 0 and 20 is satisfied, as shown by the graph of $f(x)$, figure 1.3.

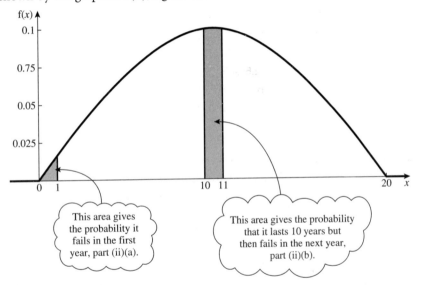

Figure 1.3

The other condition is that the area under the curve is 1.

$$\text{Area} = \int_{-\infty}^{\infty} f(x)\,dx = \int_{0}^{20} \frac{3x(20 - x)}{4000}\,dx$$

$$= \frac{3}{4000} \int_{0}^{20} (20x - x^2)\,dx$$

$$= \frac{3}{4000} \left[10x^2 - \frac{x^3}{3} \right]_{0}^{20}$$

$$= \frac{3}{4000} \left[10 \times 20^2 - \frac{20^3}{3} \right]$$

$$= 1, \text{ as required.}$$

(ii) (a) *It fails in the first year.*

This is given by $P(X < 1) = \int_0^1 \dfrac{3x(20 - x)}{4000}\,dx$

$$= \frac{3}{4000} \int_0^1 (20x - x^2)\,dx$$

$$= \frac{3}{4000} \left[10x^2 - \frac{x^3}{3} \right]_0^1$$

$$= \frac{3}{4000} \left(10 \times 1^2 - \frac{1^3}{3} \right)$$

$$= 0.007\,25$$

(b) *It fails in the 11th year.*

This is given by $P(10 \leqslant X < 11)$

$$= \int_{10}^{11} \frac{3x(20 - x)}{4000}\,dx$$

$$= \frac{3}{4000} \left[10x^2 - \frac{1}{3}x^3 \right]_{10}^{11}$$

$$= \frac{3}{4000} \left(10 \times 11^2 - \frac{1}{3} \times 11^3 \right) - \frac{3}{4000} \left(10 \times 10^2 - \frac{1}{3} \times 10^3 \right)$$

$$= 0.074\,75$$

EXAMPLE 1.2

The continuous random variable X represents the amount of sunshine in hours between noon and 4 pm at a skiing resort in the high season. The probability density function, $f(x)$, of X is modelled by

$$f(x) = \begin{cases} kx^2 & \text{for } 0 \leqslant x \leqslant 4 \\ 0 & \text{otherwise.} \end{cases}$$

(i) Find the value of k.

(ii) Find the probability that on a particular day in the high season there is more than two hours of sunshine between noon and 4 pm.

SOLUTION

(i) To find the value of k you must use the fact that the area under the graph of $f(x)$ is equal to 1.

$$\int_{-\infty}^{\infty} f(x)\,dx = \int_0^4 kx^2\,dx = 1$$

Therefore

$$\left[\frac{kx^3}{3} \right]_0^4 = 1$$

$$\frac{64k}{3} = 1$$

So $$k = \frac{3}{64}$$

(ii)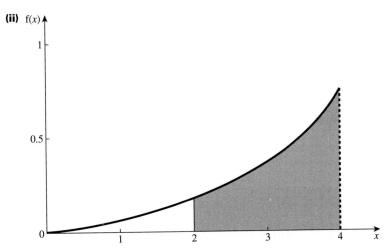

Figure 1.4

The probability of more than 2 hours of sunshine is given by

$$P(X > 2) = \int_2^\infty f(x)\,dx = \int_2^4 \frac{3x^2}{64}\,dx$$

$$= \left[\frac{x^3}{64}\right]_2^4$$

$$= \frac{64 - 8}{64}$$

$$= \frac{56}{64}$$

$$= 0.875$$

EXAMPLE 1.3

The number of hours Darren spends each day working in his garden is modelled by the continuous random variable X, with p.d.f. $f(x)$ defined by

$$f(x) = \begin{cases} kx & \text{for } 0 \leqslant x < 3 \\ k(6 - x) & \text{for } 3 \leqslant x \leqslant 6 \\ 0 & \text{otherwise.} \end{cases}$$

(i) Find the value of k.
(ii) Sketch the graph of $f(x)$.
(iii) Find the probability that Darren will work between 2 and 5 hours in his garden on a randomly selected day.

SOLUTION

(i) To find the value of k you must use the fact that the area under the graph of $f(x)$ is equal to 1. You may find the area by integration, as shown below.

$$\int_{-\infty}^{\infty} f(x)\,dx = \int_{0}^{3} kx\,dx + \int_{3}^{6} k(6-x)\,dx = 1$$

$$\left[\frac{kx^2}{2}\right]_{0}^{3} + \left[6kx - \frac{kx^2}{2}\right]_{3}^{6} = 1$$

Therefore $$\frac{9k}{2} + (36k - 18k) - \left(18k - \frac{9k}{2}\right) = 1$$

$$9k = 1$$

So $$k = \tfrac{1}{9}$$

Note

In this case you could have found k without integration because the graph of the p.d.f. is a triangle, with area given by $\frac{1}{2} \times$ base $\times$ height, resulting in the equation

$$\tfrac{1}{2} \times 6 \times k(6-3) = 1$$

hence $$9k = 1$$

and $$k = \tfrac{1}{9}.$$

(ii) Sketch the graph of $f(x)$.

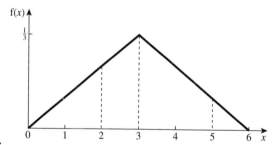

Figure 1.5

(iii) To find $P(2 \leqslant X \leqslant 5)$, you need to find both $P(2 \leqslant X < 3)$ and $P(3 \leqslant X \leqslant 5)$ because there is a different expression for each part.

$$P(2 \leqslant X \leqslant 5) = P(2 \leqslant X < 3) + P(3 \leqslant X \leqslant 5)$$

$$= \int_{2}^{3} \frac{1}{9} x\,dx + \int_{3}^{5} \frac{1}{9}(6-x)\,dx$$

$$= \left[\frac{x^2}{18}\right]_{2}^{3} + \left[\frac{2x}{3} - \frac{x^2}{18}\right]_{3}^{5}$$

$$= \frac{9}{18} - \frac{4}{18} + \left(\frac{10}{3} - \frac{25}{18}\right) - \left(2 - \frac{1}{2}\right)$$

$$= 0.72 \text{ to two decimal places.}$$

The probability that Darren works between 2 and 5 hours in his garden on a randomly selected day is 0.72.

1 The continuous random variable X has probability density function $f(x)$ where

$$f(x) = kx \quad \text{for } 1 \leqslant x \leqslant 6$$
$$= 0 \quad \text{otherwise.}$$

(i) Find the value of the constant k.
(ii) Sketch $y = f(x)$.
(iii) Find $P(X > 5)$.
(iv) Find $P(2 \leqslant X \leqslant 3)$.

2 The continuous random variable X has p.d.f. $f(x)$ where

$$f(x) = k(5 - x) \quad \text{for } 0 \leqslant x \leqslant 4$$
$$= 0 \quad \text{otherwise.}$$

(i) Find the value of the constant k.
(ii) Sketch $y = f(x)$.
(iii) Find $P(1.5 \leqslant X \leqslant 2.3)$.

3 The continuous random variable X has p.d.f. $f(x)$ where

$$f(x) = ax^3 \quad \text{for } 0 \leqslant x \leqslant 3$$
$$= 0 \quad \text{otherwise.}$$

(i) Find the value of the constant a.
(ii) Sketch $y = f(x)$.
(iii) Find $P(X \leqslant 2)$.

4 The continuous random variable X has p.d.f. $f(x)$ where

$$f(x) = kx \quad \text{for } 0 \leqslant x \leqslant 2$$
$$= 4k - kx \quad \text{for } 2 < x \leqslant 4$$
$$= 0 \quad \text{otherwise.}$$

(i) Find the value of the constant k.
(ii) Sketch $y = f(x)$.
(iii) Find $P(1 \leqslant X \leqslant 3.5)$.

5 The continuous random variable X has p.d.f. $f(x)$ where

$$f(x) = c \quad \text{for } -3 \leqslant x \leqslant 5$$
$$= 0 \quad \text{otherwise.}$$

(i) Find c.
(ii) Sketch $y = f(x)$.
(iii) Find $P(|X| < 1)$.
(iv) Find $P(|X| > 2.5)$.

6 A continuous random variable X has p.d.f.

$$f(x) = k(x-1)(6-x) \quad \text{for } 1 \leqslant x \leqslant 6$$
$$= 0 \quad \text{otherwise.}$$

(i) Find the value of k.

(ii) Sketch $y = f(x)$.

(iii) Find $P(2 \leqslant X \leqslant 3)$.

7 A random variable X has p.d.f.

$$f(x) = \begin{cases} (x-1)(2-x) & \text{for } 1 \leqslant x < 2 \\ a & \text{for } 2 \leqslant x \leqslant 4 \\ 0 & \text{otherwise.} \end{cases}$$

(i) Find the value of the constant a.

(ii) Sketch $y = f(x)$.

(iii) Find $P(1.5 \leqslant X \leqslant 2.5)$.

(iv) Find $P(|X - 2| < 1)$.

8 A random variable X has p.d.f.

$$f(x) = \begin{cases} kx(3-x) & \text{for } 0 \leqslant x \leqslant 3 \\ 0 & \text{otherwise.} \end{cases}$$

(i) Find the value of k.

(ii) The lifetime (in years) of an electronic component is modelled by this distribution. Two such components are fitted in a radio which will only function if both devices are working. Find the probability that the radio will still function after two years, assuming that their failures are independent.

9 The planning officer in a council needs information about how long cars stay in the car park, and asks the attendant to do a check on the times of arrival and departure of 100 cars. The attendant provides the following data.

Length of stay	Under 1 hour	1–2 hours	2–4 hours	4–10 hours	More than 10 hours
Number of cars	20	14	32	34	0

The planning officer suggests that the length of stay in hours may be modelled by the continuous random variable X with probability density function of the form

$$f(x) = \begin{cases} k(20 - 2x) & \text{for } 0 \leqslant x \leqslant 10 \\ 0 & \text{otherwise.} \end{cases}$$

(i) Find the value of k.

(ii) Sketch the graph of $f(x)$.

(iii) According to this model, how many of the 100 cars would be expected to fall into each of the four categories?

(iv) Do you think the model fits the data well?

(v) Are there any obvious weaknesses in the model? If you were the planning officer, would you be prepared to accept the model as it is, or would you want any further information?

10 A fish farmer has a very large number of trout in a lake. Before deciding whether to net the lake and sell the fish, she collects a sample of 100 fish and weighs them. The results (in kg) are as follows.

Weight, W	Frequency	Weight, W	Frequency
$0 < W \leqslant 0.5$	2	$2.0 < W \leqslant 2.5$	27
$0.5 < W \leqslant 1.0$	10	$2.5 < W \leqslant 3.0$	12
$1.0 < W \leqslant 1.5$	23	$3.0 < W$	0
$1.5 < W \leqslant 2.0$	26		

(i) Illustrate these data on a histogram, with the number of fish on the vertical scale and W on the horizontal scale. Is the distribution of the data symmetrical, positively skewed or negatively skewed?

A friend of the farmer suggests that W can be modelled as a continuous random variable and proposes four possible probability density functions.

$f_1(w) = \frac{2}{9} w(3 - w)$ $\qquad$ $f_2(w) = \frac{10}{81} w^2(3 - w)^2$

$f_3(w) = \frac{4}{27} w^2(3 - w)$ $\qquad$ $f_4(w) = \frac{4}{27} w(3 - w)^2$

in each case for $0 \leqslant w \leqslant 3$.

(ii) Using your calculator (or otherwise), sketch the curves of the four p.d.f.s and state which one matches the data most closely in general shape.

(iii) Use this p.d.f. to calculate the number of fish which that model predicts should fall within each group.

(iv) Do you think it is a good model?

11 During a war the crew of an aeroplane has to destroy an enemy railway line by dropping bombs. The distance between the railway line and where the bomb hits the ground is X m, where X has the following p.d.f.

$$f(x) = \begin{cases} 10^{-4}(a + x) & \text{for } -a \leqslant x < 0 \\ 10^{-4}(a - x) & \text{for } 0 \leqslant x \leqslant a \\ 0 & \text{otherwise.} \end{cases}$$

(i) Find the value of a.

(ii) Find $P(50 \leqslant X \leqslant 60)$.

(iii) Find $P(|X| < 20)$.

[MEI]

12 A random variable X has a probability density function f given by

$$f(x) = \begin{cases} cx(5-x) & 0 \leqslant x \leqslant 5 \\ 0 & \text{otherwise.} \end{cases}$$

Show that $c = \frac{6}{125}$.

The lifetime X (in years) of an electric light bulb has this distribution. Given that a standard lamp is fitted with two such new bulbs and that their failures are independent, find the probability that neither bulb fails in the first year and the probability that exactly one bulb fails within two years.

[MEI]

13 This graph shows the probability distribution function, $f(x)$, for the heights, X, of waves at the point with Latitude 44°N Longitude 41°W.

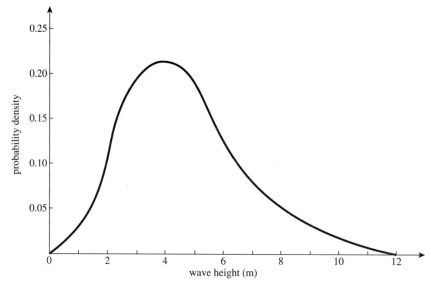

(i) Write down the values of $f(x)$ when $x = 0, 2, 4, \ldots, 12$.

(ii) Hence estimate the probability that the height of a randomly selected wave is in the interval

    (a) 0–2 m   **(b)** 2–4 m   **(c)** 4–6 m

    (d) 6–8 m   **(e)** 8–10 m   **(f)** 10–12 m.

A model is proposed in which

$$\begin{aligned} f(x) &= kx(12-x)^2 \quad \text{for } 0 \leqslant x \leqslant 12 \\ &= 0 \quad\quad\quad\quad \text{otherwise.} \end{aligned}$$

(iii) Find the value of k.

(iv) Find, according to this model, the probability that a randomly selected wave is in the interval

    (a) 0–2 m   **(b)** 2–4 m   **(c)** 4–6 m

    (d) 6–8 m   **(e)** 8–10 m   **(f)** 10–12 m.

(v) By comparing the figures from the model with the real data, state whether you think it is a good model or not.

Expectation and variance

You will recall that, for a discrete random variable, expectation and variance are given by:

$$E(X) = \sum_i x_i p_i$$

$$\text{Var}(X) = \sum_i (x_i - \mu)^2 p_i = \sum_i x_i^2 p_i - [E(X)]^2$$

where μ is the mean and p_i is the probability of the outcome x_i for $i = 1, 2, 3, \ldots$, with the various outcomes covering all possibilities.

The expressions for the expectation and variance of a continuous random variable are equivalent, but with summation replaced by integration.

$$E(X) = \int_{\substack{\text{All} \\ \text{values} \\ \text{of } x}} x f(x) \, dx$$

$$\text{Var}(X) = \int_{\substack{\text{All} \\ \text{values} \\ \text{of } x}} (x - \mu)^2 f(x) \, dx = \int_{\substack{\text{All} \\ \text{values} \\ \text{of } x}} x^2 f(x) \, dx - [E(X)]^2$$

$E(X)$ is the same as the population mean, μ, and is often called the mean of X.

EXAMPLE 1.4

The response time, in seconds, for a contestant in a general knowledge quiz is modelled by a continuous random variable X whose p.d.f. is

$$f(x) = \frac{x}{50} \quad \text{for } 0 < x \leqslant 10.$$

The rules state that a contestant who makes no answer is disqualified from the whole competition. This has the consequence that everybody gives an answer, if only a guess, to every question. Find

(i) the mean time in seconds for a contestant to respond to a particular question

(ii) the standard deviation of the time taken.

The organiser estimates the proportion of contestants who are guessing by assuming that they are those whose time is at least one standard deviation greater than the mean.

(iii) Using this assumption, estimate the probability that a randomly selected response is a guess.

SOLUTION

(i) Mean time: $\quad E(X) = \int_0^{10} x \frac{x}{50}\, dx$

$$= \left[\frac{x^3}{150}\right]_0^{10} = \frac{1000}{150} = \frac{20}{3}$$

$$= 6\frac{2}{3}$$

The mean time is $6\frac{2}{3}$ seconds.

(ii) Variance: $\quad Var(X) = \int_0^{10} x^2 f(x)\, dx - [E(X)]^2$

$$= \int_0^{10} \frac{x^3}{50}\, dx - (6\frac{2}{3})^2$$

$$= \left[\frac{x^4}{200}\right]_0^{10} - (6\frac{2}{3})^2$$

$$= 5\frac{5}{9}$$

Standard deviation $= \sqrt{\text{Variance}} = \sqrt{5.\dot{5}}$

The standard deviation of the times is 2.357 seconds (to 3 d.p.).

(iii) All those with response times greater than $6.667 + 2.357 = 9.024$ seconds are taken to be guessing. The longest possible time is 10 seconds.

The probability that a randomly selected response is a guess is given by

$$\int_{9.024}^{10} \frac{x}{50}\, dx$$

$$= \left[\frac{x^2}{100}\right]_{9.024}^{10}$$

$$= 0.186$$

So just under 1 in 5 answers are deemed to be guesses.

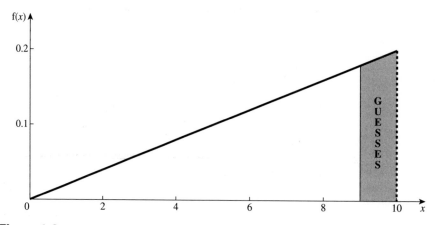

Figure 1.6

Note

Although the intermediate answers have been given rounded to three decimal places, more figures have been carried forward into subsequent calculations.

EXAMPLE 1.5

The number of hours per day that Darren spends in his garden is modelled (as on page 7) by the continuous random variable X, the p.d.f. of which is

$$f(x) = \frac{1}{9}x \qquad \text{for } 0 \leqslant x \leqslant 3$$

$$= \frac{6 - x}{9} \qquad \text{for } 3 < x \leqslant 6$$

$$= 0 \qquad \text{otherwise.}$$

Find $E(X)$, the mean number of hours per day that Darren spends in his garden.

SOLUTION

$$E(X) = \int_{-\infty}^{\infty} x f(x)\, dx$$

$$= \int_0^3 x \frac{1}{9} x\, dx + \int_3^6 x \frac{6 - x}{9}\, dx$$

$$= \left[\frac{x^3}{27} \right]_0^3 + \left[\frac{x^2}{3} - \frac{x^3}{27} \right]_3^6$$

$$= 1 + (12 - 8) - (3 - 1)$$

$$= 3$$

Darren spends a mean of 3 hours per day in his garden.

Notice that in this case $E(X)$ can be found from the line of symmetry of the graph of $f(x)$. This situation often arises and you should be alert to the possibility of finding $E(X)$ by symmetry; see figure 1.7.

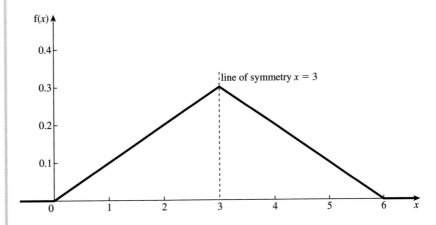

Figure 1.7

The median

The median value of a continuous random variable X with p.d.f. $f(x)$ is the value m for which

$$P(X < m) = P(X > m) = 0.5.$$

Consequently $\displaystyle\int_{-\infty}^{m} f(x)\,dx = 0.5$ and $\displaystyle\int_{m}^{\infty} f(x)\,dx = 0.5$.

The median is the value m such that the line $x = m$ divides the area under the curve $f(x)$ into two equal parts. In figure 1.8 a is the smallest possible value of X, b the largest. The line $x = m$ divides the shaded region into two regions A and B, both with area 0.5.

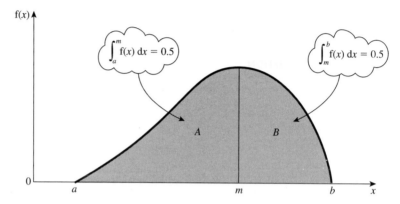

Figure 1.8

 In general the *mean* does not divide the area into two equal parts but it will do so if the curve is symmetrical about it because, in that case, it is equal to the median.

The mode

The mode of a continuous random variable X whose p.d.f. is $f(x)$ is the value for which $f(x)$ has the greatest value. Thus the mode is the value of X where the curve is at its highest.

If the mode is at a local maximum of $f(x)$, then it may often be found by differentiating $f(x)$ and solving the equation

$$f'(x) = 0.$$

 For which of the distributions in figure 1.9 could the mode be found by differentiating the p.d.f.?

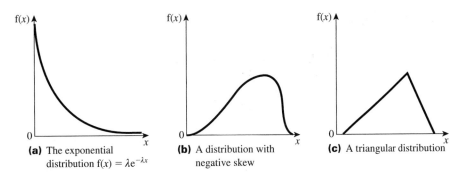

(a) The exponential distribution $f(x) = \lambda e^{-\lambda x}$

(b) A distribution with negative skew

(c) A triangular distribution

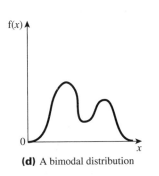

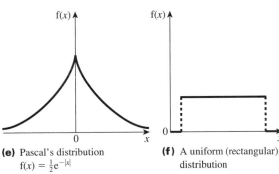

(d) A bimodal distribution

(e) Pascal's distribution $f(x) = \tfrac{1}{2}e^{-|x|}$

(f) A uniform (rectangular) distribution

Figure 1.9

EXAMPLE 1.6

The continuous random variable X has p.d.f. $f(x)$ where

$$f(x) = 4x(1 - x^2) \quad \text{for } 0 \leqslant x \leqslant 1$$
$$= 0 \qquad\qquad \text{otherwise.}$$

Find **(i)** the mode

(ii) the median.

SOLUTION

(i) The mode is found by differentiating $f(x) = 4x - 4x^3$

$$f'(x) = 4 - 12x^2$$

Solving $f'(x) = 0$

> $x = -0.577$ is also a root of $f'(x) = 0$ but is outside the range $0 \leqslant x \leqslant 1$.

$$x = \frac{1}{\sqrt{3}} = 0.577 \text{ to 3 decimal places.}$$

It is easy to see from the shape of the graph (see figure 1.10 overleaf) that this must be a maximum, and so the mode is 0.577.

(ii) The median, m, is given by $\displaystyle\int_{-\infty}^{m} f(x)\,dx = 0.5$

$$\Rightarrow \int_{0}^{m} (4x - 4x^3)\,dx = 0.5 \qquad \longleftarrow \boxed{\text{Since } x \geqslant 0}$$

$$\left[2x^2 - x^4\right]_{0}^{m} = 0.5$$

$$2m^2 - m^4 = 0.5$$

Rearranging gives

$$2m^4 - 4m^2 + 1 = 0.$$

This is a quadratic equation in m^2. The formula gives

$$m^2 = \frac{4 \pm \sqrt{16 - 8}}{4}$$

$$m = 0.541 \text{ or } 1.307 \text{ to 3 decimal places.}$$

Since 1.307 is outside the domain of X, the median is 0.541.

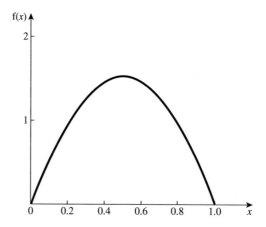

Figure 1.10

The uniform (rectangular) distribution

It is common to describe distributions by the shapes of the graphs of their p.d.f.s: U-shaped, J-shaped, etc.

The *uniform (rectangular) distribution* is particularly simple since its p.d.f. is constant over a range of values and zero elsewhere.

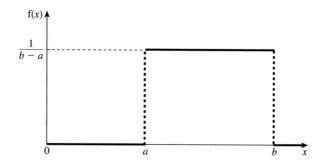

Figure 1.11

In figure 1.11, X may take values between a and b, and is zero elsewhere. Since the area under the graph must be 1, the height is $\dfrac{1}{b-a}$. The term uniform distribution can be applied to both discrete and continuous variables so in the continuous case it is often written as uniform (rectangular).

EXAMPLE 1.7

A junior gymnastics league is open to children who are at least five years old but have not yet had their ninth birthday. The age, X years, of a member is modelled by the uniform (rectangular) distribution over the range of possible values between five and nine. Age is measured in years and decimal parts of a year, rather than just completed years. Find

(i) the p.d.f. $f(x)$ of X

(ii) $P(6 \leqslant X \leqslant 7)$

(iii) $E(X)$

(iv) $Var(X)$

(v) the percentage of the children whose ages are within one standard deviation of the mean.

SOLUTION

(i) The p.d.f. $f(x) = \dfrac{1}{9-5} = \dfrac{1}{4}$ for $5 \leqslant x < 9$

$= 0$ otherwise.

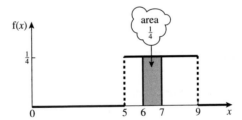

Figure 1.12

(ii) $P(6 \leqslant X \leqslant 7) = \frac{1}{4}$ by inspection of the rectangle above.
Alternatively, using integration

$$P(6 \leqslant X \leqslant 7) = \int_6^7 f(x)\,dx = \int_6^7 \frac{1}{4}\,dx$$

$$= \left[\frac{x}{4}\right]_6^7$$

$$= \frac{7}{6} - \frac{6}{4}$$

$$= \frac{1}{4}.$$

(iii) By the symmetry of the graph $E(X) = 7$. Alternatively, using integration

$$E(X) = \int_{-\infty}^{\infty} x f(x) \, dx = \int_5^9 \frac{x}{4} \, dx$$

$$= \left[\frac{x^2}{8} \right]_5^9$$

$$= \frac{81}{8} - \frac{25}{8} = 7.$$

(iv) $\mathrm{Var}(X) = \int_{-\infty}^{\infty} x^2 f(x) \, dx - [E(X)]^2 = \int_5^9 \frac{x^2}{4} \, dx - 7^2$

$$= \left[\frac{x^3}{12} \right]_5^9 - 49$$

$$= \frac{729}{12} - \frac{125}{12} - 49$$

$$= 1.333 \text{ to 3 decimal places.}$$

(v) Standard deviation $= \sqrt{\mathrm{Variance}} = \sqrt{1.333} = 1.155.$

So the percentage within 1 standard deviation of the mean is

$$\frac{2 \times 1.155}{4} \times 100\% = 57.7\%.$$

? What percentage would be within 1 standard deviation of the mean for a Normal distribution? Why is the percentage less in this example?

The mean and variance of the uniform (rectangular) distribution

In the previous example the mean and variance of a particular uniform distribution were calculated. This can easily be extended to the general uniform distribution given by:

$$f(x) = \frac{1}{b-a} \quad \text{for } a \leqslant x \leqslant b$$

$$= 0 \qquad \text{otherwise.}$$

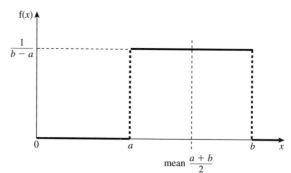

Figure 1.13

Mean   By symmetry the mean is $\dfrac{a+b}{2}$.

Variance $\text{Var}(X) = \displaystyle\int_{-\infty}^{\infty} x^2 f(x)\,dx - [E(X)]^2$

$$= \int_{a}^{b} x^2 f(x)\,dx - [E(X)]^2$$

$$= \int_{a}^{b} \frac{x^2}{b-a}\,dx - \left(\frac{a+b}{2}\right)^2$$

$$= \left[\frac{x^3}{3(b-a)}\right]_{a}^{b} - \frac{1}{4}(a^2 + 2ab + b^2)$$

$$= \frac{b^3 - a^3}{3(b-a)} - \frac{1}{4}(a^2 + 2ab + b^2)$$

$$= \frac{(b-a)}{3(b-a)}(b^2 + ab + a^2) - \frac{1}{4}(a^2 + 2ab + b^2)$$

$$= \frac{1}{12}(b^2 - 2ab + a^2)$$

$$= \frac{1}{12}(b-a)^2$$

❻ The exponential distribution

This distribution is often used to model the waiting times between events, such as earthquakes, radioactive emissions, telephone calls, etc., when the events being counted occur at random, singly and independently, at a constant overall rate.

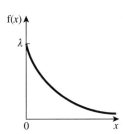

Figure 1.14

The random variable X has p.d.f. $f(x)$ as shown in figure 1.14, given by:

$$\begin{aligned} f(x) &= \lambda e^{-\lambda x} && \text{for } x \geqslant 0 \\ &= 0 && \text{otherwise.} \end{aligned}$$

The mean is $\dfrac{1}{\lambda}$ and the variance is $\dfrac{1}{\lambda^2}$.

Proof

(i) Show that, for $x \geqslant 0$, $f(x)$ satisfies the requirements for a p.d.f., that is $f(x) \geqslant 0$ for all x and

$$\int_{\substack{\text{All} \\ \text{values} \\ \text{of } x}} f(x)\,dx = 1.$$

The graph in figure 1.14 shows that $f(x) \geqslant 0$ for all x.

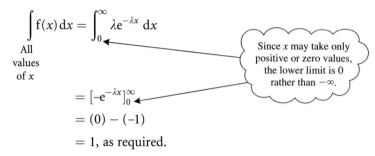

$$\int_{\substack{\text{All} \\ \text{values} \\ \text{of } x}} f(x)\,dx = \int_0^\infty \lambda e^{-\lambda x}\,dx$$

Since x may take only positive or zero values, the lower limit is 0 rather than $-\infty$.

$$= [-e^{-\lambda x}]_0^\infty$$

$$= (0) - (-1)$$

$$= 1, \text{ as required.}$$

(ii) Show that $E(X) = \dfrac{1}{\lambda}$.

$$E(X) = \int_0^\infty x f(x)\,dx = \int_0^\infty \lambda x e^{-\lambda x}\,dx$$

Integrating by parts gives

$$E(X) = [-x e^{-\lambda x}]_0^\infty + \int_0^\infty e^{-\lambda x}\,dx$$

$$= 0 - \left[\frac{e^{-\lambda x}}{\lambda}\right]_0^\infty$$

$$= -\left(-\frac{1}{\lambda}\right)$$

$$= \frac{1}{\lambda}, \text{ as required.}$$

(iii) Show that $\mathrm{Var}(X) = \dfrac{1}{\lambda^2}$.

$$\mathrm{Var}(X) = \int_0^\infty x^2 f(x)\,dx - [E(X)]^2 = \int_0^\infty x^2 \lambda e^{-\lambda x}\,dx - \left(\frac{1}{\lambda}\right)^2$$

Integrating by parts gives

$$\mathrm{Var}(X) = [-x^2 e^{-\lambda x}]_0^\infty + \int_0^\infty e^{-\lambda x} 2x\,dx - \frac{1}{\lambda^2}$$

$$= 0 + 2 \int_0^\infty x e^{-\lambda x}\,dx - \frac{1}{\lambda^2}.$$

Since it has been shown in part (ii) that

$$\int_0^\infty \lambda x e^{-\lambda x} \, dx = \frac{1}{\lambda}$$

it follows that

$$2 \int_0^\infty x e^{-\lambda x} \, dx = \frac{2}{\lambda^2}$$

and so

$$\text{Var}(X) = \frac{2}{\lambda^2} - \frac{1}{\lambda^2}$$

$$= \frac{1}{\lambda^2}, \text{ as required.}$$

1 The continuous random variable X has p.d.f. $f(x)$ where

$$f(x) = \tfrac{1}{8}x \quad \text{for } 0 \leqslant x \leqslant 4$$
$$= 0 \qquad \text{otherwise.}$$

Find
(i) $E(X)$
(ii) $\text{Var}(X)$
(iii) the median value of X.

2 The continuous random variable T has p.d.f. defined by

$$f(t) = \frac{6 - t}{18} \quad \text{for } 0 \leqslant t \leqslant 6$$
$$= 0 \qquad \text{otherwise.}$$

Find
(i) $E(T)$
(ii) $\text{Var}(T)$
(iii) the median value of T.

3 The continuous random variable Y has p.d.f. $f(y)$ defined by

$$f(y) = 12y^2(1 - y) \quad \text{for } 0 \leqslant y \leqslant 1$$
$$= 0 \qquad\qquad \text{otherwise.}$$

(i)   Find $E(Y)$.
(ii) Find $\text{Var}(Y)$.
(iii) Show that, to 2 decimal places, the median value of Y is 0.61.

4 The random variable X has p.d.f.

$$f(x) = \tfrac{1}{6} \quad \text{for } -2 \leqslant x \leqslant 4$$
$$= 0 \quad \text{otherwise.}$$

(i)   Sketch the graph of $f(x)$.
(ii) Find $P(X < 2)$.
(iii) Find $E(X)$.
(iv) Find $P(|X| < 1)$.

5 The continuous random variable X has p.d.f. $f(x)$ defined by

$$f(x) = \begin{cases} \frac{2}{9}x(3-x) & \text{for } 0 \leqslant x \leqslant 3 \\ 0 & \text{otherwise.} \end{cases}$$

(i) Find $E(X)$.

(ii) Find $Var(X)$.

(iii) Find the mode of X.

(iv) Find the median value of X.

(v) Draw a sketch graph of $f(x)$ and comment on your answers to parts (i), (iii) and (iv) in the light of what it shows you.

6 The random variable X has a uniform (rectangular) distribution over the interval $(-2, 5)$. Find

(i) the p.d.f. of X

(ii) $E(X)$

(iii) $Var(X)$

(iv) $P(X$ is positive$)$.

7 The function $f(x) = \begin{cases} k(3+x) & \text{for } 0 \leqslant x \leqslant 2 \\ 0 & \text{otherwise.} \end{cases}$

is the probability density function of the random variable X.

(i) Show that $k = \frac{1}{8}$.

(ii) Find the mean and variance of X.

(iii) Find the probability that a randomly selected value of X lies between 1 and 2.

8 A continuous random variable X has a uniform (rectangular) distribution over the interval $(4, 7)$. Find

(i) the p.d.f. of X

(ii) $E(X)$

(iii) $Var(X)$

(iv) $P(4.1 \leqslant X \leqslant 4.8)$.

9 The distribution of the lengths of adult Martian lizards is uniform between 10 cm and 20 cm. There are no adult lizards outside this range.

(i) Write down the p.d.f. of the lengths of the lizards.

(ii) Find the mean and variance of the lengths of the lizards.

(iii) What proportion of the lizards have lengths within

(a) one standard deviation of the mean

(b) two standard deviations of the mean?

10 The p.d.f. of the lifetime, X hours, of a brand of electric light bulb is modelled by

$$f(x) = \begin{cases} \dfrac{1}{60\,000}x & \text{for } 0 \leqslant x \leqslant 300 \\ \dfrac{1}{50} - \dfrac{1}{20\,000}x & \text{for } 300 < x \leqslant 400 \\ 0 & \text{for } x > 400. \end{cases}$$

(i)   Sketch the graph of f(x).

(ii) Show that f(x) fulfils the conditions for it to be a p.d.f.

(iii) Find the expected lifetime of a bulb.

(iv) Find the variance of the lifetimes of the bulbs.

(v)   Find the probability that a randomly selected bulb will last less than 100 hours.

11 The marks of candidates in an examination are modelled by the continuous random variable X with p.d.f.

$$f(x) = kx(x - 50)^2(100 - x) \quad \text{for } 0 \leqslant x \leqslant 100$$
$$= 0 \qquad\qquad\qquad\quad \text{otherwise.}$$

(i)   Find the value of k.

(ii) Sketch the graph of f(x).

(iii) Describe the shape of the graph and give an explanation of how such a graph might occur, in terms of the examination and the candidates.

(iv) Is it permissible to model a mark, which is a discrete variable going up in steps of 1, by a continuous random variable like X, as defined in this question?

12 The municipal tourism officer at a Mediterranean resort on the Costa Del Sol wishes to model the amount of sunshine per day during the holiday season. She denotes by X the number of hours of sunshine per day between 8 am and 8 pm and she suggests the following probability density function for X:

$$f(x) = k[(x - 3)^2 + 4] \quad \text{for } 0 \leqslant x \leqslant 12$$
$$= 0 \qquad\qquad\qquad\quad \text{otherwise.}$$

(i)   Show that $k = \frac{1}{300}$ and sketch the graph of the p.d.f. f(x).

(ii) Assuming that the model is accurate, find the mean and standard deviation of the number of hours of sunshine per day. Find also the probability of there being more than eight hours of sunshine on a randomly chosen day.

(iii) Obtain a cubic equation for m, the median number of hours of sunshine, and verify that m is about 9.74 to 2 decimal places.

[MEI]

13 The continuous random variable X has p.d.f. f(x) defined by

$$f(x) = ae^{-kx} \quad \text{for } x \geqslant 0$$
$$= 0 \qquad\quad \text{otherwise.}$$

Find, in terms of k,

(i) a

(ii) $E(X)$

(iii) $\text{Var}(X)$

(iv) the median value of X

(v)   There are many situations where this random variable might be used as a model. Describe one such situation.

14 A statistician is also a keen cyclist. He believes that the distance which he cycles between punctures may be modelled by the random variable, X km, with p.d.f. $f(x)$ given by

$$f(x) = 0.005e^{-0.005x} \quad \text{for } x > 0$$
$$= 0 \quad \text{otherwise.}$$

(i) Find the mean distance he cycles between punctures.

(ii) He has just repaired one puncture. What is the probability that he will travel at least 500 km before having another one?

(iii) He has just repaired one puncture. What is the probability that he will travel less than 30 km before having another one?

On one occasion he starts a race with new tyres but then has a puncture after 30 km. When he starts again he has another puncture after k km. He says that according to his model the combined probability of first a puncture within 30 km and then one within k km is 0.005.

(iv) What is the value of k?

15 The continuous random variable X has p.d.f. $f(x)$ defined by

$$f(x) = \begin{cases} \dfrac{a}{x} & \text{for } 1 \leqslant x \leqslant 2 \\ 0 & \text{otherwise.} \end{cases}$$

(i) Find the value of a.

(ii) Sketch the graph of $f(x)$.

(iii) Find the mean and variance of X.

(iv) Find the proportion of values of X between 1.5 and 2.

(v) Find the median value of X.

16 An examination is taken by a large number of candidates. The marks scored are modelled by the continuous random variable X with probability density function

$$f(x) = kx^3(120 - x), \quad 0 \leqslant x \leqslant 100.$$

(You should assume throughout this question that marks are on a continuous scale. Hence there is no need to consider continuity corrections.)

(i) Sketch the graph of this probability density function. What does the model suggest about the abilities of the candidates in relation to this examination?

(ii) Show that $k = 10^{-9}$.

(iii) The pass mark is set at 50. Find what proportion of candidates fail the examination.

(iv) The top 20% of candidates are awarded a distinction. Determine whether a mark of 90 is sufficient for a distinction. Find the least whole number mark which is sufficient for a distinction.

[MEI]

The expectation and variance of a function of *X*

There are times when one random variable is a function of another random variable. For example:

- as part of an experiment you are measuring temperatures in Celsius but then need to convert them to Fahrenheit: $F = 1.8C + 32$;
- you are measuring the lengths of the sides of square pieces of material and deducing their areas: $A = L^2$;
- you are estimating the ages, A years, of hedgerows by counting the number, n, of types of shrubs and trees in 30 m lengths: $A = 100n - 50$.

In fact in any situation where you are entering the value of a random variable into a formula, the outcome will be another random variable which is a function of the one you entered. Under these circumstances you may need to find the expectation and variance of such a function of a random variable.

For a discrete random variable, X, the expectation of a function $g[X]$ is given by:

$$E(g[X]) = \Sigma g[x_i] p_i,$$

$$Var(g[X]) = \Sigma (g[x_i])^2 p_i - \{E(g[X])\}^2.$$

The equivalent results for a continuous random variable, X, with p.d.f. $f(x)$ are:

$$E(g[X]) = \int_{\substack{\text{All} \\ \text{values} \\ \text{of } x}} g[x]\, f(x)\, dx,$$

$$Var(g[X]) = \int_{\substack{\text{All} \\ \text{values} \\ \text{of } x}} (g[x])^2\, f(x)\, dx - \{E(g[X])\}^2.$$

You may find it helpful to think of the function $g[X]$ as a new variable, say Y.

EXAMPLE 1.8

The continuous random variable X has p.d.f. $f(x)$ given by:

$$f(x) = \frac{x}{50} \quad \text{for } 0 < x \leqslant 10$$

$$= 0 \quad \text{otherwise.}$$

(This random variable was used to model response times in Example 1.4.)

(i) Find $E(3X + 4)$.

(ii) Find $3E(X) + 4$.

(iii) Find $Var(3X + 4)$.

(iv) Verify that $Var(3X + 4) = 3^2 Var(X)$.

SOLUTION

(i) $E(3X + 4) = \displaystyle\int_0^{10} (3x + 4)\frac{x}{50}\,dx$

$= \displaystyle\int_0^{10} \frac{1}{50}(3x^2 + 4x)\,dx$

$= \left[\dfrac{x^3}{50} + \dfrac{x^2}{25}\right]_0^{10}$

$= 20 + 4$

$= 24$

(ii) $3E(X) + 4 = 3\displaystyle\int_0^{10} x\frac{x}{50}\,dx + 4$

$= \left[\dfrac{3}{150}x^3\right]_0^{10} + 4$

$= 20 + 4$

$= 24$

Notice here that $E(3X + 4) = 24 = 3E(X) + 4$.

(iii) To find $\mathrm{Var}(3X + 4)$, use

$$\mathrm{Var}[g(X)] = \int [g(x)]^2 f(x)\,dx - \{E[g(X)]\}^2$$

with $\qquad\qquad g(X) = 3X + 4.$

$\mathrm{Var}(3X + 4) = \displaystyle\int_0^{10} (3x + 4)^2 \frac{1}{50}x\,dx - 24^2$

$= \displaystyle\int_0^{10} \frac{1}{50}(9x^3 + 24x^2 + 16x)\,dx - 576$

$= \dfrac{1}{50}\left[\dfrac{9x^4}{4} + 8x^3 + 8x^2\right]_0^{10} - 576$

$= 50$

(iv) $\mathrm{Var}(X) = E(X^2) - [E(X)]^2$

$E(X^2) = \displaystyle\int_0^{10} x^2\frac{1}{50}x\,dx \qquad\qquad E(X) = \displaystyle\int_0^{10} x\frac{1}{50}x\,dx$

$E(X^2) = \displaystyle\int_0^{10} \frac{1}{50}x^3\,dx \qquad\qquad E(X) = \displaystyle\int_0^{10} \frac{1}{50}x^2\,dx$

$E(X^2) = \left[\dfrac{1}{200}x^4\right]_0^{10} \qquad\qquad E(X) = \left[\dfrac{1}{150}x^3\right]_0^{10}$

$E(X^2) = 50 \qquad\qquad\qquad E(X) = 6.\dot{6}$

$\mathrm{Var}(X) = 50 - 6.\dot{6}^2 = 5.\dot{5}$

$3^2\,\mathrm{Var}(X) = 9 \times 5.\dot{5} = 50$

From part (iii), $\mathrm{Var}(3X + 4) = 50$

So $\quad \mathrm{Var}(3X + 4) = 3^2\mathrm{Var}(X)$ as required.

General results

This example illustrates a number of general results for random variables, continuous or discrete.

$$E(c) = c \qquad\qquad Var(c) = 0$$
$$E(aX) = aE(X) \qquad\qquad Var(aX) = a^2Var(X)$$
$$E(aX + b) = aE(X) + b \qquad Var(aX + b) = a^2Var(X)$$
$$E[g(X) + h(X)] = E[g(X)] + E[h(X)]$$

where a, b and c are constants and $g(X)$ and $h(X)$ are functions of X.

Note

The result $Var(aX) = a^2Var(X)$ should not surprise you. It follows from the fact that if the standard deviation of a set of data is k then the standard deviation of the set formed by multiplying all the data by a constant, a, is ak. That is,

$$\text{standard deviation}(aX) = a \times \text{standard deviation}(X)$$

Since variance = (standard deviation)^2

then $Var(aX) = [\text{standard deviation}(aX)]^2$

$= [a \times \text{standard deviation}(X)]^2$

$= a^2[\text{standard deviation}(X)]^2$

$= a^2 Var(X).$

EXAMPLE 1.9

The continuous random variable X has p.d.f. $f(x)$ given by

$$f(x) = \frac{3}{125}x^2 \quad \text{for } 0 \leqslant x \leqslant 5$$
$$= 0 \qquad \text{otherwise.}$$

Find **(i)** $E(X)$ **(ii)** $Var(X)$ **(iii)** $E(7X - 3)$ **(iv)** $Var(7X - 3)$.

SOLUTION

(i) $E(X) = \displaystyle\int_{-\infty}^{\infty} xf(x)\,dx$

$= \displaystyle\int_{0}^{5} x\frac{3}{125}x^2\,dx$

$= \left[\dfrac{3}{500}x^4\right]_{0}^{5}$

$= 3.75$

(ii) $\text{Var}(X) = \int_{-\infty}^{\infty} x^2 f(x)\,dx - [E(X)]^2$

$$= \int_0^5 x^2 \frac{3}{125} x^2 \, dx - 3.75^2$$

$$= \left[\frac{3}{625} x^5\right]_0^5 - 14.0625$$

$$= 15 - 14.0625$$

$$= 0.9375$$

(iii) $E(7X - 3) = 7E(X) - 3$
$$= 7 \times 3.75 - 3$$
$$= 23.25$$

(iv) $\text{Var}(7X - 3) = 7^2 \text{Var}(X)$
$$= 49 \times 0.9375$$
$$= 45.94 \text{ to 2 decimal places.}$$

EXERCISE 1C

1 The number of kilograms of metal extracted from 10 kg of ore from a certain mine is modelled by a continuous random variable X with probability density function $f(x)$, where $f(x) = cx(2 - x)^2$ if $0 \leqslant x \leqslant 2$ and $f(x) = 0$ otherwise, where c is a constant.

Show that c is $\frac{3}{4}$, and find the mean and variance of X.

The cost of extracting the metal from 10 kg of ore is £10x. Find the expected cost of extracting the metal from 10 kg of ore.

2 A continuous random variable X has the p.d.f.:

$$f(x) = k \quad \text{for } 0 \leqslant x \leqslant 5$$
$$= 0 \quad \text{otherwise.}$$

(i) Find the value of k.
(ii) Sketch the graph of $f(x)$.
(iii) Find $E(X)$.
(iv) Find $E(4X - 3)$ and show that your answer is the same as $4E(X) - 3$.

3 The continuous random variable X has p.d.f.

$$f(x) = 4x^3 \quad \text{for } 0 \leqslant x \leqslant 1$$
$$= 0 \quad \text{otherwise.}$$

(i) Find $E(X)$.
(ii) Find $E(X^2)$.
(iii) Find $\text{Var}(X)$.
(iv) Verify that $E(5X + 1) = 5E(X) + 1$.

4 A continuous random variable Y has p.d.f.

$$f(y) = \tfrac{2}{9}y(3 - y) \quad \text{for } 0 \leqslant y \leqslant 3$$
$$= 0 \qquad\qquad \text{otherwise.}$$

(i) Find $E(Y)$.

(ii) Find $E(Y^2)$.

(iii) Find $E(Y^2) - [E(Y)]^2$.

(iv) Find $E(2Y^2 + 3Y + 4)$.

(v) Find $\int_0^3 (y - E(Y))^2 f(y)\,dy$.

Why is the answer the same as that for part (iii)?

5 A continuous random variable X has p.d.f. $f(x)$, where

$$f(x) = 12x^2(1 - x) \quad \text{for } 0 \leqslant x \leqslant 1$$
$$= 0 \qquad\qquad \text{otherwise.}$$

(i) Find μ, the mean of X.

(ii) Find $E(6X - 7)$ and show that your answer is the same as $6E(X) - 7$.

(iii) Find the standard deviation of X.

(iv) What is the probability that a randomly selected value of X lies within one standard deviation of μ?

6 The continuous random variable X has p.d.f.

$$f(x) = \tfrac{2}{25}(7 - x) \quad \text{for } 2 \leqslant x \leqslant 7$$
$$= 0 \qquad\qquad \text{otherwise.}$$

The function $g(X)$ is defined by $g(x) = 3x^2 + 4x + 7$.

(i) Find $E(X)$.

(ii) Find $E[g(X)]$.

(iii) Find $E(X^2)$ and hence find $3E(X^2) + 4E(X) + 7$.

(iv) Use your answers to parts (ii) and (iii) to verify that

$$E[g(X)] = 3E(X^2) + 4E(X) + 7.$$

7 A toy company sells packets of coloured plastic equilateral triangles. The triangles are actually offcuts from the manufacture of a totally different toy, and the length, X, of one side of a triangle may be modelled as a random variable with a uniform (rectangular) distribution for $2 \leqslant x \leqslant 8$.

(i) Find the p.d.f. of X.

(ii) An equilateral triangle of side x has area a. Find the relationship between a and x.

(iii) Find the probability that a randomly selected triangle has area greater than 15 cm^2. (Hint: What does this imply about x?)

(iv) Find the expectation and variance of the area of a triangle.

8 A continuous random variable has probability density function f defined by

$$f(x) = kx(4 - x) \quad \text{for } 0 \leqslant x \leqslant 4$$
$$= 0 \qquad\qquad \text{otherwise.}$$

Evaluate k and the mean of the distribution.

A particle moves along a straight line in such a way that during the first four seconds of its motion its velocity at time t seconds is $v\,\text{ms}^{-1}$, where $v = 2(t + 1)$.

The particle is observed at time t seconds, where t denotes a random value from a distribution whose probability density function is the function f defined above. Calculate the probability that at the time of observation the velocity of the particle is less than $4\,\text{ms}^{-1}$. [JMB]

9 Every day I travel to and from work on the local shuttle bus, which runs every 10 minutes. The time I have to wait for the bus is modelled by the random variable T, which has a uniform (rectangular) distribution on the interval $[0, 10]$.

(i) Write down the probability density function for T, and state its mean and variance.

The *total* time I have to wait for a bus, going to and coming from work, is modelled by the random variable X whose probability density function is given by

$$\begin{aligned}
f(x) &= 0.01x && \text{for } 0 \leqslant x \leqslant 10 \\
&= 0.01(20 - x) && \text{for } 10 < x \leqslant 20 \\
&= 0 && \text{otherwise.}
\end{aligned}$$

(ii) Sketch the graph of the probability density function for X.

(iii) State $E(X)$ and use integration to find $Var(X)$.

The times I wait for the bus when going to work and coming home from work are represented by independent random variables T_1 and T_2 respectively, so that $X = T_1 + T_2$.

(iv) Find $P(X \geqslant 14)$. Give a reason why you would expect $P(X \geqslant 14)$ to be greater than $P(T_1 \geqslant 7) \times P(T_2 \geqslant 7)$.

[MEI]

10 The continuous random variable X has probability density function

$$f(x) = \tfrac{3}{1024}x(x - 8)^2 \quad 0 \leqslant x \leqslant 8.$$

A sketch of $f(x)$ is shown in the diagram.

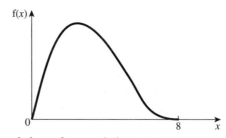

(i) Find $E(X)$ and show that $Var(X) = 2.56$.

The times, in minutes, taken by a doctor to see her patients are modelled by the continuous random variable $T = X + 2$.

(ii) Sketch the distribution of T and describe in words what this model implies about the lengths of the doctor's appointments.

[MEI]

11 A canon fires balls at a fixed angle of elevation with an initial speed U in ☆ ms^{-1}. The horizontal distance they travel R (in m), is given by

$$R = 0.1U^2.$$

The initial speed of the canon balls depends on the charge and so is somewhat variable.

(i) The initial speed U is modelled as having a uniform (rectangular) distribution between 80 and 120 in ms^{-1}.

    (a) Find the mean and standard deviation of U.

    (b) Find the mean and standard deviation of R.

(ii) An alternative model is considered for U and this is shown in the diagram below.

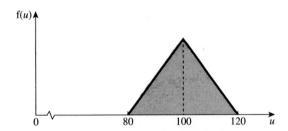

    (a) Find the p.d.f. for U under this model.

    (b) Find the mean and variance of U.

    (c) Find the mean and variance of R.

12 A company specialises in extinguishing oil fires. For much of the time its ☆ personnel have no work to do but they have to be available to travel anywhere at a moment's notice. The company reckons its overhead costs are £5000 per day, whether they have work or not.

The company model the waiting time, t days, between jobs by the exponential distribution

$$f(t) = \frac{1}{100} e^{-\left(\frac{1}{100}\right)t}.$$

(i) Find the mean time that they wait between jobs.

(ii) Find the probability that they go for one year or more between jobs.

(iii) Find the number of days, x, within which they have a 95% probability of getting another job.

When they work, they take an average of 20 days to put out a fire. They aim to make enough profit during that time to be able to meet their costs for the next x days, so that there is a probability of 0.95 that they will have another job before their profit from the last one has run out.

(iv) How much should they charge per day when on a job?

(v) What is the expectation of their profit per day?

The cumulative distribution function

500 enter Avonford half-marathon

There was a record entry for this year's Avonford half-marathon, including several famous names who were treating it as a training run in preparation for the London marathon. Overall winner was Reuben Mhango in 1 hour 4 minutes and 2 seconds; the first woman home was 37-year-old Lynn Barber in 1 hour 20 minutes exactly. There were many fun runners but everybody completed the course within 4 hours.

Record numbers, but no record times this year

£150 prize to be won

Mike Harrison, chair of the Avonford Half Committee, says: 'This year we restricted entries to 500 but this meant disappointing many people. Next year we intend to allow everybody to run and expect a much bigger entry. In order to allow us to marshall the event properly we need a statistical model to predict the flow of runners, and particularly their finishing times. We are offering a prize of £150 for the best such model submitted.'

This year's percentages of runners finishing in given times were as shown in the table. Entries should be submitted to Mike Harrison at Harrison Sports, High St, Avonford.

Time (hours)	Finished (%)
$1\frac{1}{4}$	3
$1\frac{1}{2}$	15
$1\frac{3}{4}$	33
2	49
$2\frac{1}{4}$	57
$2\frac{1}{2}$	75
3	91
$3\frac{1}{2}$	99
4	100

An entrant for the competition proposed a model in which a runner's time, X hours, is a continuous random variable with p.d.f.

$$f(x) = \tfrac{4}{27}(x-1)(4-x)^2 \quad 1 \leqslant x \leqslant 4$$
$$= 0 \qquad\qquad\qquad \text{otherwise}$$

According to this model the mode is at 2 hours, and everybody finishes in between 1 hour and 4 hours; see figure 1.15.

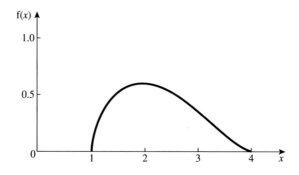

Figure 1.15

How does this model compare with the figures you were given for the actual race?

Those figures gave the *cumulative distribution*, the total numbers (expressed as percentages) of runners who had finished by certain times. To obtain the equivalent figures from the model, you must find the relevant area under the graph in figure 1.16.

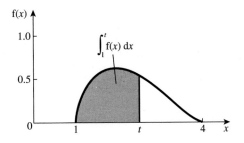

Figure 1.16

In this model, the proportion finishing by time t hours is given by

$$\int_1^t f(x)\,dx = \int_1^t \tfrac{4}{27}(x-1)(4-x)^2\,dx$$

$$= \tfrac{4}{27}\int_1^t (x^3 - 9x^2 + 24x - 16)\,dx$$

$$= \tfrac{4}{27}\left[\tfrac{1}{4}x^4 - 3x^3 + 12x^2 - 16x\right]_1^t$$

$$= \tfrac{4}{27}\left(\tfrac{1}{4}t^4 - 3t^3 + 12t^2 - 16t\right) - (-1)$$

$$= \tfrac{1}{27}t^4 - \tfrac{4}{9}t^3 + \tfrac{16}{9}t^2 - \tfrac{64}{27}t + 1$$

This is called the *cumulative distribution function* and denoted by $F(t)$.
In this case,

$$F(t) = 0 \qquad\qquad\qquad\qquad\qquad\qquad\text{for } t < 1$$

$$= \tfrac{1}{27}t^4 - \tfrac{4}{9}t^3 + \tfrac{16}{9}t^2 - \tfrac{64}{27}t + 1 \quad \text{for } 1 \leqslant t \leqslant 4$$

$$= 1 \qquad\qquad\qquad\qquad\qquad\qquad\text{for } t > 4.$$

To find the proportions of runners finishing by any time, substitute that value for t; so when $t = 2$

$$F(2) = \tfrac{1}{27} \times 2^4 - \tfrac{4}{9} \times 2^3 + \tfrac{16}{9} \times 2^2 - \tfrac{64}{27} \times 2 + 1$$

$$= 0.41 \text{ to 2 decimal places.}$$

Here is the complete table, with all the values worked out.

Time (hours)	Model	Runners
1.00	0.00	0.00
1.25	0.04	0.03
1.50	0.13	0.15
1.75	0.26	0.33
2.00	0.41	0.49
2.25	0.55	0.57
2.50	0.69	0.75
3.00	0.89	0.91
3.50	0.98	0.99
4.00	1.00	1.00

Notice the distinctive shape of the curves of these functions (figure 1.17), sometimes called an *ogive*. You have probably met this already, when drawing cumulative frequency curves, for example in *Statistics 1*.

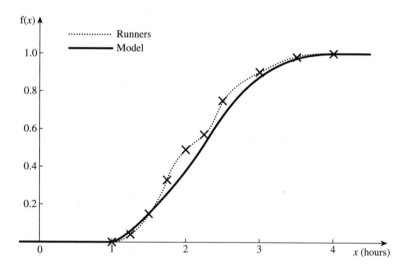

Figure 1.17

Do you think that this model is worth the £150 prize? If you were on the organising committee what more might you look for in a model?

Notes

1 Notice the use of lower and upper case letters here. The probability density function is denoted by the lower case f, whereas the cumulative distribution function is given the upper case F.

2 F was derived here as a function of *t* rather than *x*, to avoid using the same variable in the expression to be integrated. In this case *t* was a natural variable to use because time was involved, but that is not always the case.

It is more usual to write F as a function of *x*, F(*x*), but you would not be correct to write down an expression like

$$F(x) = \int_1^x \frac{4}{27}(x-1)(4-x)^2 \, dx \qquad \text{INCORRECT}$$

since *x* would then be both a limit of the integral and the variable used within it.

To overcome this problem a dummy variable, *u*, is used in the rest of this section, so that F(*x*) is now written,

$$F(x) = \int_1^x \frac{4}{27}(u-1)(4-u)^2 \, du \qquad \text{CORRECT}$$

You may of course use another symbol, like *y* or *p*, rather than *u*, anything except *x*.

3 The term cumulative distribution function is often abbreviated to c.d.f.

Properties of the cumulative distribution function, F(*x*)

The graphs, figure 1.18, show the probability density function f(*x*) and the cumulative distribution function F(*x*) of a typical continuous random variable X. You will see that the values of the random variable always lie between *a* and *b*.

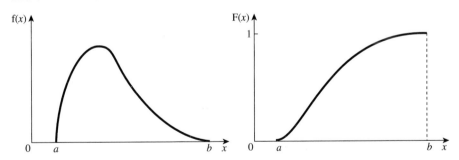

Figure 1.18

These graphs illustrate a number of general results for cumulative distribution functions.

1 $F(x) = 0$ for $x \leqslant a$, the lower limit of *x*.

The probability of X taking a value less than or equal to *a* is zero; the value of X must be greater than or equal to *a*.

2 $F(x) = 1$ for $x \geqslant b$, the upper limit of x.
X cannot take values greater than b.

3 $P(c \leqslant X \leqslant d) = F(d) - F(c)$
$P(c \leqslant X \leqslant d) = P(X \leqslant d) - P(X \leqslant c)$

This is very useful when finding
probabilities from a p.d.f. or a c.d.f.

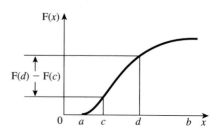

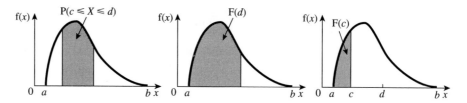

Figure 1.19

4 The median, m, satisfies the equation $F(m) = 0.5$.
$P(X \leqslant m) = 0.5$ by definition of the median.

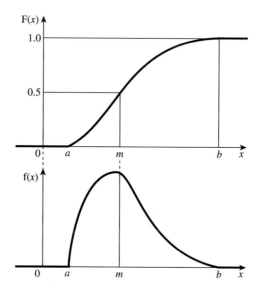

Figure 1.20

5 $f(x) = \dfrac{d}{dx} F(x) = F'(x)$

Since you integrate $f(x)$ to obtain $F(x)$, the reverse must also be true:
differentiating $F(x)$ gives $f(x)$.

6 $F(x)$ is a continuous function: the graph of $y = F(x)$ has no gaps.

EXAMPLE 1.10

A machine saws planks of wood to a nominal length. The continuous random variable X represents the error in millimetres of the actual length of a plank coming off the machine. The variable X has p.d.f. $f(x)$ where

$$f(x) = \frac{10 - x}{50} \quad \text{for } 0 \leqslant x \leqslant 10$$

$$= 0 \qquad \text{otherwise.}$$

(i) Sketch $f(x)$.

(ii) Find the cumulative distribution function $F(x)$.

(iii) Sketch $F(x)$ for $0 \leqslant x \leqslant 10$.

(iv) Find $P(2 \leqslant X \leqslant 7)$.

(v) Find the median value of X.

A customer refuses to accept planks for which the error is greater than 8 mm.

(vi) What percentage of planks will he reject?

SOLUTION

(i)

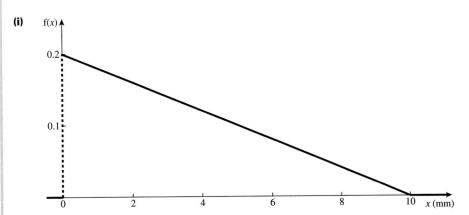

Figure 1.21

(ii) $F(x) = \displaystyle\int_0^x \frac{(10 - u)}{50} \, du$

$$= \frac{1}{50} \left[10u - \frac{u^2}{2} \right]_0^x$$

$$= \frac{1}{5} x - \frac{1}{100} x^2$$

The full definition of $F(x)$ is:

$$F(x) = 0 \qquad\qquad\qquad \text{for } x < 0$$

$$= \frac{1}{5} x - \frac{1}{100} x^2 \quad \text{for } 0 \leqslant x \leqslant 10$$

$$= 1 \qquad\qquad\qquad \text{for } x > 10.$$

(iii) The graph F(x) is shown in figure 1.22.

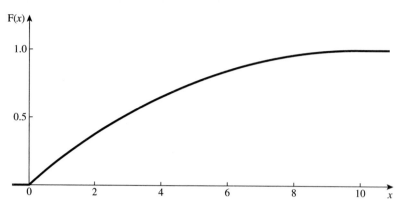

Figure 1.22

(iv) $P(2 \leqslant X \leqslant 7) = F(7) - F(2)$
$$= \left[\tfrac{7}{5} - \tfrac{49}{100}\right] - \left[\tfrac{2}{5} - \tfrac{4}{100}\right]$$
$$= 0.91 - 0.36$$
$$= 0.55.$$

(v) The median value of X is found by solving the equation
$$F(m) = 0.5$$
$$\tfrac{1}{5}m - \tfrac{1}{100}m^2 = 0.5.$$

This is rearranged to give
$$m^2 - 20m + 50 = 0$$
$$m = \frac{20 \pm \sqrt{20^2 - 4 \times 50}}{2}$$
$$m = 2.93 \text{ (or 17.07, outside the domain for } X\text{)}.$$

The median error is 2.93 mm.

(vi) The customer rejects those planks for which $8 \leqslant X \leqslant 10$
$$P(8 \leqslant X \leqslant 10) = F(10) - F(8)$$
$$= 1 - 0.96$$

so 4% of planks are rejected.

EXAMPLE 1.11

The p.d.f. of a continuous random variable X is given by:
$$f(x) = \frac{x}{24} \qquad \text{for } 0 \leqslant x \leqslant 4$$
$$= \frac{(12 - x)}{48} \qquad \text{for } 4 \leqslant x \leqslant 12$$
$$= 0 \qquad \text{otherwise.}$$

(i) Sketch $f(x)$.

(ii) Find the cumulative distribution function $F(x)$.

(iii) Sketch $F(x)$.

SOLUTION

(i) The graph of $f(x)$ is shown in figure 1.23.

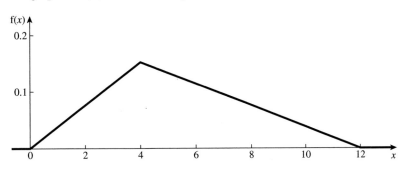

Figure 1.23

(ii) For $0 \leqslant x \leqslant 4$, $F(x) = \displaystyle\int_0^x \frac{u}{24} \, du$

$$= \left[\frac{u^2}{48} \right]_0^x$$

$$= \frac{x^2}{48}$$

and so $F(4) = \frac{1}{3}$.

For $4 \leqslant x \leqslant 12$, a second integration is required:

$$F(x) = \int_0^4 \frac{u}{24} \, du + \int_4^x \left(\frac{12 - u}{48} \right) du$$

$$= F(4) + \left[\frac{u}{4} - \frac{u^2}{96} \right]_4^x$$

$$= \frac{1}{3} + \frac{x}{4} - \frac{x^2}{96} - \frac{5}{6}$$

$$= -\frac{1}{2} + \frac{x}{4} - \frac{x^2}{96}$$

So the full definition of $F(x)$ is

$$\begin{aligned} F(x) &= 0 & \text{for } x < 0 \\[2mm] &= \frac{x^2}{48} & \text{for } 0 \leqslant x \leqslant 4 \\[2mm] &= -\frac{1}{2} + \frac{x}{4} - \frac{x^2}{96} & \text{for } 4 \leqslant x \leqslant 12 \\[2mm] &= 1 & \text{for } x > 12. \end{aligned}$$

(iii) The graph of F(x) is shown in figure 1.24.

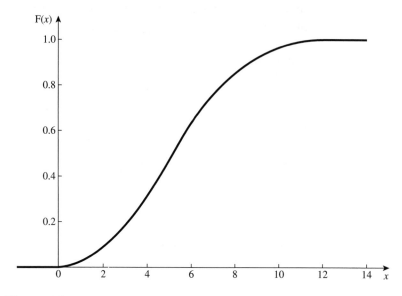

Figure 1.24

EXAMPLE 1.12

The continuous random variable X has cumulative distribution function F(x) given by:

$$F(x) = \begin{cases} 0 & \text{for } x < 2 \\ \dfrac{x^2}{32} - \dfrac{1}{8} & \text{for } 2 \leqslant x \leqslant 6 \\ 1 & \text{for } x > 6. \end{cases}$$

Find the p.d.f. f(x).

SOLUTION

$$f(x) = \frac{d}{dx} F(x)$$

$$f(x) = \begin{cases} \dfrac{d}{dx} F(x) = 0 & \text{for } x < 2 \\ \dfrac{d}{dx} F(x) = \dfrac{x}{16} & \text{for } 2 \leqslant x \leqslant 6 \\ \dfrac{d}{dx} F(x) = 0 & \text{for } x > 6. \end{cases}$$

e **Finding the p.d.f. of a function of a continuous random variable**

The cumulative distribution function provides you with a stepping stone between the p.d.f. of a continuous random variable and that of a function of that variable. Example 1.13 shows how it is done.

EXAMPLE 1.13

A company make metal boxes to order. The basic process consists of cutting four squares off the corners of a sheet of metal, which is then folded and welded along the joins. Consequently, for every box there are four square offcuts of waste metal.

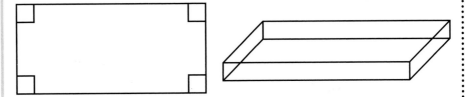

Figure 1.25

The company is looking for ways to cut costs and the designers wonder if anything can be done with these square pieces. They decide in the first place to investigate the distribution of their sizes. A survey of the large pile in their scrap area shows that they vary in length up to a maximum of 2 decimetres. It is suggested their lengths can be modelled as a continuous random variable L with probability density function

$$f(l) = \frac{l}{4}(4 - l^2) \quad \text{for } 0 < l \leqslant 2$$
$$= 0 \quad \text{otherwise.}$$

Assume this model to be accurate.

(i) Find the cumulative distribution function for the length of a square.

(ii) Hence derive the cumulative distribution function for the area of a square.

(iii) Find the p.d.f. for the area of a square.

(iv) Sketch the graphs of the probability density functions and the cumulative distribution functions of the length and the area.

(v) Find the mean area of the square offcuts when making a box.

SOLUTION

(i) The c.d.f. is

$$F(l) = \int_0^l \frac{u}{4}(4 - u^2)\, du$$

$$= \left[\frac{u^2}{2} - \frac{u^4}{16} \right]_0^l$$

Notice the use of u as a dummy variable for L.

and so

$$F(l) = 0 \qquad \text{for } l < 0$$
$$= \frac{l^2}{2} - \frac{l^4}{16} \quad \text{for } 0 < l \leqslant 2$$
$$= 1 \qquad \text{for } l > 2.$$

(ii) The area, a, and length, l, of a square are related by

$$a = l^2$$

and since $0 < l \leqslant 2$

it follows that $0 < a \leqslant 2^2$, that is, $0 < a \leqslant 4$.

Substituting a for l^2 in the answer to part (i), and using the appropriate range of values for a, gives the cumulative distribution function $H(a)$, because

$$\begin{aligned} H(a) &= P(A \leqslant a) \\ &= P(L^2 \leqslant l^2) \\ &= P(L \leqslant l) \qquad \text{(as } L > 0) \\ &= F(l) \end{aligned}$$

Since $$F(l) = \frac{l^2}{2} - \frac{l^4}{16} \quad \text{for } 0 < l \leqslant 2$$

it follows that $$H(a) = \frac{a}{2} - \frac{a^2}{16} \quad \text{for } 0 < a \leqslant 4$$

$$= 1 \qquad \text{for } a > 4$$

(iii) The p.d.f. for the area of a square is found by differentiating $H(a)$

$$h(a) = \frac{d}{da} H(a) = \frac{1}{2} - \frac{a}{8} \quad \text{for } 0 < a \leqslant 4$$

$$= 0 \qquad \text{otherwise.}$$

Note

Notice the use of H and h for the c.d.f. and the p.d.f. of the area, in place of F and f. The different letters are used to distinguish these from the corresponding functions for the length.

(iv) The graphs of the p.d.f.s of the length and the area are shown in figure 1.26.

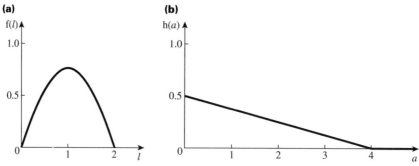

(a)

(b)

Figure 1.26

(a) $f(l) = \dfrac{1}{4} l(4 - l^2)$ for $0 < l \leqslant 2$

$= 0$ otherwise

(b) $h(a) = \dfrac{1}{2} - \dfrac{a}{8}$ for $0 < a \leqslant 4$

$= 0$ otherwise

The graphs of the c.d.f.s of the length and the area are shown in figure 1.27.

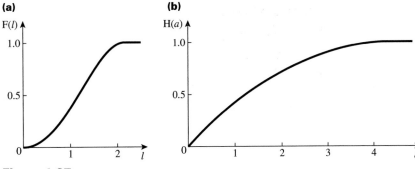

Figure 1.27

(a) $F(l) = \dfrac{l^2}{2} - \dfrac{l^4}{16}$ for $0 < l \leqslant 2$

        $= 1$ for $l > 2$.

(b) $H(a) = \dfrac{a}{2} - \dfrac{a^2}{16}$ for $0 < a \leqslant 4$

        $= 1$ for $a > 4$.

(v)   Mean $= E(A) = \displaystyle\int_0^4 ah(a)\,da$

$$= \int_0^4 \left(\frac{a}{2} - \frac{a^2}{8} \right) da$$

$$= \left[\frac{a^2}{4} - \frac{a^3}{24} \right]_0^4$$

$$= \frac{4}{3}$$

Note

This could also have been found as the mean of a function of a continuous random variable, using the general result

$$E[g(X)] = \int_{\substack{\text{All} \\ \text{values} \\ \text{of } x}} g(x)\,f(x)\,dx$$

where x is the length (not the area) of one of the squares.

In this case $g(x) = x^2$ $f(x) = \dfrac{x}{4}(4 - x^2)$ and $0 < x \leqslant 2$,

giving $E[g(X)] = \displaystyle\int_0^2 x^2 \frac{x}{4}(4 - x^2)\,dx$

$$= \int_0^2 \left(x^3 - \frac{x^5}{4} \right) dx$$

$$= \left[\frac{x^4}{4} - \frac{x^6}{24} \right]_0^2$$

$$= 4 - \frac{64}{24} = \frac{4}{3}$$

i.e. the same answer.

e The Normal distribution

The continuous random variable with which you are probably most familiar is Z, which has the standardised Normal distribution.

Remember that a value z is calculated from the actual data value, x, by using the transformation

$$z = \frac{x - \mu}{\sigma}$$

where μ is the population mean and σ is the population standard deviation.

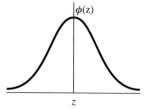

Figure 1.28

The p.d.f. of the Normal curve is given the special notation $\phi(z)$ and is given by

$$\phi(z) = \frac{1}{\sqrt{2\pi}}\, e^{-\frac{1}{2}z^2} \quad \text{for} \quad -\infty < z < \infty.$$

Consequently the cumulative distribution function, which is given the notation $\Phi(z)$, is given by

$$\Phi(z) = \frac{1}{\sqrt{2\pi}} \int_{-\infty}^{z} e^{-\frac{1}{2}u^2}\, du.$$

The function $\Phi(z)$ represents the probability of a value of Z less than or equal to z. That is

$$\Phi(z) = P(Z \leqslant z)$$

Unfortunately the integration cannot be carried out algebraically and so there is no neat expression for $\Phi(z)$. Instead the integration has been performed numerically for different values of z, and the results are given in the form of the well-known Normal distribution tables, see figure 1.29.

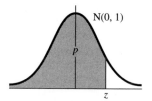

ADD

z	.00	.01	.02	.03	.04	.05	.06	.07	.08	.09	1	2	3	4	5	6	7	8	9
0.0	.5000	5040	5080	5120	5160	5199	5239	5279	5319	5359	4	8	12	16	20	24	28	32	36
0.1	.5398	5438	5478	5517	5557	5596	5636	5675	5714	5753	4	8	12	16	20	24	28	32	35
0.2	.5793	5832	5871	5910	5948	5987	6026	6064	6103	6141	4	8	12	15	19	23	27	31	35
0.3	.6179	6217	6255	6293	6331	6368	6406	6443	6480	6517	4	8	11	15	19	23	26	30	34
0.4	.6554	6591	6628	6664	6700	6736	6772	6808	6844	6879	4	7	11	14	18	22	25	29	32
0.5	.6915	6950	6985	7019	7054	7088	7123	7157	7190	7224	3	7	10	14	17	21	24	27	31
0.6	.7257	7291	7324	7357	7389	7422	7454	7486	7517	7549	3	6	10	13	16	19	23	26	29
0.7	.7580	761				7764	7794	7823	7852		3	6	9	12	15	18	21	24	27
0.8	7						78	8106	8133		3	6					19	22	25
							65	8280											23

Figure 1.29

The table gives the probability p of a random variable distributed as N(0, 1) being less than z.

1 The continuous random variable X has p.d.f. $f(x)$ where

$$f(x) = 0.2 \quad \text{for } 0 \leqslant x \leqslant 5$$
$$= 0 \quad \text{otherwise.}$$

   (i)   Find $E(X)$.
   (ii) Find the cumulative distribution function, $F(x)$.
   (iii) Find $P(0 \leqslant x \leqslant 2)$ using **(a)** $F(x)$ **(b)** $f(x)$
         and show your answer is the same by each method.

2 The continuous random variable U has p.d.f. $f(u)$ where

$$f(u) = ku \quad \text{for } 5 \leqslant u \leqslant 8$$
$$= 0 \quad \text{otherwise.}$$

   (i)   Find the value of k.
   (ii) Sketch $f(u)$.
   (iii) Find $F(u)$.
   (iv) Sketch the graph of $F(u)$.

3 A continuous random variable X has p.d.f. $f(x)$ where

$$f(x) = cx^2 \quad \text{for } 1 \leqslant x \leqslant 4$$
$$= 0 \quad \text{otherwise.}$$

   (i)   Find the value of c.
   (ii) Find $F(x)$.
   (iii) Find the median of X.
   (iv) Find the mode of X.

4 The continuous random variable X has p.d.f. $f(x)$ given by

$$f(x) = \frac{k}{(x+1)^4} \quad \text{for } x \geqslant 0$$
$$= 0 \quad \text{for } x < 0$$

   where k is a constant.
   (i)   Show that $k = 3$, and find the cumulative distribution function.
   (ii) Find also the value of x such that $P(X < x) = \frac{7}{8}$.

   [Cambridge]

5 The continuous random variable X has c.d.f. given by

$$F(x) = \begin{cases} 0 & \text{for } x < 0 \\ 2x - x^2 & \text{for } 0 \leqslant x \leqslant 1 \\ 1 & \text{for } x > 1. \end{cases}$$

   (i)   Find $P(X > 0.5)$.
   (ii) Find the value of q such that $P(X < q) = \frac{1}{4}$.
   (iii) Find the p.d.f. $f(x)$ of X, and sketch its graph.

   [Cambridge]

6 The continuous random variable X has p.d.f. $f(x)$ given by

$$f(x) = \begin{cases} k(4 - x^2) & \text{for } 0 \leqslant x \leqslant 2 \\ 0 & \text{otherwise} \end{cases}$$

where k is a constant.

Show that $k = \frac{3}{16}$ and find the values of $E(X)$ and $Var(X)$.

Find the cumulative distribution function for X, and verify by calculation that the median value of X is between 0.69 and 0.70.

[Cambridge]

7 A random variable X has p.d.f. $f(x)$ where

$$f(x) = 12x^2(1 - x) \quad \text{for } 0 \leqslant x \leqslant 1$$

and $\qquad\quad f(x) = 0 \qquad\qquad\qquad$ for all other x.

Find μ, the mean of X, and show that σ, the standard deviation of X, is $\frac{1}{5}$.
Show that $F(x)$, the probability that $X \leqslant x$ (for any value of x between 0 and 1), satisfies

$$F(x) = \begin{cases} 0 & \text{for } x < 0 \\ 4x^3 - 3x^4 & \text{for } 0 \leqslant x \leqslant 1 \\ 1 & \text{for } x > 1. \end{cases}$$

Use this result to show that $P(|X - \mu| < \sigma) = 0.64$.

What would this probability be if, instead, X were Normally distributed?

[MEI]

8 The temperature in degrees Celsius in a refrigerator which is operating properly has probability density function given by

$$f(t) = \begin{cases} kt^2(12 - t) & 0 < t < 12 \\ 0 & \text{otherwise.} \end{cases}$$

(i) Show that the value of k is $\frac{1}{1728}$.
(ii) Find the cumulative distribution function $F(t)$.
(iii) Show, by substitution, that the median temperature is about $7.37\,°C$.
(iv) The temperature in a refrigerator is too high if it is over $10\,°C$. Find the probability that this occurs.

[MEI]

9 The probability that a randomly chosen flight from Stanston Airport is delayed by more than x hours is

$$\frac{(x - 10)^2}{100} \quad \text{for } 0 \leqslant x \leqslant 10.$$

No flights leave early, and none is delayed for more than 10 hours. The delay, in hours, for a randomly chosen flight is denoted by X.

(i) Find the median, m, of X, correct to three significant figures.
(ii) Find the cumulative distribution function, F, of X and sketch the graph of F.
(iii) Find the probability density function, f, of X, and sketch the graph of f.
(iv) Show that $E(X) = \frac{10}{3}$.

[Cambridge]

10 A random variable X has p.d.f. $f(x)$, where

$$f(x) = k\sin 2x \quad \text{for } 0 \leqslant x \leqslant \frac{\pi}{2}$$

$$= 0 \qquad \text{otherwise.}$$

By integration find, in terms of x and the constant k, an expression for the cumulative distribution function of X for $0 \leqslant x \leqslant \frac{\pi}{2}$.

Hence show that $k = 1$ and find the probability that $X < \frac{\pi}{8}$.

[MEI]

11 On any day, the amount of time, measured in hours, that Mr Goggle spends watching television is a continuous random variable T, with cumulative distribution function given by

$$F(t) = \begin{cases} 0 & t < 0 \\ 1 - k(15 - t)^2 & 0 \leqslant t \leqslant 15 \\ 1 & t > 15 \end{cases}$$

where k is a constant.

(i) Show that $k = \frac{1}{225}$ and find $P(5 \leqslant T \leqslant 10)$.

(ii) Show that, for $0 \leqslant t \leqslant 15$, the probability density function of T is given by

$$f(t) = \frac{2}{15} - \frac{2t}{225}.$$

(iii) Find the median of T.

(iv) Find $\text{Var}(T)$.

[Cambridge]

12 The time, T minutes, between customer arrivals at a country store, from Monday to Friday, can be modelled, for $t \geqslant 0$, by the probability density function $f(t)$ defined by

$$f(t) = 0.1\,e^{-0.1t}.$$

(i) Find the probability that the time between arrivals is

(a) less than 5 minutes   **(b)** more than 15 minutes

illustrating these probabilities on a sketch of the graph of $f(t)$.

(ii) Obtain the cumulative distribution function for T. Hence find the median time between arrivals.

The time, T minutes, between customer arrivals at the country store on Saturdays can be modelled by the probability density function $g(t)$ defined by

$$g(t) = \lambda e^{-\lambda t}$$

where λ is a positive constant.

(iii) On Saturdays, the probability of the time between customer arrivals exceeding 5 minutes is 0.4. Estimate the value of λ.

[MEI]

13 A firm has a large number of employees. The distance in miles they have to travel each day from home to work can be modelled by a continuous random variable X whose **cumulative distribution function** is given by

$$F(1) = 0$$

$$F(x) = k\left(1 - \frac{1}{x}\right) \quad 1 \leqslant x \leqslant b$$

$$F(b) = 1$$

where b represents the farthest distance anybody lives from work.

The diagram below shows a sketch of this cumulative distribution function.

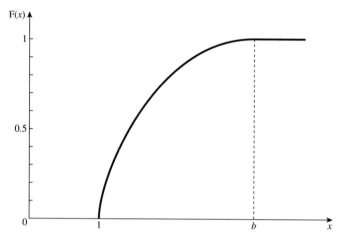

A survey suggests that $b = 5$. Use this parameter for parts (i) to (iv).

(i) Show that $k = 1.25$.

(ii) Write down and solve an equation to find the median distance travelled to work.

(iii) Find the probability that an employee lives within half a mile of the median.

(iv) Derive the probability density function for X and illustrate it with a sketch.

(v) Show that, for any value of b greater than 1, the median distance travelled does not exceed 2.

[MEI]

14 The wages department of a large company models the incomes of the employees by the continuous random variable X with cumulative distribution function

$$F(x) = 1 - \left(\frac{3}{x}\right)^4 \quad 3 \leqslant x < \infty$$

where X is measured in an arbitrary currency unit. (X is said to have a Pareto distribution.)

(i) Find the median income. Find also the smallest income of an employee in the top 10% of incomes.

(ii) Find the probability density function of X and hence show that the mean income is 4.

(iii) Find the probability that a randomly chosen employee earns more than the mean income.

[MEI]

15 A continuous random variable X has probability density function $f(x)$. The probability that $X \leqslant x$ is given by the function $F(x)$.

Explain why $F'(x) = f(x)$.

A rod of length $2a$ is broken into two parts at a point whose position is random. State the form of the probability distribution of the length of the smaller part, and state also the mean value of this length.

Two equal rods, each of length $2a$, are broken into two parts at points whose positions are random. X is the length of the shortest of the four parts thus obtained. Find the probability, $F(x)$, that $X \leqslant x$, where $0 < x \leqslant a$. Hence, or otherwise, show that the probability density function of X is given by

$$f(x) = \frac{2(a - x)}{a^2} \quad \text{for } 0 < x \leqslant a$$
$$= 0 \quad \text{for } x \leqslant 0, \ x > a.$$

Show that the mean value of X is $\frac{1}{3}a$.

Write down the mean value of the sum of the two smaller parts and show that the mean values of the four parts are in the proportions $1 : 2 : 4 : 5$.

[JMB]

16 (i) Explain the significance of the results:

(a) $\displaystyle\int_{-\infty}^{\infty} \frac{1}{\sqrt{2\pi}}\, e^{-\frac{1}{2}z^2}\, dz = 1$ **(b)** $\displaystyle\int_{-\infty}^{\infty} \frac{1}{\sqrt{2\pi}}\, z e^{-\frac{1}{2}z^2}\, dz = 0.$

The random variable Y is given by $Y = Z^2$ (where Z is the standardised Normal variable).

(ii) Using the results in part (i), find

    (a) $E(Y)$ **(b)** Var (Y).

    (You will need to use integration by parts.)

17 The random variable Y is given by $Y = Z^2$ (where Z is the standardised Normal variable).

(i) State the range of values Y may take.

(ii) Explain carefully why $P(Y \leqslant y) = 2P(0 \leqslant Z \leqslant \sqrt{y})$.

Let $G(y)$ denote the cumulative distribution function for Y.

(iii) Show that $G(y) = 2(\Phi(\sqrt{y}) - \frac{1}{2})$.

(iv) Differentiate the result in part (iii) to show that the p.d.f. of Y is

$$g(y) = \frac{1}{\sqrt{2\pi y}}\, e^{-\frac{1}{2}y} \quad y \geqslant 0.$$

Note: for interest, the random variable Y has the χ^2 distribution with $v = 1$.

1 If X is a continuous random variable with p.d.f. $f(x)$

- $\int f(x)\,dx = 1$
- $f(x) \geqslant 0$ for all x
- $P(c \leqslant x \leqslant d = \int_c^d f(x)\,dx$
- $E(X) = \int x f(x)\,dx$
- $\text{Var}(X) = \int x^2 f(x)\,dx - [E(X)]^2$
- The mode of X is the value for which $f(x)$ has its greatest magnitude.

2 If $g[X]$ is a function of X then

- $E(g[X]) = \int g[x]f(x)\,dx$
- $\text{Var}(g[X]) = \int (g[x])^2 f(x)\,dx - [E(g[X])]^2$

3 **The cumulative distribution function**

- $F(x) = \int_a^x f(u)\,du$ where the constant a is the lower limit of X.
- $f(x) = \dfrac{d}{dx} F(x)$
- For the median, m, $F(m) = 0.5$

4 **The uniform (rectangular) distribution over the interval (a, b)**

- $f(x) = \dfrac{1}{b-a}$
- $E(X) = \frac{1}{2}(a+b)$
- $\text{Var}(X) = \dfrac{(b-a)^2}{12}$

e **The exponential distribution**

- $f(x) = \lambda e^{-\lambda x}$ for $x \geqslant 0$
- $E(X) = \dfrac{1}{\lambda}$
- $\text{Var}(X) = \dfrac{1}{\lambda^2}$

e **The Normal distribution**

- $f(z) = \phi(z) = \dfrac{1}{\sqrt{2\pi}} e^{-\frac{1}{2}z^2}$ $-\infty < z < \infty$
- $F(z) = \Phi(z) = \displaystyle\int_{-\infty}^z \dfrac{1}{\sqrt{2\pi}} e^{-\frac{1}{2}u^2}\,du$ $-\infty < z < \infty$

Expectation algebra

To approach zero defects, you must have statistical control of processes.

David Wilson

THE AVONFORD STAR

Unfair dismissal

'It was just one of those days', Janice Baptiste told the court. 'Everything went wrong. First the school bus arrived 5 minutes late to pick up my little boy. Then it was wet and slippery and there were so many people about that I just couldn't walk at my normal speed; usually I take 15 minutes but that day it took me 18 to get to work. And then when I got to work I had to wait $3\frac{1}{2}$ minutes for the lift instead of the usual $\frac{1}{2}$ minute. So instead of arriving my normal 10 minutes early I was 1 minute late.'

'Mrs Dickens just wouldn't listen', Janice went on. 'She said she did not employ people to make excuses and told me to leave there and then.'

Mrs Baptiste's bad morning turned a lot worse when her boss fired her

Like Janice, we all have days when everything goes wrong at once. There were three random variables involved in her arrival time at work: the time she had to wait for the school bus, S; the time she took to walk to work, W, and the time she had to wait for the lift, L.

Her total time for getting to work, T, was the sum of all three:

$$T = S + W + L.$$

Janice's case was essentially that the probability of T taking such a large value was very small. To estimate that probability you would need information about the distributions of the three random variables involved. You would also need to know how to handle the sum of two or more (in this case three) random variables.

The expectation of a function of *X*, E(g[*X*])

However, before you can do this, you need to extend some of the work you did in *Statistics 1* on random variables. There you learnt that, for a discrete random variable X with $P(X = x_i) = p_i$,

its expectation $= E(X) = \mu = \Sigma x_i \times P(X = x_i) = \Sigma x_i p_i$

and its variance $= \sigma^2 = E[(X - \mu)^2] = \Sigma(x_i - \mu)^2 \times P(X = x_i) = \Sigma(x_i - \mu)^2 p_i$

$$= E(X^2) - E[(X)]^2 = \Sigma x_i^2 \times P(X = x_i) - \mu^2 = \Sigma x_i^2 p_i - \mu^2$$

This only finds the expected value and variance of a particular random variable.

Sometimes you will need to find the expectation of a function of a random variable. That sounds rather forbidding and you may think the same of the definition given below at first sight. However, as you will see in the next two examples, the procedure is straightforward and common sense.

If $g[X]$ is a function of the discrete random variable X then $E(g[X])$ is given by

$$E(g[X]) = \sum_i g[x_i] \times P(X = x_i).$$

EXAMPLE 2.1

What is the expectation of the square of the number that comes up when a fair die is rolled?

SOLUTION

Let the random variable X be the number that comes up when the die is rolled.

$$g[X] = X^2$$

$$E(g[X]) = E(X^2) = \sum_i x_i^2 \times P(X = x_i)$$

$$= 1^2 \times \tfrac{1}{6} + 2^2 \times \tfrac{1}{6} + 3^2 \times \tfrac{1}{6} + 4^2 \times \tfrac{1}{6} + 5^2 \times \tfrac{1}{6} + 6^2 \times \tfrac{1}{6}$$

$$= 1 \times \tfrac{1}{6} + 4 \times \tfrac{1}{6} + 9 \times \tfrac{1}{6} + 16 \times \tfrac{1}{6} + 25 \times \tfrac{1}{6} + 36 \times \tfrac{1}{6}$$

$$= \tfrac{91}{6}$$

$$= 15.17$$

Note

This calculation could also have been set out in table form as shown below.

X_i	$P(X = x_i)$	x_i^2	$x_i^2 \times P(X = x)$
1	$\frac{1}{6}$	1	$\frac{1}{6}$
2	$\frac{1}{6}$	4	$\frac{4}{6}$
3	$\frac{1}{6}$	9	$\frac{9}{6}$
4	$\frac{1}{6}$	16	$\frac{16}{6}$
5	$\frac{1}{6}$	25	$\frac{25}{6}$
6	$\frac{1}{6}$	36	$\frac{36}{6}$
Total			$\frac{91}{6}$

$$E(g[X]) = \tfrac{91}{6} = 15.17$$

? $E(X^2)$ is not the same as $[E(X)]^2$. In this case $15.57 \neq 3.5^2$ which is 12.25. In fact, the difference between $E(X^2)$ and $[E(X)]^2$ is very important in statistics. Why is this?

EXAMPLE 2.2

A random variable X has the following probability distribution.

Outcome	1	2	3
Probability	0.4	0.4	0.2

(i) Calculate $E(4X + 5)$.

(ii) Calculate $4E(X) + 5$.

(iii) Comment on the relationship between your answers to parts (i) and (ii).

SOLUTION

(i) $E(g[X]) = \sum_i g[x_i] \times P(X = x_i)$ with $g[X] = 4X + 5$

x_i	1	2	3
$g[x_i]$	9	13	17
$P(X = x_i)$	0.4	0.4	0.2

$$E(4X + 5) = E(g[X])$$
$$= 9 \times 0.4 + 13 \times 0.4 + 17 \times 0.2$$
$$= 12.2$$

(ii) $E(X) = 1 \times 0.4 + 2 \times 0.4 + 3 \times 0.2 = 1.8$

and so
$$E(X) + 5 = 4 \times 1.8 + 5$$
$$= 12.2$$

(iii) Clearly $E(4X + 5) = 4E(X) + 5$, both having the value 12.2.

Expectation: algebraic results

In Example 2.2 above you found that $E(4X + 5) = 4E(X) + 5$.

The working was numerical, showing that both expressions came out to be 12.2, but it could also have been shown algebraically. This would have been set out as follows.

Proof	*Reasons (general rules)*
$E(4X + 5) = E(4X) + E(5)$	$E(X \pm Y) = E(X) \pm E(Y)$
$= 4E(X) + E(5)$	$E(aX) = aE(X)$
$= 4E(X) + 5$	$E(c) = c$

Look at the general rules on the right-hand side of the page. (X and Y are random variables, a and c are constants.) They are important but they are also common sense.

Notice the last one, which in this case means the expectation of 5 is 5. Of course it is; 5 cannot be anything else but 5. It is so obvious that sometimes people find it confusing!

These rules can be extended to take in the expectation of the sum of two functions of a random variable.

$$E(f[X] + g[X]) = E(f[X]) + E(g[X])$$

where f and g are both functions of X.

Proof

By definition

$$E(f[X] + g[X]) = \sum_i (f[x_i] + g[x_i]) \times P(X = x_i)$$

$$= \sum_i f[x_i] \times P(X = x_i) + \sum_i g[x_i] \times P(X = x_i)$$

$$= E(f[X]) + E(g[X])$$

EXAMPLE 2.3

The random variable X has the following probability distribution.

x	1	2	3	4
$P(X = x)$	0.6	0.2	0.1	0.1

Find

(i) $\text{Var}(X)$ **(ii)** $\text{Var}(7)$ **(iii)** $\text{Var}(3X)$ **(iv)** $\text{Var}(3X+7)$.

What general results do the answers to parts (ii) to (iv) illustrate?

SOLUTION

(i)

x	1	2	3	4
x^2	1	4	9	16
$P(X = x)$	0.6	0.2	0.1	0.1

$$E(X) = 1 \times 0.6 + 2 \times 0.2 + 3 \times 0.1 + 4 \times 0.1$$
$$= 1.7$$
$$E(X^2) = 1 \times 0.6 + 4 \times 0.2 + 9 \times 0.1 + 16 \times 0.1$$
$$= 3.9$$
$$\text{Var}(X) = E(X^2) - [E(X)]^2$$
$$= 3.9 - 1.7^2$$
$$= 1.01$$

(ii) $\text{Var}(7) = \text{E}(7^2) - [\text{E}(7)]^2$

$= \text{E}(49) - [7]^2$

$= 49 - 49$

$= 0$

General result

$\text{Var}(c) = 0$ for a constant c.

This result is obvious; a constant is constant and so can have no spread.

(iii) $\text{Var}(3X) = \text{E}[(3X)^2] - \mu^2$

$= \text{E}(9X^2) - [\text{E}(3X)]^2$

$= 9\text{E}(X^2) - [3\text{E}(X)]^2$

$= 9 \times 3.9 - (3 \times 1.7)^2$

$= 35.1 - 26.01$

$= 9.09$

General result

$\text{Var}(aX) = a^2\text{Var}(X)$.

Notice that it is a^2 and not a on the right-hand side, but that taking the square root of each side gives the standard deviation $(aX) = a \times$ standard deviation (X) as you would expect from common sense.

(iv) $\text{Var}(3X + 7)$

$= \text{E}[(3X + 7)^2]$

$\quad - [\text{E}(3X + 7)]^2$

$= \text{E}(9X^2 + 42X + 49)$

$\quad - [3\text{E}(X) + 7]^2$

$= \text{E}(9X^2) + \text{E}(42X) + \text{E}(49)$

$\quad - [3 \times 1.7 + 7]^2$

$= 9\text{E}(X^2) + 42\text{E}(X)$

$\quad + 49 - 12.1^2$

$= 9 \times 3.9 + 42 \times 1.7$

$\quad + 49 - 146.41$

$= 9.09$

General result

$\text{Var}(aX + c) = a^2\text{Var}(X)$.

Notice that the constant c does not appear on the right-hand side.

1 The probability distribution of random variable X is as follows.

x	1	2	3	4	5
$P(X = x)$	0.1	0.2	0.3	0.3	0.1

(i) Find **(a)** $\text{E}(X)$ **(b)** $\text{Var}(X)$.

(ii) Verify that $\text{Var}(2X) = 4\text{Var}(X)$.

2 The probability distribution of a random variable X is as follows.

x	0	1	2
$P(X = x)$	0.5	0.3	0.2

(i) Find **(a)** $\text{E}(X)$ **(b)** $\text{Var}(X)$.

(ii) Verify that $\text{Var}(5X + 2) = 25\text{Var}(X)$.

3 Prove that $\text{Var}(aX - b) = a^2 \text{Var}(X)$ where a and b are constants.

4 A coin is biased so that the probability of obtaining a tail is 0.75. The coin is tossed four times and the random variable X is the number of tails obtained. Find

(i) $\text{E}(2X)$

(ii) $\text{Var}(3X)$.

5 A discrete random variable W has the following distribution.

x	1	2	3	4	5	6
$\mathbf{P}(W = w)$	0.1	0.2	0.1	0.2	0.1	0.3

Find the mean and variance of

(i) $W + 7$

(ii) $6W - 5$.

6 The random variable X is the number of heads obtained when four unbiased coins are tossed. Construct the probability distribution for X and find

(i) $\text{E}(X)$

(ii) $\text{Var}(X)$

(iii) $\text{Var}(3X + 4)$.

7 The discrete random variable X has probability distribution given by

$$P(X = x) = \frac{(4x + 7)}{68} \quad \text{for } x = 1, 2, 3, 4.$$

(i) Find **(a)** $\text{E}(X)$ **(b)** $\text{E}(X^2)$ **(c)** $\text{E}(X^2 + 5X - 2)$.

(ii) Verify that $\text{E}(X^2 + 5X - 2) = \text{E}(X^2) + 5\text{E}(X) - 2$.

8 A bag contains four balls, numbered 2, 4, 6, 8 but identical in all other respects. One ball is chosen at random and the number on it is denoted by N, so that $P(N = 2) = P(N = 4) = P(N = 6) = P(N = 8) = \frac{1}{4}$. Show that $\mu = \text{E}(N) = 5$ and $\sigma^2 = \text{Var}(N) = 5$.

Two balls are chosen at random one after the other, with the first ball being replaced after it has been drawn. Let $\overline{N}$ be the arithmetic mean of the numbers on the two balls. List the possible values of $\overline{N}$ and their probabilities of being obtained. Hence evaluate $\text{E}(\overline{N})$ and $\text{Var}(\overline{N})$.

[MEI]

The sums and differences of independent random variables

Sometimes, as in the case of Janice in the *Avonford Star* article on page 53, you may need to add or subtract a number of independent random variables. This process is illustrated in the next example.

EXAMPLE 2.4

The possible lengths (in cm) of the blades of cricket bats form a discrete uniform distribution:

$$38, 40, 42, 44, 46.$$

The possible lengths (in cm) of the handles of cricket bats also form a discrete uniform distribution:

$$22, 24, 26.$$

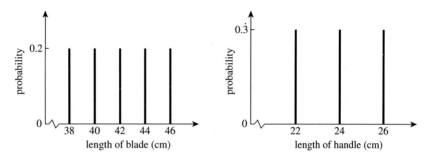

Figure 2.1

The blades and handles can be joined together to make bats of various lengths, and it may be assumed that the lengths of the two sections are independent.

(i) How many different (total) bat lengths are possible?

(ii) Work out the mean and variance of random variable X_1, the length (in cm) of the blades.

(iii) Work out the mean and variance of random variable X_2, the length (in cm) of the handles.

(iv) Work out the mean and variance of random variable $X_1 + X_2$, the total length of the bats.

(v) Verify that

$$\mathrm{E}(X_1 + X_2) = \mathrm{E}(X_1) + \mathrm{E}(X_2)$$

and $\qquad \mathrm{Var}(X_1 + X_2) = \mathrm{Var}(X_1) + \mathrm{Var}(X_2).$

SOLUTION

(i) The number of different bat lengths is 7. This can be seen from the sample space diagram below.

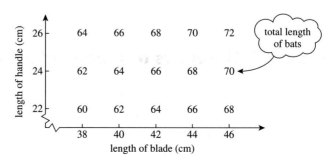

Figure 2.2

(ii)

Length of blade (cm)	38	40	42	44	46
Probability	0.2	0.2	0.2	0.2	0.2

$E(X_1), \mu_1 = \Sigma xp = (38 \times 0.2) + (40 \times 0.2) + (42 \times 0.2) + (44 \times 0.2)$
$$+ (46 \times 0.2)$$
$$= 42 \, \text{cm}$$

$Var(X_1) = E(X_1^2) - \mu_1^2$

$E(X_1^2) = (38^2 \times 0.2) + (40^2 \times 0.2) + (42^2 \times 0.2) + (44^2 \times 0.2)$
$$+ (46^2 \times 0.2)$$
$$= 1772$$

$Var(X_1) = 1772 - 42^2 = 8$

(iii)

Length of handle (cm)	22	24	26
Probability	$\frac{1}{3}$	$\frac{1}{3}$	$\frac{1}{3}$

$E(X_2), \mu_2 = (22 \times \frac{1}{3}) + (24 \times \frac{1}{3}) + (26 \times \frac{1}{3}) = 24 \, \text{cm}$

$Var(X_2) = E(X_2^2) - \mu_2^2$

$E(X_2^2) = (22^2 \times \frac{1}{3}) + (24^2 \times \frac{1}{3}) + (26^2 \times \frac{1}{3}) = 578.667 \text{ to 3 d.p.}$

$Var(X_2) = 578.667 - 24^2 = 2.667 \text{ to 3 d.p.}$

(iv) The probability distribution of $X_1 + X_2$ can be obtained from figure 2.2.

Total length of cricket bat (cm)	60	62	64	66	68	70	72
Probability	$\frac{1}{15}$	$\frac{2}{15}$	$\frac{3}{15}$	$\frac{3}{15}$	$\frac{3}{15}$	$\frac{2}{15}$	$\frac{1}{15}$

$E(X_1 + X_2) = (60 \times \frac{1}{15}) + (62 \times \frac{2}{15}) + (64 \times \frac{3}{15}) + (66 \times \frac{3}{15}) + (68 \times \frac{3}{15})$
$$+ (70 \times \frac{2}{15}) + (72 \times \frac{1}{15})$$
$$= 66 \, \text{cm}$$

$Var(X_1 + X_2) = E[(X_1 + X_2)^2] - 66^2$

$E[(X_1 + X_2)^2] = (60^2 \times \frac{1}{15}) + (62^2 \times \frac{2}{15}) + (64^2 \times \frac{3}{15}) + (66^2 \times \frac{3}{15})$
$$+ (68^2 \times \frac{3}{15}) + (70^2 \times \frac{2}{15}) + (72^2 \times \frac{1}{15})$$
$$= \frac{65\,500}{15} = 4366.667 \text{ to 3 d.p.}$$

$Var(X_1 + X_2) = 4366.667 - 66^2 = 10.667 \text{ to 3 d.p.}$

(v) $E(X_1 + X_2) = 66 = 42 + 24 = E(X_1) + E(X_2)$, as required.

$Var(X_1 + X_2) = 10.667 = 8 + 2.667 = Var(X_1) + Var(X_2)$, as required.

Note

You should notice that the standard deviations of X_1 and X_2 do not add up to the standard deviation of $X_1 + X_2$

$$\sqrt{8} + \sqrt{2.667} \neq \sqrt{10.667}$$

i.e. $\qquad 2.828 + 1.633 \neq 3.266$

General results

Example 2.4 has illustrated the following general results for the sums and differences of random variables.

For any two random variables X_1 and X_2

- $E(X_1 + X_2) = E(X_1) + E(X_2)$

Replacing X_2 by $-X_2$ in this result gives

$\qquad E(X_1 + (-X_2)) = E(X_1) + E(-X_2)$

- $E(X_1 - X_2) = E(X_1) - E(X_2)$

If the variables X_1 and X_2 are independent then

- $\mathrm{Var}(X_1 + X_2) = \mathrm{Var}(X_1) + \mathrm{Var}(X_2)$

Replacing X_2 by $-X_2$ gives

$\qquad \mathrm{Var}(X_1 + (-X_2)) = \mathrm{Var}(X_1) + \mathrm{Var}(-X_2)$
$\qquad \mathrm{Var}(X_1 + (-X_2)) = \mathrm{Var}(X_1) + (-1)^2\mathrm{Var}(X_2)$

- $\mathrm{Var}(X_1 - X_2) = \mathrm{Var}(X_1) + \mathrm{Var}(X_2)$

The sums and differences of Normal variables

If the variables X_1 and X_2 are Normally distributed, then the distributions of $(X_1 + X_2)$ and $(X_1 - X_2)$ are also Normal. The means of these distributions are $E(X_1) + E(X_2)$ and $E(X_1) - E(X_2)$.

You must, however, be careful when you come to their variances, since you may only use the result that

$$\mathrm{Var}(X_1 \pm X_2) = \mathrm{Var}(X_1) + \mathrm{Var}(X_2)$$

to find the variances of these distributions if the variables X_1 and X_2 are independent.

This is the situation in the next two examples.

EXAMPLE 2.5

Robert Fisher, a keen chess player, visits his local club most days. The total time taken to drive to the club and back is modelled by a Normal variable with mean 25 minutes and standard deviation 3 minutes. The time spent at the chess club is also modelled by a Normal variable with mean 120 minutes and standard deviation 10 minutes. Find the probability that on a certain evening Mr Fisher is away from home for more than $2\frac{1}{2}$ hours.

SOLUTION

Let the random variable $X_1 \sim N(25, 3^2)$ represent the driving time, and the random variable $X_2 \sim N(120, 10^2)$ represent the time spent at the chess club.

Then the random variable T, where $T = X_1 + X_2 \sim N(145, (\sqrt{109})^2)$, represents his total time away.

So the probability that Mr Fisher is away for more than $2\frac{1}{2}$ hours (150 minutes) is given by

$$P(T > 150) = 1 - \Phi\left(\frac{150 - 145}{\sqrt{109}}\right)$$

$$= 1 - \Phi(0.479)$$

$$= 0.316$$

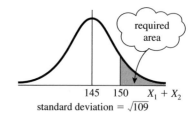

Figure 2.3

EXAMPLE 2.6

In the manufacture of a bridge made entirely from wood, circular pegs have to fit into circular holes. The diameters of the pegs are Normally distributed with mean 1.60 cm and standard deviation 0.01 cm, while the diameters of the holes are Normally distributed with mean 1.65 cm and standard deviation of 0.02 cm. What is the probability that a randomly chosen peg will not fit into a randomly chosen hole?

SOLUTION

Let the random variable X be the diameter of a hole:

$$X \sim N(1.65, 0.02^2) = N(1.65, 0.0004).$$

Let the random variable Y be the diameter of a peg:

$$Y \sim N(1.60, 0.01^2) = N(1.6, 0.0001).$$

Let $F = X - Y$. F represents the gap remaining between the peg and the hole and so the sign of F determines whether or not a peg will fit in a hole.

$$E(F) = E(X) - E(Y) = 1.65 - 1.60 = 0.05$$

$$Var(F) = Var(X) + Var(Y) = 0.0004 + 0.0001 = 0.0005$$

$$F \sim N(0.05, 0.0005)$$

If for any combination of peg and hole the value of F is negative, then the peg will not fit into the hole.

The probability that $F < 0$ is given by

$$\Phi\left(\frac{0 - 0.05}{\sqrt{0.0005}}\right) = \Phi(-2.236)$$

$$= 1 - 0.9873$$

$$= 0.0127.$$

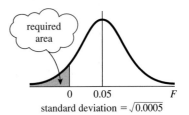

standard deviation $= \sqrt{0.0005}$

Figure 2.4

1 The menu at a cafe is shown below.

Main course		*Dessert*	
Fish and Chips	£3	Ice Cream	£1
Bacon and Eggs	£3.50	Apple Pie	£1.50
Pizza	£4	Sponge Pudding	£2
Steak and Chips	£5.50		

The owner of the cafe says that all the main-course dishes sell equally well, as do all the desserts, and that customers' choice of dessert is not influenced by the main course they have just eaten.

The variable M denotes the cost of the items for the main course, in pounds, and the variable D the cost of the items for the dessert. The variable T denotes the total cost of a two-course meal: $T = M + D$.

(i) Find the mean and variance of M.

(ii) Find the mean and variance of D.

(iii) List all the possible two-course meals, giving the price for each one.

(iv) Use your answer to part (iii) to find the mean and variance of T.

(v) Hence verify that for these figures

$$\text{mean } (T) = \text{mean } (M) + \text{mean } (D)$$

and variance $(T) = $ variance $(M) + $ variance (D).

2 X_1 and X_2 are independent random variables with distributions N(50, 16) and N(40, 9) respectively. Write down the distributions of

(i) $X_1 + X_2$ (ii) $X_1 - X_2$ (iii) $X_2 - X_1$.

3 A play is enjoying a long run at a theatre. It is found that the playing time may be modelled as a Normal variable with mean 130 minutes and standard deviation 3 minutes, and that the length of the intermission in the middle of the performance may be modelled by a Normal variable with mean 15 minutes and standard deviation 5 minutes. Find the probability that the performance is completed in less than 140 minutes.

4 The time Melanie spends on her history assignments may be modelled as being Normally distributed, with mean 40 minutes and standard deviation 10 minutes. The times taken on assignments may be assumed to be independent. Find
(i) the probability that a particular assignment will last longer than an hour
(ii) the time in which 95% of all assignments can be completed
(iii) the probability that two assignments will be completed in less than 75 minutes.

5 The weights of full cans of a particular brand of pet food may be taken to be Normally distributed, with mean 260 g and standard deviation 10 g. The weights of the empty cans may be taken to be Normally distributed, with mean 30 g and standard deviation 2 g. Find
(i) the mean and standard deviation of the weights of the contents of the cans
(ii) the probability that a full can weighs more than 270 g
(iii) the probability that two full cans together weigh more than 540 g.

6 The independent random variables X_1 and X_2 are distributed as follows:

$$X_1 \sim N(30, 9); \quad X_2 \sim N(40, 16).$$

Find the distributions of the following:
(i) $X_1 + X_2$
(ii) $X_1 - X_2$.

7 In a vending machine the capacity of cups is Normally distributed, with mean 200 cm^3 and standard deviation 4 cm^3. The volume of coffee discharged per cup is Normally distributed, with mean 190 cm^3 and standard deviation 5 cm^3. Find the percentage of drinks which overflow.

8 On a distant island the heights of adult men and women may both be taken to be Normally distributed, with means 173 cm and 165 cm and standard deviations 10 cm and 8 cm respectively.
(i) Find the probability that a randomly chosen woman is taller than a randomly chosen man.
(ii) Do you think that this is equivalent to the probability that a married woman is taller than her husband?

9 The lifetimes of a certain brand of refrigerator are approximately Normally distributed, with mean 2000 days and standard deviation 250 days. Mrs Chudasama and Mr Poole each buy one on the same date.

What is the probability that Mr Poole's refrigerator is still working one year after Mrs Chudasama's refrigerator has broken down?

10 A random sample of size 2 is chosen from a Normal distribution N(100, 10). Find the probability that
(i) the sum of the sample numbers exceeds 225
(ii) the first observation is at least 12 more than the second observation.

More than two independent random variables

The results on page 61 may be generalised to give the mean and variance of the sums and differences of n random variables, $X_1, X_2, \ldots, X_n$.

- $E(X_1 \pm X_2 \pm \ldots \pm X_n) = E(X_1) \pm E(X_2) \pm \ldots \pm E(X_n)$

and, provided $X_1, X_2, \ldots, X_n$ are independent,

- $\text{Var}(X_1 \pm X_2 \pm \ldots \pm X_n) = \text{Var}(X_1) + \text{Var}(X_2) + \ldots + \text{Var}(X_n)$.

If $X_1, X_2, \ldots, X_n$ is a set of Normally distributed variables, then the distribution of $(X_1 \pm X_2 \pm \ldots \pm X_n)$ is also Normal.

EXAMPLE 2.7

The mass, X, of a suitcase at an airport is modelled as being Normally distributed, with mean 15 kg and standard deviation 3 kg. Find the probability that a random sample of ten suitcases weighs more than 154 kg.

SOLUTION

The mass X of one suitcase is given by

$$X \sim N(15, 9).$$

Then the mass of each of the ten suitcases has the distribution of X; call them $X_1, X_2, \ldots, X_{10}$.

Let the random variable T be the total weight of ten suitcases.

$$T = X_1 + X_2 + \ldots + X_{10}.$$
$$E(T) = E(X_1) + E(X_2) + \ldots + E(X_{10})$$
$$= 15 + 15 + \ldots + 15$$
$$= 150$$

Similarly
$$\text{Var}(T) = \text{Var}(X_1) + \text{Var}(X_2) + \ldots + \text{Var}(X_{10})$$
$$= 9 + 9 + \ldots + 9$$
$$= 90$$

So $T \sim N(150, 90)$

The probability that T exceeds 154 is given by

$$1 - \Phi\left(\frac{154 - 150}{\sqrt{90}}\right)$$
$$= 1 - \Phi(0.422)$$
$$= 1 - 0.6635$$
$$= 0.3365$$

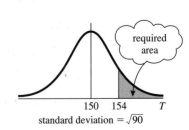

required area

150 154 T

standard deviation $= \sqrt{90}$

Figure 2.5

EXAMPLE 2.8

The running times of the four members of a 4×400 m relay race may all be taken to be Normally distributed, as follows.

Member	Mean time (s)	Standard deviation (s)
Adil	52	1
Brian	53	1
Colin	55	1.5
Dexter	51	0.5

Assuming that no time is lost during changeovers, find the probability that the team finishes the race in less than 3 minutes 28 seconds.

SOLUTION

Let the total time be T.

$$E(T) = 52 + 53 + 55 + 51 = 211$$
$$Var(T) = 1^2 + 1^2 + 1.5^2 + 0.5^2$$
$$= 1 + 1 + 2.25 + 0.25 = 4.5$$

So $T \sim N(211, 4.5)$.

The probability of a total time of less than 3 minutes 28 seconds (208 seconds) is given by

$$\Phi\left(\frac{208 - 211}{\sqrt{4.5}}\right) = \Phi(-1.414)$$
$$= 1 - 0.9213$$
$$= 0.0787$$

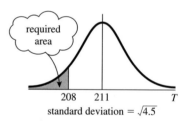

Figure 2.6

Linear combinations of two or more independent random variables

The results given on page 61 can also be generalised to include linear combinations of random variables.

For any random variables X and Y,

- $E(aX + bY) = aE(X) + bE(Y)$, where a and b are constants.

If X and Y are independent

- $Var(aX + bY) = a^2 Var(X) + b^2 Var(Y)$.

If the distributions of X and Y are Normal, then the distribution of $(aX + bY)$ is also Normal.

These results may be extended to any number of random variables.

EXAMPLE 2.9

In a workshop joiners cut out rectangular sheets of laminated board, of length L cm and width W cm, to be made into work surfaces. Both L and W may be taken to be Normally distributed with standard deviation 1.5 cm. The mean of L is 150 cm, that of W is 60 cm, and the lengths of L and W are independent. Both of the short sides and one of the long sides have to be covered by a protective strip (the other long side is to lie against a wall and so does not need protection).

What is the probability that a protecting strip 275 cm long will be too short for a randomly selected work surface?

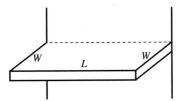

Figure 2.7

SOLUTION

Denoting the length and width by the independent random variables L and W and the total length of strip required by T:

$$T = L + 2W$$
$$E(T) = E(L) + 2E(W)$$
$$= 150 + 2 \times 60$$
$$= 270$$
$$Var(T) = Var(L) + 2^2 Var(W)$$
$$= 1.5^2 + 4 \times 1.5^2$$
$$= 11.25$$

The probability of a strip 275 cm long being too short is given by

$$1 - \Phi\left(\frac{275 - 270}{\sqrt{11.25}}\right) = 1 - \Phi(1.491)$$
$$= 1 - 0.932$$
$$= 0.068.$$

Note

You have to distinguish carefully between the random variable $2W$, which means twice the size of one observation of the random variable W, and the random variable $W_1 + W_2$, which is the sum of two independent observations of the random variable W.

In the last example $\quad E(2W) = 2E(W) = 120$

and $\quad Var(2W) = 2^2 Var(W) = 4 \times 2.25 = 9.$

In contrast, $\quad E(W_1 + W_2) = E(W_1) + E(W_2) = 60 + 60 = 120$

and $\quad Var(W_1 + W_2) = Var(W_1) + Var(W_2) = 2.25 + 2.25 = 4.5.$

EXAMPLE 2.10

A machine produces sheets of paper the thicknesses of which are Normally distributed with mean 0.1 mm and standard deviation 0.006 mm.

(i) State the distribution of the total thickness of eight randomly selected sheets of paper.

(ii) Single sheets of paper are folded three times (to give eight thicknesses). State the distribution of the total thickness.

SOLUTION

Denote the thickness of one sheet (in mm) by the random variable W, and the total thickness of eight sheets by T.

(i) *Eight separate sheets*

In this situation $\quad T = W_1 + W_2 + W_3 + W_4 + W_5 + W_6 + W_7 + W_8$

where $W_1, W_2, \ldots, W_8$ are eight independent observations of the variable W. The distribution of W is Normal with mean 0.1 and variance 0.006^2. So the distribution of T is Normal with

$$\text{mean} = 0.1 + 0.1 + \ldots + 0.1 = 8 \times 0.1 = 0.8$$
$$\text{variance} = 0.006^2 + 0.006^2 + \ldots + 0.006^2 = 8 \times 0.006^2$$
$$= 0.000\,288$$
$$\text{standard deviation} = \sqrt{0.000\,288} = 0.017.$$

The distribution is $N(0.8, 0.017^2)$.

(ii) *Eight thicknesses of the same sheet*

In this situation $T = W_1 + W_1 + W_1 + W_1 + W_1 + W_1 + W_1 + W_1 = 8W_1$ where W_1 is a single observation of the variable W.

So the distribution of T is Normal with

$$\text{mean} = 8 \times E(W) = 0.8$$
$$\text{variance} = 8^2 \times \text{Var}(W) = 8^2 \times 0.006^2 = 0.002\,304$$
$$\text{standard deviation} = \sqrt{0.002\,304} = 0.048.$$

The distribution is $N(0.8, 0.048^2)$.

? Notice that in both cases the mean thickness is the same but for the folded paper the variance is greater. Why is this?

EXERCISE 2C

1 A garage offers motorists 'MOT While U Wait' and claims that an average test takes only 20 minutes. Assuming that the time taken can be modelled as a Normal variable with mean 20 minutes and standard deviation 2 minutes, find the distribution of the total time taken to conduct six MOTs in succession at this garage. State any assumptions you make.

2   A company manufactures floor tiles of mean length 20 cm with standard deviation 0.2 cm. Assuming the distribution of the lengths of the tiles is Normal, find the probability that, when 12 randomly selected floor tiles are laid in a row, their total length exceeds 241 cm.

3   The masses of Christmas cakes produced at a bakery are independent and may be modelled as being Normally distributed with mean 4 kg and standard deviation 100 g. Find the probability that a set of eight Christmas cakes has a total mass between 32.3 kg and 32.7 kg.

4   A random sample of 15 items is chosen from a Normal population with mean 30 and variance 9. Find the probability that the sum of the variables in the sample is less than 440.

5   The distributions of four independent random variables X_1, X_2, X_3 and X_4 are N(7, 9), N(8, 16), N(9, 4) and N(10, 1) respectively.
Find the distributions of
   (i) $X_1 + X_2 + X_3 + X_4$ (ii) $X_1 + X_2 - X_3 - X_4$ (iii) $X_1 + X_2 + X_3$.

6   The distributions of X and Y are N(100, 25) and N(110, 36), and X and Y are independent. Find
   (i) the probability that $8X + 2Y < 1000$
   (ii) the probability that $8X - 2Y > 600$.

7   The distributions of the independent random variables A, B and C are N(35, 9), N(30, 8) and N(35, 9). Write down the distributions of
   (i) $A + B + C$ (ii) $5A + 4B$ (iii) $A + 2B + 3C$ (iv) $4A - B - 5C$.

8   The distributions of the independent random variables X and Y are N(60, 4) and N(90, 9). Find the probability that
   (i) $X - Y < -35$ (ii) $3X + 5Y > 638$ (iii) $3X > 2Y$.

9   If $X \sim$ N(60, 4) and $Y \sim$ N(90, 9) and X and Y are independent, find the probability that
   (i)   when one item is sampled from each population, the one from the Y population is more than 35 greater than the one from the X population
   (ii) the sum of a sample consisting of three items from population X and five items from population Y exceeds 638
   (iii) the sum of a sample of three items from population X exceeds that of two items from population Y.
   (iv) Comment on your answers to questions 8 and 9.

10   If $X_1 \sim$ N(600, 400) and $X_2 \sim$ N(1000, 900) and X_1 and X_2 are independent, write down the distributions of
   (i) $4X_1 + 5X_2$
   (ii) $7X_1 - 3X_2$
   (iii) $aX_1 + bX_2$, where a and b are constants.

11 The distribution of the weights of those rowing in a very large regatta may be taken to be Normal with mean 80 kg and standard deviation 8 kg.

(i) What total weight would you expect 70% of randomly chosen crews of four oarsmen to exceed?

(ii) State what assumption you have made in answering this question and comment on whether you consider it reasonable.

12 The quantity of fuel used by a coach on a return trip of 200 km is modelled as a Normal variable with mean 45 l and standard deviation 1.5 l.

(i) Find the probability that in nine return journeys the coach uses between 400 and 406 l of fuel.

(ii) Find the volume of fuel which is 95% certain to be sufficient to cover the total fuel requirements for two return journeys.

13 The weekly takings at three cinemas are modelled as independent Normally distributed random variables with means and standard deviations as shown in the table, in £.

	Mean	Standard deviation
Cinema A	6000	400
Cinema B	9000	800
Cinema C	5100	180

(i) Find the probability that the weekly takings at cinema A will be less than those at cinema C.

(ii) Find the probability that the weekly takings at cinema B will be at least twice those at cinema C.

(iii) The parent company receives a weekly levy consisting of 12% of the weekly takings at cinema A, 20% of those at cinema B and 8% of those at cinema C. Find the probability that this levy exceeds £3000 in any given week. Hence find the probability that in a 4-week period the weekly levy exceeds £3000 at least twice.

[MEI]

14 Assume that the weights of men and women may be taken to be Normally distributed, men with mean 75 kg and standard deviation 4 kg, and women with mean 65 kg and standard deviation 3 kg.

At a village fair, tug-of-war teams consisting of either five men or six women are chosen at random. The competition is then run on a knock-out basis, with teams drawn out of a hat. If in the first round a women's team is drawn against a men's team, what is the probability that the women's team is the heavier? State any assumptions you have made and explain how they can be justified.

15 A school student investigated how long he actually had to spend on homework assignments, which were nominally for half-hour periods. He found that the times were approximately Normally distributed, with mean 35 minutes and standard deviation 8 minutes. Using this model, and assuming independence between assignments, find

   (i) the probability that three assignments each take more than 40 minutes

   (ii) the probability that three assignments will take more than 2 hours altogether.

[Cambridge]

16 The length, in centimetres, of a rectangular tile is a Normal variable with mean 19.8 and standard deviation 0.1. The breadth, in centimetres, is an independent Normal variable with mean 9.8 and standard deviation 0.1.

   (i) Find the probability that the sum of the lengths of five randomly chosen tiles exceeds 99.4 cm.

   (ii) Find the probability that the breadth of a randomly chosen tile is less than one half of the length.

   (iii) S denotes the sum of the lengths of 50 randomly chosen tiles and T denotes the sum of the breadths of 90 randomly chosen tiles. Find the mean and variance of $S - T$.

[Cambridge]

17 The weights of pamphlets are Normally distributed with mean 40 g and standard deviation 2 g. What is the distribution of the total weight of

   (i) a random sample of 2 pamphlets?

   (ii) a random sample of n pamphlets?

Pamphlets are stacked in piles nominally containing 25. To save time, the following method of counting is used. A pile of pamphlets is weighed and is accepted (i.e. assumed to contain 25 pamphlets) if its weight lies between 980 g and 1020 g. Assuming each pile is a random sample, determine to three decimal places the probabilities that

   (iii) a pile actually containing 24 pamphlets will be accepted

   (iv) a pile actually containing 25 pamphlets will be rejected.

Justify the choice of the limits as 980 g and 1020 g.

[MEI]

18 The four runners in a relay team have individual times, in seconds, which are Normally distributed, with means 12.1, 12.2, 12.3, 12.4, and standard deviations 0.2, 0.25, 0.3, 0.35 respectively. Find the probability that, in a randomly chosen race,

   (i) the total time of the four runners is less than 48 seconds

   (ii) runners 1 and 2 take longer in total than do runners 3 and 4.

What assumption have you made and how realistic is the model?

19 A petrol company issues a voucher with every 12 litres of petrol that a customer buys. Customers who send 50 vouchers to Head Office are entitled to a 'free gift'. After this promotion has been running some time the company receives several hundred bundles of vouchers in each day's post. It would take a long time, and so be costly, for somebody to count each bundle and so they weigh them instead. The weight of a single voucher is a Normal variable with mean 40 mg and standard deviation 5 mg.

(i) What is the distribution of the weights of bundles of 50 vouchers?

(ii) Find the weight W mg which is exceeded by 95% of bundles.

The company decides to count only the number of vouchers in those bundles which weigh less than W mg. A man has only 48 vouchers but decides to send them in, claiming that there are 50.

(iii) What is the probability that the man is detected?

20 Jim Longlegs is an athlete whose specialist event is the triple jump. This is made up of a *hop*, a *step* and a *jump*. Over a season the lengths of the *hop*, *step* and *jump* sections, denoted by H, S and J respectively, are measured, from which the following models are proposed:

$$H \sim N(5.5, 0.5^2) \quad S \sim N(5.1, 0.6^2) \quad J \sim N(6.2, 0.8^2)$$

where all distances are in metres. Assume that H, S and J are independent.

(i) In what proportion of his triple jumps will Jim's total distance exceed 18 metres?

(ii) In six successive independent attempts, what is the probability that at least one total distance will exceed 18 m?

(iii) What total distance will Jim exceed 95% of the time?

(iv) Find the probability that, in Jim's next triple jump, his step will be greater than his hop.

[MEI]

21 A country baker makes biscuits whose masses are Normally distributed with mean 30 g and standard deviation 2.3 g. She packs them by hand into either a small carton (containing 20 biscuits) or a large carton (containing 30 biscuits).

(i) State the distribution of the total mass, S, of biscuits in a small carton and find the probability that S is greater than 615 g.

(ii) Six small and four large cartons are placed in a box. Find the probability that the total mass of biscuits in the ten cartons lies between 7150 g and 7250 g.

(iii) Find the probability that three small cartons contain at least 25 g more than two large ones.

The label on a large carton of biscuits reads 'Net mass 900 g'. A trading standards officer insists that 90% of such cartons should contain biscuits with a total mass of at least 900 g.

(iv) Assuming the standard deviation remains unchanged, find the least value of the mean mass of a biscuit consistent with this requirement.

[MEI]

22 The continuous random variables X and Y represent the masses of male and female students who attend my local college.

Both X and Y are Normally distributed such that $X \sim N(75, 6^2)$ and $Y \sim N(65, 5^2)$, where all masses are given in kilograms.

(i) Find the probability that, if a male student and a female student are chosen at random, they each have a mass exceeding 70 kg.

(ii) State carefully the distribution of the combined mass of a random sample of m male and f female students.

A lift in the college has a notice

> **MAXIMUM 8 PEOPLE or 650 kg**

Find the probability that the combined mass of a random sample of eight students will exceed the mass restriction if it consists of

(a) eight males

(b) five males and three females.

(iii) What is the probability that a randomly selected female student has a greater mass than a randomly selected male student?

[MEI]

23 During the hour from 10.00 am to 11.00 am on a Wednesday morning, customers enter a large store at a constant average rate of 6.2 per minute.

(i) Use a suitable distribution to find the probability that more than six customers enter the store in any given minute. What assumption have you made about customers' behaviour?

(ii) Give a suitable approximating distribution for the total number of customers entering during the hour. Use this distribution to find the probability that more than 350 customers enter the store during the hour.

Suppose now that during this hour customers leave the store at a constant average rate of 5.7 per minute.

(iii) Obtain a distribution for the increase in the number of customers during the hour. Use this distribution to find the probability that more customers leave than enter during the hour.

[MEI]

24 The Reverend Thomas, a clergyman in the north of England who is also a keen statistician, has been monitoring the lengths of his sermons. He aims for each sermon to be between 10 and 15 minutes long, but in fact the sermons' lengths are given by the random variable X which is Normally distributed with mean $13\frac{1}{2}$ minutes and standard deviation 2 minutes. The lengths of different sermons are independent of one another.

(i) Find the probability that an individual sermon lasts between 10 and 15 minutes.

(ii) During a particular week, Rev. Thomas gives four sermons. Find the probability that their total length is more than an hour.

(iii) Rev. Thomas is asked to provide a series of sermons to be broadcast in religious radio programmes but is instructed that he must reduce their length. Suppose he is successful to the extent that the random variable giving the sermons' lengths is now $\frac{1}{2}X$. Find the time interval required in a radio programme to ensure that, with probability 0.9, there is time for a sermon.

(iv) Because of other variable elements in the radio programmes, the time available for a reduced-length sermon is itself a random variable, Normally distributed with mean 8 minutes and standard deviation 0.5 minutes. Find the probability that there is time for a sermon.

[MEI]

25 Bricks of a certain type are meant to be 65 mm in height, but in fact their heights are Normally distributed with mean 64.4 mm and standard deviation 1.4 mm. A warehouse keeps a large stock of these bricks, stored on shelves. The bricks are stacked one on top of another. The heights of the bricks may be regarded as statistically independent.

(i) Find the probability that an individual brick has height greater than 65 mm.

(ii) Find the probability that the height of a stack of six bricks is greater than 390 mm.

(iii) Find the vertical gap required between shelves to ensure that, with probability 0.99, there is room for a stack of six bricks.

(iv) The vertical gap between shelves is Normally distributed with a mean of 400 mm and standard deviation 7 mm. Find the probability that such a gap has room for a stack of six bricks.

(v) A workman buys ten bricks which can be considered to be a random sample from all the bricks in the warehouse. Find the probability that the average height of these bricks is between 64.8 mm and 65.2 mm.

[MEI]

26 The members of a dining club pay an annual subscription which is meant to cover the costs of four meals and leave a small margin for administrative expenses. The cost of each meal is taken as a Normally distributed random variable X with mean £10.50 (i.e. 1050 pence) and standard deviation 40 pence. The total cost of four meals in a year is the sum of four independent random variables each distributed as X.

(i) Find the probability that the cost of an individual meal is less than £10.

(ii) Find the probability that the total cost of four meals is less than £41.50.

(iii) Find the required annual subscription so that it is $97\frac{1}{2}\%$ certain that there will be a margin of at least £2 for administrative expenses.

(iv) Suppose instead that it is decided to budget for the administrative expenses to be 5% of the total cost of four meals. Find the required annual subscription so that it is $97\frac{1}{2}\%$ certain that the total cost of the meals and administration will be covered.

[MEI]

The distribution of the sample mean

In many practical situations you do not know the true value of the mean of a variable that you are investigating, that is the parent population mean (usually just called the *population mean*). Indeed that may be one of the things you are trying to establish.

In such cases you will usually take a random sample, $x_1, x_2, \ldots, x_n$, of size n from the population and work out the sample mean $\bar{x}$,

$$\bar{x} = \frac{x_1 + x_2 + \ldots + x_n}{n}$$

to use as an estimate for the true population mean μ.

How accurate is this estimate likely to be and how does its reliability vary with n, the sample size?

Each of the sample values $x_1, x_2, \ldots, x_n$ can be thought of as a value of an independent random variable $X_1, X_2, \ldots, X_n$. The variables $X_1, X_2, \ldots, X_n$ have the same distribution as the population and so $E(X_1) = \mu$, $Var(X_1) = \sigma^2$, etc.

So the sample mean is a value of the random variable $\bar{X}$ given by

$$\bar{X} = \frac{1}{n}(X_1 + X_2 + \ldots + X_n)$$

$$= \frac{1}{n}X_1 + \frac{1}{n}X_2 + \ldots + \frac{1}{n}X_n$$

and so

$$E(\bar{X}) = \frac{1}{n}E(X_1) + \frac{1}{n}E(X_2) + \ldots + \frac{1}{n}E(X_n)$$

$$= \frac{1}{n}\mu + \frac{1}{n}\mu + \ldots + \frac{1}{n}\mu$$

$$= n\left(\frac{1}{n}\mu\right)$$

$$= \mu, \text{ the population mean.}$$

Further, using the fact that $X_1, X_2, \ldots, X_n$ are independent,

$$Var(\bar{X}) = Var\left(\frac{X_1}{n}\right) + Var\left(\frac{X_2}{n}\right) + \ldots + Var\left(\frac{X_n}{n}\right)$$

$$= \frac{1}{n^2}Var(X_1) + \frac{1}{n^2}Var(X_2) + \ldots + \frac{1}{n^2}Var(X_n)$$

$$= \frac{1}{n^2}\sigma^2 + \frac{1}{n^2}\sigma^2 + \ldots + \frac{1}{n^2}\sigma^2$$

$$= n\left(\frac{1}{n^2}\sigma^2\right)$$

$$= \frac{\sigma^2}{n}$$

Thus the distribution of the means of samples of size n, drawn from a parent population with mean μ and variance σ^2, has mean μ and variance $\dfrac{\sigma^2}{n}$. The distribution of the sample means is called the *sampling distribution of the means*, or just the *sampling distribution*.

Notice that $\text{Var}(\overline{X}) = \dfrac{\sigma^2}{n}$ means that as n increases the variance of the sample means decreases. In other words, the value obtained for $\overline{X}$ from a large sample is more reliable as an estimate for μ than one obtained from a smaller sample. This result, simple though it is, lies at the heart of statistics: it says that you are likely to get more accurate results if you take a larger sample.

The standard deviation of sample means of size n is $\dfrac{\sigma}{\sqrt{n}}$ and this is called the *standard error of the mean*, or often just the *standard error*. It gives a measure of the degree of accuracy of $\overline{X}$ as an estimate for μ.

Note

The derivation has required no assumptions about the distribution of the parent population, other than that μ and σ are finite. If, in fact, the parent distribution is Normal, then the sampling distribution will also be Normal, whatever the size of n.

If the parent population is not Normal, the sampling distribution will still be approximately Normal, and will be more accurately so for larger values of n.

This result is called the Central Limit Theorem and will be developed in Chapter 4.

The derivation does require that the sample items are independent (otherwise the result for $\text{Var}(X)$ would not have been valid).

EXAMPLE 2.11

The discrete random variable X has a probability distribution as shown.

X	1	2	3
Probability	0.5	0.4	0.1

A random sample of size 2 is chosen, with replacement after each selection.
(i) Find μ and σ^2.
(ii) Verify that $\text{E}(\overline{X}) = \mu$ and $\text{Var}(\overline{X}) = \dfrac{\sigma^2}{2}$.

SOLUTION

(i)
$$\mu = \text{E}(X) = 1 \times 0.5 + 2 \times 0.4 + 3 \times 0.1$$
$$= 1.6$$
$$\text{E}(X^2) = 1^2 \times 0.5 + 2^2 \times 0.4 + 3^2 \times 0.1$$
$$= 3$$
$$\sigma^2 = \text{Var}(X) = \text{E}(X^2) - [\text{E}(X)]^2$$
$$= 3 - 1.6^2 = 0.44$$

(ii) The table below lists all the possible samples of size 2, their means and probabilities.

Sample	1, 1	1, 2	1, 3	2, 1	2, 2	2, 3	3, 1	3, 2	3, 3
Mean	1	1.5	2	1.5	2	2.5	2	2.5	3
Probability	0.25	0.2	0.05	0.2	0.16	0.04	0.05	0.04	0.01

This gives the following probability distribution of the sample mean.

$\overline{X}$	1	1.5	2	2.5	3
Probability	0.25	0.4	0.26	0.08	0.01

Using this table gives

$$E(\overline{X}) = 1 \times 0.25 + 1.5 \times 0.4 + 2 \times 0.26 + 2.5 \times 0.08 + 3 \times 0.01$$
$$= 1.6 = \mu, \text{ as required.}$$
$$E(\overline{X}^2) = 1^2 \times 0.25 + 1.5^2 \times 0.4 + 2^2 \times 0.26 + 2.5^2 \times 0.08 + 3^2 \times 0.01$$
$$= 2.78$$
$$\text{Var}(\overline{X}) = E(\overline{X}^2) - [E(\overline{X})]^2$$
$$= 2.78 - (1.6)^2$$
$$= 0.22$$
$$= \frac{0.44}{2} = \frac{\sigma^2}{2}, \text{ as required.}$$

ⓔ The χ^2 (chi-squared) distribution

You have seen that if n independent Normal variables, $X_1, X_2, X_3, \ldots, X_n$ are added together, the resulting variable

$$T = X_1 + X_2 + X_3 + \ldots + X_n$$

is itself Normal. If the Normal variables have been standardised so that each has mean 0 and variance 1, then the variable T has mean 0 and variance n.

A different, but important, distribution is formed when the squares of a set of independent standardised Normal variables are added. This is the χ^2 (chi-squared) distribution which is used in the χ^2 test (the subject of Chapter 7 of this book) which evaluates how well a model fits data.

If $\qquad U = Z_1^{\,2} + Z_2^{\,2} + Z_3^{\,2} + \ldots + Z_n^{\,2}$

then $\qquad U \sim \chi_n^2$

where n denotes the number of independent random variables involved, which is called the *degrees of freedom*. The Greek letter v (nu) is usually used to denote the degrees of freedom.

Figure 2.8 shows the p.d.f.s of the χ^2 distribution for various values of v.

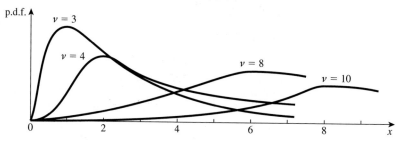

Figure 2.8

Note

As can be seen from figure 2.8, the shapes of the curves are alike and are all skewed. For large values of v they can be well approximated by the distribution $N(v, 2v)$.

The graphs of the χ^2 distribution in the cases $v = 1$ and $v = 2$ are quite different from all the others and are shown in figure 2.9.

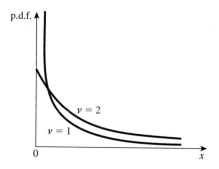

Figure 2.9

KEY POINTS

1 For a discrete random variable, X, which can assume only the values $x_1, x_2, \ldots, x_n$ with probabilities $p_1, p_2, \ldots, p_n$ respectively:

- $\sum p_i = 1 \quad p_i \geqslant 0$
- $E(X) = \sum x_i p_i = \sum x_i \times P(X = x_i)$
- $E(g[X]) = \sum g[x_i] \times p_i = \sum g[x_i] \times P(X = x_i)$
- $\text{Var}(X) = E(X^2) - [E(X)]^2$.

2 For any discrete random variable X and constants a and c:

- $E(c) = c$
- $E(aX) = aE(X)$
- $E(aX + c) = aE(X) + c$
- $E(f[X] + g[X]) = E(f[X]) + E(g[X])$
- $\text{Var}(c) = 0$
- $\text{Var}(aX) = a^2\text{Var}(X)$
- $\text{Var}(aX + c) = a^2\text{Var}(X)$.

3 For two random variables X and Y, whether independent or not, and constants a and b,

- $E(X \pm Y) = E(X) \pm E(Y)$
- $E(aX + bY) = aE(X) + bE(Y)$

and, if X and Y are independent,

- $\text{Var}(X \pm Y) = \text{Var}(X) + \text{Var}(Y)$
- $\text{Var}(aX + bY) = a^2\text{Var}(X) + b^2\text{Var}(Y)$.

4 For a set of n random variables, $X_1, X_2, \ldots, X_n$

- $E(X_1 \pm X_2 \pm \ldots \pm X_n) = E(X_1) \pm E(X_2) \pm \ldots \pm E(X_n)$

and, if the variables are independent,

- $\text{Var}(X_1 \pm X_2 \pm \ldots \pm X_n) = \text{Var}(X_1) + \text{Var}(X_2) + \ldots + \text{Var}(X_n)$.

5 If random variables are Normally distributed so are the sums, differences and other linear combinations of them.

6 **The sampling distribution of the means**

For samples of size n drawn from an infinite, or large, population with mean μ and variance σ^2, or for sampling with replacement,

- $E(\bar{X}) = \mu$
- $\text{Var}(\bar{X}) = \dfrac{\sigma^2}{n}$ where $\bar{X}$ is the sample mean.

The standard deviation of the sample means, $\dfrac{\sigma}{\sqrt{n}}$, is called the standard error of the mean.

e **The χ^2 (chi-squared) distribution**

If $U = Z_1^2 + Z_2^2 + \ldots + Z_n^2$

where Z_1^2, Z_2^2, Z_3^2, etc. are the squares of independent standardised Normal variables, then

$$U \sim \chi_n^2.$$

3

Sampling

If you wish to learn swimming you have to go into the water.

G. Polya

THE AVONFORD STAR

Independent set to become Local M.P.

Next week's Avonford by-election looks set to produce the first independent Member of Parliament for many years, according to an opinion poll conducted by the Star's research team.

When 30 potential voters were asked who they thought would make the best M.P., 12 opted for Independent candidate Mrs Curtis. The other three candidates attracted between 3 and 9 votes.

Mrs Valerie Curtis taking the polls by storm.

Assuming that the figures quoted in the article are true, does this really mean that Independent Mrs Curtis will be elected to Parliament next week?

Only time will tell that, but meanwhile the newspaper report raises a number of questions that should make you suspicious of its conclusion.

Was the sample large enough? Thirty seems a very small number.

Were those interviewed asked the right question? They were asked who they thought would make the best M.P., not who they intended to vote for.

How was the sample selected? *Was it representative of the whole electorate*?

Before addressing these questions you will find it helpful to be familiar with the language and notation associated with sampling.

Terms and notation

The *Avonford Star* took a sample of size 30. Taking samples and interpreting them is an essential part of statistics. The populations in which you are interested are often so large that it would be quite impractical to use every item; the electorate of Avonford might well number 70 000.

A *sample* provides a set of data values of a random variable, drawn from all such possible values, the *parent population*. The parent population can be finite, such as all professional footballers, or infinite, such as the points where a dart can land on a dart board.

A representation of the items available to be sampled is called the *sampling frame*. This could, for example, be a list of the sheep in a flock, a map marked with a grid or an electoral register. In many situations no sampling frame exists nor is it possible to devise one, for example, for the cod in the North Atlantic. The proportion of the available items that are actually sampled is called the *sampling fraction*.

A parent population, often just called the *population*, is described in terms of its *parameters*, such as its mean, μ, and variance, σ^2. By convention Greek letters are used to denote these parameters.

A value derived from a sample is written in Roman letters: mean, $\bar{x}$, variance, s^2, etc. Such a number is the value of a *sample statistic* (or just *statistic*). When sample statistics are used to estimate the parent population parameters they are called *estimates*.

Thus if you take a random sample in which the mean is $\bar{x}$, you can use $\bar{x}$ to estimate the parent mean, μ. If in a particular sample $\bar{x} = 23.4$, then you can use 23.4 as an estimate of the population mean. The true value of μ will generally be somewhat different from your estimated value.

Upper case letters, X, Y, etc., are used to represent the random variables, and lower case letters, x, y, etc., to denote particular values of them. In the example of the Avonford voters, you could define X to be the percentage of voters, in a sample of size 30, showing support for Mrs Curtis. The particular value from this sample, $x = \left(\frac{12}{30}\right) \times 100 = 40\%$.

Sampling

There are essentially two reasons why you might wish to take a sample.

- To estimate the values of the parameters of the parent population.
- To conduct a hypothesis test.

There are many ways you can interpret data. First you will consider how sample data are collected and the steps you can take to ensure their quality.

An estimate of a parameter derived from sample data will in general differ from its true value. The difference is called the *sampling error*. To reduce the sampling error, you want your sample to be as representative of the parent population as you can make it. This, however, may be easier said than done.

Here are a number of questions that you should ask yourself when about to take a sample.

1 Are the data relevant?

It is a common mistake to replace what you need to measure by something else for which data are more easily obtained.

You must ensure that your data are relevant, giving values of whatever it is that you really want to measure. This was clearly not the case in the example of the *Avonford Star*, where the question people were asked, 'Who would make the best M.P.?', was not the one whose answer was required. The question should have been 'Which person do you intend to vote for?'.

2 Are the data likely to be biased?

Bias is a systematic error. If, for example, you wished to estimate the mean time of young women running 100 metres and did so by timing the members of a hockey team over that distance, your result would be biased. The hockey players would be fitter and more athletic than most young women and so your estimate for the time would be too low.

You must try to avoid bias in the selection of your sample.

3 Does the method of collection distort the data?

The process of collecting data must not interfere with the data. It is, for example, very easy when designing a questionnaire to frame questions in such a way as to lead people into making certain responses 'Are you a law-abiding citizen?' and 'Do you consider your driving to be above average?' are both questions inviting the answer 'Yes'.

In the case of collecting information on voting intentions another problem arises. Where people put the cross on their ballot papers is secret and so people are being asked to give away private information. There may well be those who find this offensive and react by deliberately giving false answers.

People often give the answer they think the questioner wants to receive.

4 Is the right person collecting the data?

Bias can be introduced by the choice of those taking the sample. For example, a school's authorities want to estimate the proportion of the students who smoke, which is against the school rules. Each class teacher is told to ask five students whether they smoke. Almost certainly some smokers will say 'No' to their teacher for fear of getting into trouble, even though they might say 'Yes' to a different person.

5 Is the sample large enough?

The sample must be sufficiently large for the results to have some meaning. In this case the intention was to look for differences of support between the four candidates and for that a sample of 30 is totally inadequate. For opinion polls, a sample size of about 1000 is common.

The sample size depends on the precision required in the results. For example, in the opinion polls for elections a much larger sample is required if you want the estimate to be reliable to within 1% than if 5% will do.

6 Is the sampling procedure appropriate in the circumstances?

The method of choosing the sample must be appropriate. Suppose, for example, that you were carrying out the survey for the *Avonford Star* of people's voting intentions in the forthcoming by-election. How would you select the sample of people you are going to ask?

If you stood in the town's high street in the middle of one morning and asked passers-by you would probably get an unduly high proportion of those who, for one reason or another, were not employed. It is quite possible that this group has different voting intentions from those in work.

If you selected names from the telephone directory, you would automatically exclude those who do not have telephones: the lower income groups, students and so on.

It is actually very difficult to come up with a plan which will yield a fair sample, one that is not biased in some direction or another. There are, however, a number of established sampling techniques and these are described in the next section of this chapter.

? Each of the situations below involves a *population* and a *sample*. In each case identify both, briefly but precisely.

1 An M.P. is interested in whether her constituents support proposed legislation to restore capital punishment for murder. Her staff report that letters on the proposed legislation have been received from 361 constituents of whom 309 support it.

2 A flour company wants to know what proportion of Manchester households bake some or all of their own bread. A sample of 500 residential addresses in Manchester is taken and interviewers are sent to these addresses. The interviewers are employed during regular working hours on weekdays and interview only during these hours.

3 The Chicago Police Department wants to know how black residents of Chicago feel about police service. A questionnaire with several questions about the police is prepared. A sample of 300 postal addresses in predominantly black areas of Chicago is taken and a police officer is sent to each address to administer the questionnaire to an adult living there.

Each sampling situation contains a serious source of probable bias. In each case give the reason that bias may occur and also the direction of the bias.

[MEI]

Sampling techniques

In considering the following techniques it is worth repeating that a key aim when taking a sample is to obtain a sample that is *representative* of the parent population being investigated. It is assumed that the sampling is done without replacement, otherwise, for example, one person could give an opinion twice, or more. The fraction of the population which is selected is called the *sampling fraction*.

$$\text{Sampling fraction} = \frac{\text{sample size}}{\text{population size}}$$

Simple random sampling

In a *simple random sampling procedure*, every possible sample of a given size is equally likely to be selected. It follows that in such a procedure every member of the parent population is equally likely to be selected. However, the converse is not true. It is possible to devise a sampling procedure in which every member is equally likely to be selected but some samples are not permissible.

1 A school has 20 classes, each with 30 students. One student is chosen at random from each class, giving a sample size of 20. Why is this not a simple random sampling procedure?

2 If you write the name of each student in the school on a slip of paper, put all the slips in a box, shake it well and then take out 20, would this be a simple random sample?

Simple random sampling is fine when you can do it, but you must have a sampling frame. The selection of items within the frame is often done using tables of random numbers. Random numbers can be generated using a calculator or computer program.

Stratified sampling

You have already thought about the difficulty of conducting a survey of people's voting intentions in a particular area before an election. In that situation it is possible to identify a number of different sub-groups which you might expect to have different voting patterns: low, medium and high income groups; urban, suburban and rural dwellers; young, middle-aged and elderly voters; men and women; and so on. The sub-groups are called *strata*. In *stratified sampling*, you would ensure that all strata were sampled. You would need to sample from high income, suburban, elderly women; medium income, rural young men; etc. In this example, 54 strata ($3 \times 3 \times 3 \times 2$) have been identified. If the numbers sampled in the various strata are proportional to the size of their populations, the procedure is called *proportional stratified sampling*. If the sampling is not proportional, then appropriate weighting has to be used.

The selection of the items to be sampled within each stratum is usually done by simple random sampling. Stratified sampling will usually lead to more accurate results about the entire population, and will also give useful information about the individual strata.

Cluster sampling

Cluster sampling also starts with sub-groups, or strata, of the population, but in this case the items are chosen from one or several of the sub-groups. The sub-groups are now called clusters. It is important that each cluster should be reasonably representative of the entire population. If, for example, you were asked to investigate the incidence of a particular parasite in the puffin population of Northern Europe, it would be impossible to use simple random sampling. Rather you would select a number of sites and then catch some puffins at each place. This is cluster sampling. Instead of selecting from the whole population you are choosing from a limited number of clusters.

Systematic sampling

Systematic sampling is a method of choosing individuals from a sampling frame. If you were surveying telephone subscribers, you might select a number at random, say 66, and then sample the 66th name on every page of the directory. If the items in the sampling frame are numbered $1, 2, 3, \ldots$, you might choose a random starting point like 38 and then sample numbers 38, 138, 238 and so on.

When using systematic sampling you have to beware of any cyclic patterns within the frame. For example, a school list is made up class by class, each of exactly 25 children, in order of merit, so that numbers $1, 26, 51, 76, 101, \ldots$, in the frame are those at the top of their class. If you sample every 50th child starting with number 26, you will conclude that the children in the school are very bright.

Quota sampling

Quota sampling is the method often used by companies employing people to carry out opinion surveys. An interviewer's quota is always specified in stratified terms, how many males and how many females, etc. The choice of who is sampled is then left up to the interviewer and so is definitely non-random.

Other sampling techniques

This is by no means a complete list of sampling techniques. *Survey design*, the formulation of the most appropriate sampling procedure in a particular situation, is a major topic within statistics.

EXERCISE 3A

1 (i) An accountant is sampling from a computer file. The first number is selected randomly and is item 47; the rest of the sample is selected automatically and comprises items 97, 147, 197, 247, 297, ...

What type of sampling procedure is being used?

(ii) Pritam is a student at Avonford High School. He has been given a copy of the list of all students in the school. The list numbers the students from 1 to 2500.

Pritam generates a four-digit random number on his calculator, for example 0.4325. He multiplies the random number by 2500 and notes the integer part. For example, 0.4325×2500 results in 1081 so Pritam chooses the student listed as 1081. He repeats the process until he has a sample of 100 names.

(a) What type of sampling procedure is Pritam carrying out?

(b) What is the sampling fraction in this case?

(iii) Mr Jones wishes to find out if a mobile grocery service would be popular in Avonford. He chooses four streets at random in the town and calls at 15 randomly selected houses in each of the streets to seek the residents' views.

(a) What type of sampling procedure is he using?

(b) Is the procedure random?

(iv) Tracey is trying to encourage people to shop at her boutique. She has produced a short questionnaire and has employed four college students to administer it. The questionnaire asks people about their fashion preferences. Each student is told to question 20 women and 20 men and then to stop.

(a) What type of sampling procedure is Tracey using?

(b) Is the procedure random?

(c) Comment on the number of people that are surveyed.

2 (i) There are five year groups in the school Jane attends. She wishes to survey opinion about what to do with an unused section of field next to the playground. Because of a limited budget she has produced only 30 questionnaires.

There are 140 students in each of Years l and 2.
There are 100 students in each of Years 3 and 4.
There are 120 students in Year 5.

Jane plans to use a stratified sampling procedure.
(a) How many students from each year should Jane survey?
(b) What is the sampling fraction?

(ii) A factory safety inspector wishes to inspect a sample of vehicles to check for faulty tyres. The factory has 280 light vans, 21 company cars and 5 large-load vehicles.

The chairman has instructed that a sampling fraction of $\frac{1}{10}$ should be used and that each type of vehicle should be represented in the sample.
(a) How many of each vehicle type should be inspected?
(b) How should the inspector choose his sample? What is the sampling procedure called?

(iii) A small village has a population of 640. The population is classified by age as shown in the table below.

Age (years)	0–5	6–12	13–21	22–35	36–50	51+
Number of people	38	82	108	204	180	28

A survey of the inhabitants of the village is intended. A sample of size 80 is proposed.
(a) What is the overall sampling fraction?
(b) A stratified sample is planned. Calculate the approximate number that should be sampled from each age group.

3 Identify the sampling procedures that would be appropriate in the following situations.
(i) A local education officer wishes to estimate the mean number of children per family on a large housing estate.
(ii) A consumer protection body wishes to estimate the proportion of trains that are running late.
(iii) A marketing consultant wishes to investigate the proportion of households in a town that have a personal computer.
(iv) A local politician wishes to carry out a survey into people's views on capital punishment within your area.
(v) A health inspector wishes to investigate what proportion of people wear spectacles.

(vi) Ministry officials wish to estimate the proportion of cars with bald tyres.

(vii) A television company wishes to estimate the proportion of householders who have not paid their television licence fee.

(viii) The police want to find out how fast cars travel in the outside lane of a motorway.

(ix) A sociologist wants to know how many girlfriends the average 18-year-old boy has had.

(x) The headteacher of a large school wishes to estimate the average number of hours of homework done per week by the students.

4 You have been given the job of refurnishing the college canteen. You wish to survey student opinion on this. You are considering a number of sampling methods. In each case describe the sampling method and list the advantages and disadvantages.

(i) Select every 25th student from the college's alphabetical listing of students.

(ii) Select students as they arrive at college, ensuring proportional numbers of males and females and from classes on different courses.

(iii) Select students as they enter the canteen.

(iv) Select students at random from first and second year-group listings and in proportion to the number on each list.

5 Sampling is required in the situations below. For each situation devise, name and describe a suitable strategy. (Your answer is expected to take about five to ten lines for each part.)

(i) A company producing strip lighting wishes to find an estimate of the life expectancy of a typical strip light. Suggest how they might obtain a suitable sample.

(ii) A tree surgeon wishes to estimate the number of damaged trees in a large forest. He has available a map of the forest. Suggest how he might select a sample.

(iii) A factory produces computer chips. It has five production lines. Each production line produces, on average, 100 000 chips per week. One week the quality control manager decides to take a random sample of 500 chips from each production line.

    (a) Describe how she might arrange for a sample to be taken from a production line.

    (b) What sampling method is she employing overall?

(iv) Avonford Technical College is anxious to monitor the use of the College car park, which has parking spaces for 100 cars. It is aware that the number of staff employed by the College is greater than this but also that some staff use public transport sometimes. It is considering giving staff a choice of a parking permit (cost as yet undecided) or paying for staff to use public transport.

How would you survey staff views on these proposals?

(v) Some of your fellow students have shown concern about the lack of available space to do private study. You have been asked to represent them in approaching the Principal in order to press for some improvement in appropriate study space. Before you do this you want to be sure that you are representing a majority view, not just the feelings of a few 'complaining' individuals.

Describe how you would survey the students to gain the required information.

6 During a general election in the United Kingdom, a national TV company wishes to undertake a sample survey of the electorate.

(i) Describe the method of cluster sampling.

(ii) Explain briefly why cluster sampling might be appropriate.

An exit poll is conducted in a constituency. (An exit poll asks a sample of voters, immediately after they have voted, which party they voted for.)

(iii) Explain why an exit poll will not in practice be a simple random sample of all those who voted in this constituency. [MEI]

7 Peter is carrying out a survey for his GCSE *Media Studies* project. He wants to find out the favourite types of television programmes for students in his school. In total, there are 1000 students on the roll, the numbers in Years 7 to 11 being as follows.

Year	7	8	9	10	11
Number of students	180	180	200	240	200

Peter wants to take a sample of 50 students.

(i) Describe how a systematic sample of 50 students may be taken using the sampling frame of all 1000 students.

(ii) Name and briefly describe another method of sampling, in which each year is represented proportionately. [MEI]

8 Delightful Desserts produces pots of yoghurt in five flavours with the following proportions.

Black Cherry	Peach	Raspberry	Rhubarb	Strawberry
30%	20%	20%	10%	20%

For each flavour, an average of 5% of pots fail a taste test.

During each shift, the quality control department samples 50 pots of yoghurt for testing purposes.

(i) Give two distinct reasons why taking 50 pots from the first hour's production is an inappropriate method of sampling.

(ii) Describe a suitable method of selecting the sample of 50 pots, stating the number of pots of each flavour that should be in the sample. [MEI]

KEY POINTS

1 There are essentially two reasons why you might wish to take a sample:

- to estimate the values of the parameters of the parent population
- to conduct a hypothesis test.

2 When taking a sample you should ensure that:

- the data are relevant
- the data are unbiased
- the data are not distorted by the act of collection
- a suitable person is collecting the data
- the sample is of a suitable size
- a suitable sampling procedure is being followed.

3 Some sampling procedures are:

- simple random sampling
- stratified sampling
- cluster sampling
- systematic sampling
- quota sampling.

4

Interpreting sample data using the Normal distribution

When we spend money on testing an item, we are buying confidence in its performance.

Tony Cutler

THE AVONFORD STAR

The perfect apple grower

From our Farming Correspondent Tom Smith

Avonford fruit grower, Angie Fallon, believes that, after years of trials, she has developed trees that will produce the perfect supermarket apple. 'There are two requirements' Angie told me. 'The average weight of an apple should be 100 grams and they should all be nearly the same size. I have measured hundreds of mine and the standard deviation is a mere 5 grams.'

Angie invited me to take any ten apples off the shelf and weigh them for myself. It was quite uncanny; they were all so close to the magic 100 grams: 98, 107, 105, 98, 100, 99, 104, 93, 105, 103.

Angie is calling her apple the 'Avonford Pippin'. Will it, I wonder, spread the name of our beautiful town all round the world?

What can you conclude from the weights of the reporter's sample of ten apples?

Before going any further, it is appropriate to question whether the reporter's sample was random. Angie invited him to 'take any ten apples off the shelf'. That is not necessarily the same as taking any ten off the tree. The apples on the shelf could all have been specially selected to impress the reporter. So what follows is based on the assumption that Angie has been honest and the ten apples really do constitute a random sample.

The sample mean is

$$\bar{x} = \frac{98 + 107 + 105 + 98 + 100 + 99 + 104 + 93 + 105 + 103}{10} = 101.2$$

❓ What does that tell you about the population mean, μ

To estimate how far the value of μ is from 101.2, you need to know something about the spread of the data, the usual measure is the standard deviation, σ. In the article you are told that $\sigma = 5$.

In *Statistics 2* you met the result that if samples of size n are drawn from a population with a Normal distribution with mean μ and standard deviation σ, the distribution of the sample means is also Normal; its mean is μ and its standard deviation is $\frac{\sigma}{\sqrt{n}}$.

This is actually a special case of a more general result called the Central Limit Theorem. The Central Limit Theorem covers the case where samples are drawn from a population which is not necessarily Normal.

The Central Limit Theorem

> For samples of size n drawn from a distribution with mean μ and finite variance σ^2, the distribution of the sample mean is approximately $N\left(\mu, \dfrac{\sigma^2}{n}\right)$ for sufficiently large n.

This theorem is fundamental to much of statistics and so it is worth pausing to make sure you understand just what it is saying.

It deals with the distribution of sample means. This is called the *sampling distribution* (or more correctly the *sampling distribution of the means*). There are three aspects to it.

1 The mean of the sample means is μ, the population mean of the original distribution. That is not a particularly surprising result but it is extremely important.

2 The standard deviation of the sample means is $\dfrac{\sigma}{\sqrt{n}}$. This is often called the *standard error of the mean*.

   Within a sample you would expect some values above the population mean, others below it, so that overall the deviations would tend to cancel each other out, and the larger the sample the more this would be the case. Consequently the standard deviation of the sample means is smaller than that of individual items, by a factor of $\sqrt{n}$.

3 The distribution of sample means is approximately Normal.

This last point is the most surprising part of the theorem. Even if the underlying parent distribution is not Normal, the distribution of the means of samples of a particular size drawn from it is approximately Normal. The larger the sample size, n, the closer this distribution is to the Normal. For any given value of n the sampling distribution will be closest to Normal where the parent distribution is not unlike the Normal.

In many cases the value of n does not need to be particularly large. For most parent distributions you can rely on the distribution of sample means being Normal if n is about 20 or 25 (or more).

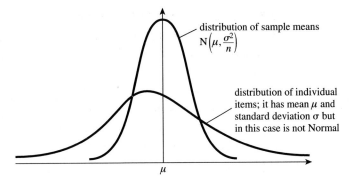

distribution of sample means $N\left(\mu, \frac{\sigma^2}{n}\right)$

distribution of individual items; it has mean μ and standard deviation σ but in this case is not Normal

μ

Figure 4.1

Confidence intervals

Returning to the figures on the Avonford Pippin apples, you would estimate the population mean to be the same as the sample mean, namely 101.2.

You can express this by saying that you estimate μ to lie within a range of values, an interval, centred on 101.2

$$101.2 - \text{a bit} < \mu < 101.2 + \text{a bit.}$$

Such an interval is called a *confidence interval.*

Imagine you take a large number of samples and use a formula to work out the interval for each of them. If you catch the true population mean in 90% of your intervals, the confidence interval is called a 90% confidence interval. Other percentages are also used and the confidence intervals are named accordingly. The width of the interval is clearly twice the 'bit'.

Finding a confidence interval involves a very simple calculation but the reasoning behind it is somewhat subtle and requires clear thinking. It is explained in the next section, but you may prefer to make your first reading of it a light one. You should, however, come back to it at some point; otherwise you will not really understand the meaning of confidence intervals.

The theory of confidence intervals

To understand confidence intervals you need to look not at the particular sample whose mean you have just found, but at the parent population from which it was drawn. For the data on the Avonford Pippin apples this does not look very promising. All you know about it is its standard deviation σ (in this case 5). You do not know its mean, μ, which you are trying to estimate, or even its shape.

It is now that the strength of the Central Limit Theorem becomes apparent. This states that the distribution of the means of samples of size n drawn from this population is approximately Normal with mean μ and standard deviation $\dfrac{\sigma}{\sqrt{n}}$.

In figure 4.2 the central 90% region has been shaded leaving the two 5% tails, corresponding to z values of ±1.645, unshaded. So if you take a large number of samples, all of size n, and work out the sample mean $\bar{x}$ for each one, you would expect that in 90% of cases the value of $\bar{x}$ would lie in the shaded region between A and B.

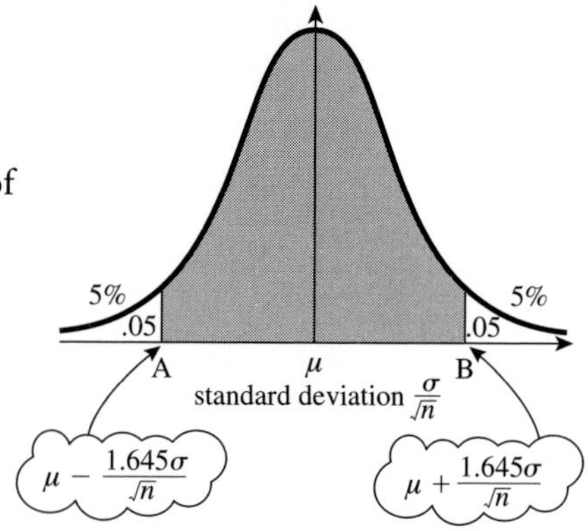

5%
.05

5%
.05

A

μ
standard deviation $\frac{\sigma}{\sqrt{n}}$

B

$\mu - \dfrac{1.645\sigma}{\sqrt{n}}$

$\mu + \dfrac{1.645\sigma}{\sqrt{n}}$

Figure 4.2

For such a value of $\bar{x}$ to be in the shaded region

it must be to the right of A:

$$\bar{x} > \mu - 1.645\frac{\sigma}{\sqrt{n}} \qquad \text{①}$$

it must be to the left of B:

$$\bar{x} < \mu + 1.645\frac{\sigma}{\sqrt{n}} \qquad \text{②}$$

Rearranging these two inequalities:

① $\qquad \bar{x} + 1.645\dfrac{\sigma}{\sqrt{n}} > \mu \qquad \text{or } \mu < \bar{x} + 1.645\dfrac{\sigma}{\sqrt{n}}$

② $\qquad \bar{x} - 1.645\dfrac{\sigma}{\sqrt{n}} < \mu$

Putting them together gives the result that in 90% of cases

$$\bar{x} - 1.645\frac{\sigma}{\sqrt{n}} < \mu < \bar{x} + 1.645\frac{\sigma}{\sqrt{n}}$$

and this is the 90% confidence interval for μ.

The numbers corresponding to the points A and B are called the 90% *confidence limits* and 90% is the *confidence level*. If you want a different confidence level, you use a different z value from 1.645.

This number is often denoted by k; commonly used values are:

Confidence level	k
90%	1.645
95%	1.96
99%	2.58

and the confidence interval is given by

$$\bar{x} - k\frac{\sigma}{\sqrt{n}} \quad \text{to} \quad \bar{x} + k\frac{\sigma}{\sqrt{n}}.$$

The P% confidence interval for the mean is an interval constructed from sample data in such a way that P% of such intervals will include the true population mean. Figure 4.3 shows a number of confidence intervals constructed from different samples, one of which fails to catch the population mean.

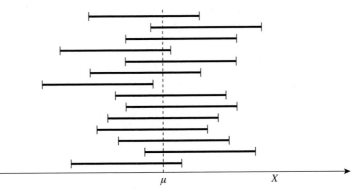

Figure 4.3

Note

Notice that this is a two-sided symmetrical confidence interval for the mean, μ. Confidence intervals do not need to be symmetrical and can be one-sided. The term confidence interval is a general one, applying not just to the mean but to other population parameters, like variance and skewness, as well. All these cases, however, are outside the scope of this book.

In the case of the data on the Avonford Pippin apples,

$$\bar{x} = 101.2, \quad \sigma = 5, \quad n = 10$$

and so the 90% confidence interval is

$$101.2 - 1.645 \times \frac{5}{\sqrt{10}} \quad \text{to} \quad 101.2 + 1.645 \times \frac{5}{\sqrt{10}}$$

$$98.6 \quad \text{to} \quad 103.8.$$

Known and estimated standard deviation

Notice that you can only use this procedure if you already know the value of the standard deviation of the parent population, σ. In this example, Angie Fallon said that she knew from hundreds of measurements of her apples, that its value is 5.

It is more often the situation that you do not know the population standard deviation or variance, and have to estimate it from your sample data. If that is the case, the procedure is different in that you use the t distribution rather than the Normal provided that the parent population is Normally distributed, and this results in different values of k. The use of the t distribution is the subject of the next chapter.

However, if the sample is large, for example over 50, confidence intervals worked out using the Normal distribution will be reasonably accurate even though the standard deviation used is an estimate from the sample. So it is quite acceptable to use the Normal distribution for large samples whether the standard deviation is known or not.

Paired samples

Very often you want to find an estimate of the difference between the means of two populations. For example, the senior tutor at a flying school is interested to see if there is a difference between the percentage marks achieved on Paper 1 and Paper 2 of the theory examination. She considers that her 200 students are sufficiently typical for them to be regarded as a random sample of all those taking the examination.

For each student she calculates the difference, d = Paper 1 mark − Paper 2 mark and the mean and standard deviation of d: $\bar{d} = 5.62$ and $s = 16.45$.

Based on previous results, she assumes that these differences are distributed Normally so she can find a 95% confidence interval for the difference in marks between the two papers.

$$5.62 - 1.96\frac{16.45}{\sqrt{200}} \quad \text{to} \quad 5.62 + 1.96\frac{16.45}{\sqrt{200}}$$

$$3.34 \quad \text{to} \quad 7.90$$

This whole interval is positive, so she concludes that Paper 1 appears to be easier.

(Note that as the sample size of 200 is quite large, it is reasonable to use s as an estimate for σ.)

You can see that the process here is exactly the same as for finding a confidence interval for the mean of a population with the extra initial step of finding the differences.

The situation in this example in which the data are paired (there are two marks for each student) is best for comparisons if you can obtain a suitable sample. Such a sample is called a *paired sample* or a *matched sample*. In practice, however, it is often impossible to obtain paired data. Instead you have to resort to taking a random sample from each population with no link between members of each sample. This is called a two-sample experiment; the design is described as unpaired. It involves slightly more complicated procedures which you will meet in *Statistics 4*.

EXPERIMENTS

These experiments are designed to help you understand confidence intervals, rather than to teach you anything new about dice.

When a single die is thrown, the possible outcomes, 1, 2, 3, 4, 5, 6, are all equally likely with probability $\frac{1}{6}$. Consequently the expectation or mean score from throwing a die is

$$\mu = 1 \times \tfrac{1}{6} + 2 \times \tfrac{1}{6} + \ldots + 6 \times \tfrac{1}{6} = 3.5.$$

Similarly the standard deviation is

$$\sigma = \sqrt{\left(1^2 \times \tfrac{1}{6} + 2^2 \times \tfrac{1}{6} + \ldots + 6^2 \times \tfrac{1}{6}\right) - 3.5^2} = 1.708.$$

Imagine that you know σ but don't know μ and wish to construct a 90% confidence interval for it.

Converging confidence intervals

Start by throwing a die once. Suppose you get a 5. You have a sample of size 1, namely {5}, which you could use to work out a sort of 90% confidence interval (but see the warning below).

This confidence interval is given by

$$5 - 1.645 \times \frac{1.708}{\sqrt{1}} \quad \text{to} \quad 5 + 1.645 \times \frac{1.708}{\sqrt{1}}$$
$$2.19 \quad \text{to} \quad 7.81.$$

 So far the procedure is not valid. The sample is small and the underlying distribution is not Normal. However, things will get better. The more times you throw the die, the larger the sample size and so the more justifiable the procedure.

Now throw the die again. Suppose this time you get a 3. You now have a sample of size 2, namely {5, 3}, with mean 4, and can work out another confidence interval.

The confidence interval is given by

$$4 - 1.645 \times \frac{1.708}{\sqrt{2}} \quad \text{to} \quad 4 + 1.645 \times \frac{1.708}{\sqrt{2}}$$
$$2.79 \quad \text{to} \quad 5.21.$$

Now throw the die again and find a third confidence interval, and a fourth, fifth and so on. You should find them converging on the population mean of 3.5; but it may take some time to get close, particularly if you start with, say, two 6s. This demonstrates that, the larger the sample you take, the narrower the range of values within the confidence interval.

Catching the population mean

Organise a group of friends to throw five dice (or one die five times), and to do this 100 times. Each of these gives a sample of size 5 and so you can use it to work out a 90% confidence interval for μ.

You know that the real value of μ is 3.5 and it should be that this is caught within 90% of 90% confidence intervals.

 Out of your 100 confidence intervals, how many actually enclose 3.5?

How large a sample do you need?

You are now in a position to start to answer the question of how large a sample needs to be. The answer, as you will see in Example 4.1, depends on the precision you require, and the confidence level you are prepared to accept.

EXAMPLE 4.1

A trading standards officer is investigating complaints that a coal merchant is giving short measure. Each sack should contain 25 kg but some variation will inevitably occur because of the size of the lumps of coal; the officer knows from experience that the standard deviation should be 1.5 kg.

The officer plans to take, secretly, a random sample of n sacks, find the total weight of the coal inside them and thereby estimate the mean weight of the coal per sack. He wants to present this figure correct to the nearest kilogram with 95% confidence. What value of n should he choose?

SOLUTION

The 95% confidence interval for the mean is given by

$$\bar{x} - 1.96\frac{\sigma}{\sqrt{n}} \quad \text{to} \quad \bar{x} + \frac{1.96\sigma}{\sqrt{n}}$$

and so, since $\sigma = 1.5$, the inspector's requirement is that

$$\frac{1.96 \times 1.5}{\sqrt{n}} \leqslant 0.5$$

$$\Rightarrow \qquad \frac{1.96 \times 1.5}{0.5} \leqslant \sqrt{n}$$

$$\Rightarrow \qquad\qquad n \geqslant 34.57$$

So the inspector needs to take 35 sacks.

Large samples

Given that the width of a confidence interval decreases with sample size, why is it not standard practice to take very large samples?

The answer is that the cost and time involved has to be balanced against the quality of information produced. Because the width of a confidence interval depends on $\frac{1}{\sqrt{n}}$ and not on $\frac{1}{n}$, increasing the sample size does not produce a proportional reduction in the width of the interval. You have, for example, to increase the sample size by a factor of 4 to halve the width of the interval. In the previous example the inspector had to weigh 35 sacks of coal to achieve a class interval of $2 \times 0.5 = 1$ kg with 95% confidence. That is already quite a daunting task; does the benefit from reducing the interval to 0.5 kg justify the time, cost and trouble involved in weighing another 105 sacks?

1 A biologist studying a colony of beetles selects and weighs a random sample of 20 adult males. She knows that, because of natural variability, the weights of such beetles are Normally distributed with standard deviation 0.2 g. Their weights, in grams, are as follows.

| 5.2 | 5.4 | 4.9 | 5.0 | 4.8 | | 5.7 | 5.2 | 5.2 | 5.4 | 5.1 |
| 5.6 | 5.0 | 5.2 | 5.1 | 5.3 | | 5.2 | 5.1 | 5.3 | 5.2 | 5.2 |

(i) Find the mean weight of the beetles in this sample.

(ii) Find 95% confidence limits for the mean weight of such beetles.

2 An aptitude test for deep-sea divers has been designed to produce scores which are approximately Normally distributed on a scale from 0 to 100 with standard deviation 25. The scores from a random sample of people taking the test were as follows.

23   35   89   35   12   45   60   78   34   66

(i) Find the mean score of the people in this sample.

(ii) Construct a 90% confidence interval for the mean score of people taking the test.

(iii) Construct a 99% confidence interval for the mean score of people taking the test. Compare this confidence interval with the 90% confidence interval.

3 In a large city the distribution of incomes per family has a standard deviation of £5200.

(i) For a random sample of 400 families, what is the probability that the sample mean income per family is within £500 of the actual mean income per family?

(ii) Given that the sample mean income was, in fact, £8300, calculate a 95% confidence interval for the actual mean income per family.

[MEI]

4 A manufacturer of women's clothing wants to know the mean height of the women in a town (in order to plan what proportion of garments should be of each size). She knows that the standard deviation of their heights is 5 cm. She selects a random sample of 50 women from the town and finds their mean height to be 165.2 cm.

(i) Use the available information to estimate the proportion of women in the town who were
   (a) over 170 cm tall
   (b) less than 155 cm tall.

(ii) Construct a 95% confidence interval for the mean height of women in the town.

(iii) Another manufacturer in the same town wants to know the mean height of women in the town to within 0.5 cm with 95% confidence. What is the minimum sample size that would ensure this?

5   The masses of 40 men are recorded to the nearest kilogram below.

$$74 \quad 87 \quad 80 \quad 71 \quad 77 \quad 67 \quad 80 \quad 83$$
$$78 \quad 84 \quad 75 \quad 79 \quad 73 \quad 79 \quad 81 \quad 77$$
$$89 \quad 68 \quad 74 \quad 93 \quad 86 \quad 65 \quad 82 \quad 87$$
$$78 \quad 92 \quad 76 \quad 78 \quad 73 \quad 81 \quad 75 \quad 73$$
$$85 \quad 77 \quad 73 \quad 76 \quad 80 \quad 83 \quad 78 \quad 69$$

Calculate the mean and variance of these masses.

Assuming that these masses are a random sample from a population of masses distributed Normally with a variance of 40, find 95% confidence limits for the population mean. Explain carefully the meaning to be attached to these limits.

Assuming further that the population mean is 78.4, find the probability that a random sample of eight men from the population will have a total mass exceeding 640 kg.

[Cambridge]

6   An examination question, marked out of 10, is answered by a very large number of candidates. A random sample of 400 scripts are taken and the marks on this question are recorded.

Mark	0	1	2	3	4	5	6	7	8	9	10
Frequency	12	35	11	12	3	20	57	87	20	14	129

(i) Calculate the sample mean and the sample standard deviation.
(ii) Assuming that the population standard deviation has the same value as the sample standard deviation, find 90% confidence limits for the population mean.

7   An archaeologist discovers a short manuscript in an ancient language which he recognises but cannot read. There are 30 words in the manuscript and they contain a total of 198 letters. There are two written versions of the language. In the *early* form of the language the mean word length is 6.2 letters with standard deviation 2.5; in the *late* form certain words were given prefixes, raising the mean length to 7.6 letters but leaving the standard deviation unaltered. The archaeologist hopes the manuscript will help him to date the site.

(i) Construct a 95% confidence interval for the mean word length of the language.
(ii) What advice would you give the archaeologist?

8 The age, X, in years at last birthday, of 250 mothers when their first child was born is given in the following table.

Age, X	18–	20–	22–	24–	26–	28–	30–	32–	34–	36–	38–
No. of mothers	14	36	42	57	48	26	17	7	2	0	1

[The notation implies that, for example, in column 1, there are 14 mothers for whom the continuous variable X satisfies $18 \leqslant X < 20$.]

Calculate, to the nearest 0.1 of a year, estimates of the mean and the standard deviation of X.

If the 250 mothers are a random sample from a large population of mothers, find 95% confidence limits for the mean age, μ, of the total population.

[Cambridge]

9 The distribution of measurements of thicknesses of a random sample of yarns produced in a textile mill is shown in the following table.

Yarn thickness in microns (mid-interval value)	Frequency
72.5	6
77.5	18
82.5	32
87.5	57
92.5	102
97.5	51
102.5	25
107.5	9

Illustrate these data on a histogram. Estimate, to 2 decimal places, the mean and standard deviation of yarn thickness.

Hence estimate the standard error of the mean to 2 decimal places, and use it to determine approximate symmetrical 95% confidence limits, giving your answer to 1 decimal place.

[MEI]

10 In a game of patience, which involves no skill, the player scores between 0 and 52 points. The standard deviation is known to be 8; the mean is unknown but thought to be about 12.

(i) Explain why players' scores cannot be Normally distributed if the mean is indeed about 12.

A casino owner wishes to make this into a gambling event but needs to know the mean score before he can set the odds profitably. He employs a student to play the game 500 times. The student's total score is 6357.

(ii) Find 99% confidence limits for the mean score.

The student recorded all her individual scores and finds on investigation that their standard deviation is not 8 but 6.21.

(iii) What effect would accepting this value for the standard deviation have on the 99% confidence interval?

The casino owner wants to know the mean score to the nearest 0.1 with 99% confidence.

(iv) Using the value of 6.21 for the standard deviation, find the smallest sample size that would be needed to achieve this.

11 The label on a particular size of milk bottle states that it holds 1.136 litres of milk. In an investigation at the bottling plant, the contents, x litres, of 100 such bottles are carefully measured. The data are summarised by

$$\sum x = 112.4, \qquad \sum x^2 = 126.80.$$

(i) Estimate the variance of the underlying population.

(ii) Provide a 90% confidence interval for the mean of the underlying population, stating the assumptions you have made.

(iii) A manager states that 'the probability that the population mean lies in the calculated interval is 90%'. Explain why this interpretation is wrong. Give the correct interpretation of the interval.

(iv) Use the calculated interval to explain whether it appears that the target of 1.136 litres in a bottle is being met.

[MEI]

12 The manager of a supermarket is investigating the queuing situation at the check-outs. At busy periods, customers usually have to queue for some time to reach a check-out and then a further amount of time to be served.

(i) At an initial stage of the investigation, the time Q, in minutes, spent queuing to reach a check-out is modelled by a random variable having mean 5.6 and standard deviation 3.8. Similarly, the time R, in minutes, spent being served is modelled by a random variable having mean 1.8 and standard deviation 1.4. It is assumed that Q and R are independent. The total time for a customer to pass through the system is $Q + R$. Find the mean and standard deviation of $Q + R$.

100 customers, selected at random, are timed passing through the system. Their times, t minutes, are summarised by

$$\sum t = 764, \qquad \sum t^2 = 12\,248.$$

(ii) Estimate the mean and variance of the underlying population and hence comment informally on the adequacy of the model for $Q + R$ in part (i).

(iii) Provide a 90% confidence interval for the mean of the underlying population.

(iv) Explain why the confidence interval calculated in part (iii) is only approximate. Give two reasons why, with sample of size 100, the approximation is good.

[MEI]

13 In an investigation concerning acid rain, a large number of specimens of rain water were collected at different times over a wide area. These may be considered as a large random sample. They were analysed for acidity and the readings for a standard measure of acidity are summarised by

$$\text{number of specimens} = 75, \qquad \sum x = 282.6, \qquad \sum x^2 = 1096.42.$$

(i) Estimate the mean and variance of the underlying population.

(ii) Provide a 90% two-sided confidence interval for the population mean acidity of the rain water.

(iii) Explain carefully the interpretation of the interval in part (ii).

Now let $X_1, X_2, \ldots, X_n$ represent a random sample from a distribution with mean μ and variance σ^2, where n is large. Let $\overline{X} = \dfrac{1}{n}\sum X_i$ and let

$$V = \frac{1}{n-1}\sum (X_i - \overline{X})^2.$$

(iv) State the approximate distribution of $\dfrac{\overline{X} - \mu}{\dfrac{\sigma}{\sqrt{n}}}$.

(v) Suppose that σ^2 is unknown and is estimated by v, where v is the value of V as calculated from observations on the X_i. Explain whether the approximation in part (iv) is still good when σ is replaced by $\sqrt{v}$.

[MEI]

14 A football boot manufacturer did extensive testing on the wear of the front studs of its Supa range. It found that, after 30 hours use, the wear (i.e. the amount by which the length was reduced) was Normally distributed with standard deviation 1.3 mm. However, the mean wear on the studs of the boot on the dominant foot of the player was 4 mm more than on the studs of the other boot.

(i) Using the manufacturer's figure, find the standard deviation of the differences in wear between a pair of boots after 30 hours use.

The coach of a football team accepted the claim for the standard deviation but was suspicious of the claim about the mean difference. He chose ten of his squad at random. He fitted them with new boots and measured the wear after 30 hours of use with the following results.

Player	1	2	3	4	5	6	7	8	9	10
Dominant foot	6.5	8.3	4.5	6.7	9.2	5.3	7.6	8.1	9.0	8.4
Other foot	4.2	4.6	2.3	3.8	7.0	4.7	1.4	3.8	8.4	5.7

(ii) Using the value found in part (i) for the population standard deviation of the differences, calculate 95% confidence limits for the mean difference in wear based on the sample data.

(iii) Use these limits to explain whether or not you consider the coach's suspicions were justified.

15 A school decided to introduce a new P.E. programme for its Year 7 entry to try to improve the fitness of the students. In order to see whether the programme was effective, several tests were done. For one of these, the students were timed on a run of 1 kilometre in their first week in the school and again ten weeks later. A random sample of 100 of the students did both runs. The differences of their mean times, subtracting the time of the second run from that of the first, were calculated. The mean and standard deviation were found to be 0.75 minutes and 1.62 minutes respectively.

Calculate a 90% confidence interval for the population mean difference. You may assume that the differences are distributed Normally. What assumption have you made in finding this confidence interval?

The organiser of the programme considers that it should lead to an improvement of at least half a minute in the average times. Explain whether or not this aim has been achieved.

16 In an experiment to see if reaction times were affected by whether or not individuals are hungry, 2000 randomly chosen soldiers were tested before and after they had eaten a substantial lunch. The test used was to drop a metre rule, which was held vertically so that its lower end was level with the thumb and first finger of each person, and to measure how far the rule fell before it was caught. For each person, the difference, d, of the distance measured after lunch minus the distance measured before lunch was found. From these it was calculated that $\sum d = 1626$ and $\sum d^2 = 258\,632$.

Use these data to provide a 98% confidence interval for the population mean difference, stating any assumptions you have made.

What does your confidence interval suggest about reaction times before and after a meal?

For situations where the population mean, μ, is unknown but the population variance, σ^2 (or standard deviation, σ), is known:

The Central Limit Theorem

1 For samples of size n drawn from a distribution with mean μ and finite variance σ^2, the distribution of the sample mean is approximately $N\left(\mu, \dfrac{\sigma^2}{n}\right)$ for sufficiently large n.

The standard error of the mean

2 The standard error of the mean (i.e. the standard deviation of the sample means) is given by $\dfrac{\sigma}{\sqrt{n}}$.

Confidence intervals

3 Two-sided confidence intervals for μ are given by

$$\bar{x} - k\frac{\sigma}{\sqrt{n}} \quad \text{to} \quad \bar{x} + k\frac{\sigma}{\sqrt{n}}.$$

4 The value of k for any confidence level can be found using Normal distribution tables.

Confidence level	k
90%	1.645
95%	1.96
99%	2.58

5 Confidence intervals for paired samples are formed in the same way but the variable is now the difference between the paired values.

Interpreting sample data using the *t* distribution

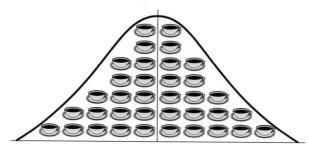

The tea distribution was quite normal.

Douglas Butler: MEI Newsletter report on
an annual general meeting

THE AVONFORD STAR
Local students find new bat

From our Science Correspondent Ama Williams

Two students and a lecturer from Avonford
Community College have found their way into
the textbooks. On a recent field trip they
discovered a small colony of a previously
unknown bat living in a cave.

'Somewhere in Britain' is all that Shakila
Mahadavan, 20, would tell me about its location.
'We don't want the general public disturbing the
bats or worse still catching them for
specimens', she explained.

The other two members of the group, lecturer
Alison Evans and 21-year-old Iain Scott, showed
me scores of photographs of the bats as well as
pages of measurements that they had gently
made on the few they had caught before
releasing them back into their cave.

*At a mystery location, Avonford students have
pushed forward the frontiers of science*

The measurements referred to in the article include the weights (in g) of eight
bats which were identified as adult males.

$$156 \quad 132 \quad 160 \quad 142 \quad 145 \quad 138 \quad 151 \quad 144$$

From these figures, the team want to estimate the mean weight of an adult male
bat, and 95% confidence limits for their figure.

It is clear from the newspaper report that these are the only measurements
available. All that is known about the parent population is what can be inferred
from these eight measurements. You know neither the mean nor the standard
deviation of the parent population, but you can estimate both.

The mean is estimated to be the same as the sample mean:

$$\frac{156 + 132 + 160 + 142 + 145 + 138 + 151 + 144}{8} = 146.$$

When it comes to estimating the standard deviation you have to be careful. The deviations of the eight numbers are as follows.

$$
\begin{aligned}
156 - 146 &= 10 \\
132 - 146 &= -14 \\
160 - 146 &= 14 \\
142 - 146 &= -4 \\
145 - 146 &= -1 \\
138 - 146 &= -8 \\
151 - 146 &= -5 \\
144 - 146 &= -2
\end{aligned}
$$

These eight deviations are not independent: they must add up to zero because of the way the mean is calculated. This means that when you have worked out the first seven deviations, it is inevitable that the final one has the value it does (in this case -2). Only seven values of the deviation are independent, and in general only $n - 1$ out of the n deviations from the sample mean are independent.

Consequently the variance is worked out using the formula:

$$\frac{S_{xx}}{n-1} \quad \text{or} \quad \sum_i \frac{(x_i - \bar{x})^2}{(n-1)}.$$

This gives the sample variance. The resulting value is an *unbiased estimate of the parent population variance*. A particular value is denoted by s^2, the associated random variable by S^2.

$$s^2 = \frac{S_{xx}}{n-1} = \sum_i \frac{(x_i - \bar{x})^2}{(n-1)}$$

In the case of the bats this gives

$$s^2 = \frac{(100 + 196 + 196 + 16 + 1 + 64 + 25 + 4)}{7} = 86.$$

The corresponding value of the standard deviation is $s = \sqrt{86} = 9.27$.

Degrees of freedom

The use of $n - 1$ in the calculation of s^2 illustrates an important idea in statistics. Much of the theory of statistics involves considering a particular sample in relation to all possible samples of the same size, subject to any restrictions. In this case there is one restriction, the mean. For a given value of the mean, $n - 1$ of the data items are free to take any reasonable value, but the value of the last one is then fixed if the mean is to work out correctly.

Consequently there are $n - 1$ *free variables* in this situation. The number of free variables within a system is called the *degrees of freedom* and denoted by v.

You need to know the degrees of freedom in many situations where you are calculating confidence intervals or conducting hypothesis tests. You may recall meeting the idea in Chapter 4 of *Statistics 2* when interpreting correlation coefficients.

Calculating the confidence intervals

Returning to the problem of estimating the mean weight of the bats, you now know that:

$$\bar{x} = 146, \quad s^2 = 86, \quad s = 9.27, \quad \text{and} \quad v = 8 - 1 = 7.$$

Before starting on further calculations there are some important and related points to notice.

1 This is a small sample. It would have been much better if they had managed to catch and weigh more than eight bats.

2 The true parent standard deviation, σ, is unknown and consequently the standard deviation of the sampling distribution given by the Central Limit Theorem, $\dfrac{\sigma}{\sqrt{n}}$, is also unknown.

3 In situations where the sample is small and the parent standard deviation or variance is unknown, there is little more that can be done unless you can assume that the parent population is Normal. (In this case that is a reasonable assumption, the bats being a naturally occurring population.) If you can assume Normality, then you may use the t distribution, estimating the value of σ from your sample.

4 It is possible to test whether a set of data could reasonably have been taken from a Normal distribution by using Normal probability paper. The method involves making a cumulative frequency table and plotting points on a graph with specially chosen axes. If the graph obtained is approximately a straight line then the data could plausibly have been drawn from a Normal population. Otherwise a Normal population is unlikely.

The t distribution looks very like the Normal distribution, and indeed for large values of v is little different from it. The larger the value of v, the closer the t distribution is to the Normal. Figure 5.1 shows the Normal distribution and t distributions $v = 2$ and $v = 10$.

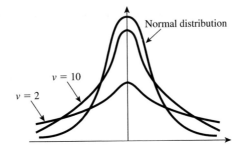

Figure 5.1

Historical note

William S. Gosset was born in Canterbury in 1876. After studying both mathematics and chemistry at Oxford he joined the Guinness breweries in Dublin as a scientist. He found an immense amount of statistical data was available, relating the brewing methods and the quality of the ingredients, particularly barley and hops, to the finished product. Much of this data was in the form of samples, and Gosset developed techniques to handle it, including the discovery of the *t* distribution. Gosset published his work under the pseudonym 'Student' and so the *t* test is often called Student's *t* test.

Gosset's name has frequently been misspelt as Gossett (with a double t), giving rise to puns about the *t* distribution.

Confidence intervals using the *t* distribution are constructed in much the same way as those using the Normal, with the confidence limits given by:

$$\bar{x} \pm k\frac{s}{\sqrt{n}}$$

where the values of k are found from a table of percentage points of the *t* distribution, for the appropriate degrees of freedom, v, and confidence level.

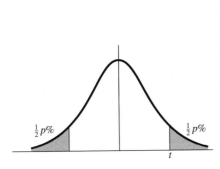

$p\%$	10	⑤	2	1
$v = 1$	6.314	12.71	31.82	63.66
2	2.920	4.303	6.965	9.925
3	2.353	3.182	4.541	5.841
4	2.132	2.776	3.747	4.604
5	2.015	2.571	3.365	4.032
6	1.943	2.447	3.143	3.707
⑦	1.895	2.365	2.998	3.499
8	1.860	2.306	2.896	3.355
9	1.833	2.262	2.821	3.250
10	1.812	2.228	2.764	3.169
11	1.796	2.201	2.718	3.106
12	1.782	2.179	2.681	3.055
13	1.771	2.160	2.650	3.012
14	1.761	2.145	2.624	2.977
15	1.753	2.131	2.602	2.947
20	1.725	2.086	2.528	2.845
30	1.697	2.042	2.457	2.750
50	1.676	2.009	2.403	2.678
100	1.660	1.984	2.364	2.626
∞	1.645	1.960	2.326	2.576

$v = 7, p = 5\%$ gives $k = 2.365$

$=$ Percentage points of the Normal distribution N(0, 1)

Figure 5.2

To construct a 95% confidence interval for the mean weight of the bats, you look under $p = 5\%$ and $v = 7$, to get $k = 2.365$; see figure 5.2. This gives a 95% confidence interval of

$$146 - 2.365 \times \frac{9.27}{\sqrt{8}} \quad \text{to} \quad 146 + 2.365 \times \frac{9.27}{\sqrt{8}}$$

$$138.2 \quad \text{to} \quad 153.8.$$

Hypothesis testing on a sample mean using the *t* distribution

THE AVONFORD STAR

Letters to the editor

Dear Sir,

It was with great interest that I read about the discovery of a previously unknown type of bat. My grandfather was a keen naturalist and I well-remember him telling us that he had found a cave containing a large colony of bats not known to science. He refused to tell anybody where the cave was but he spent months there observing and measuring them.

Unfortunately he perished when his house was hit by a stray bomb during the war, and all his notes went up in flames. I do have an old diary of his which includes a scribbled note 'Average weight of male bats 160 g, females 154.9 g'.

Could these be the same bats?

Yours faithfully,

Julia Bainton.

It will never be possible to know for certain whether the two colonies of bats are of the same type. It is even conceivable that Julia's grandfather had found the same cave and that the students had discovered the descendants of his bats, but the information has been irretrievably lost.

What you can do is to set up a hypothesis test that the newly-discovered bats are drawn from a population with the same mean weight for adult males of 160 g.

H_0: $\mu = 160$

H_1: $\mu \neq 160$

Two-tail test, 1% significance level.

The sample data may be summarised by:

$$\bar{x} = 146, \quad s = 9.27, \quad \text{and} \quad v = 8 - 1 = 7.$$

The test statistic is $\quad t = \dfrac{\overline{x} - \mu}{\dfrac{s}{\sqrt{n}}}$

and this has value $\quad t = \dfrac{146 - 160}{\dfrac{9.27}{\sqrt{8}}} = -4.27.$

This is compared with the critical value 3.499 found in the t distribution tables under $p = 1\%$ and $v = 7$ (see figure 5.3).

Since $-4.27 < -3.499$ the null hypothesis is rejected. The evidence suggests the bats were not of the same type.

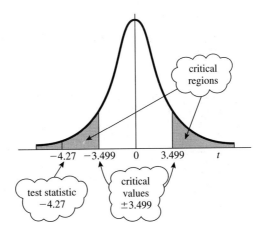

critical regions

-4.27 -3.499 0 3.499 t

test statistic -4.27

critical values ± 3.499

Figure 5.3

Note

Underlying this test is the assumption that the distribution of the weights of the students' bats is Normal. If this is not the case, the test is not valid.

EXAMPLE 5.1

Tests are being carried out on a new sleeping pill which is given one evening to a random sample of 16 people. The number of hours they sleep may be assumed to be Normally distributed and is recorded as follows.

$$8.1 \quad 6.7 \quad 3.3 \quad 7.2 \quad 8.1 \quad 9.2 \quad 6.0 \quad 7.4$$
$$6.4 \quad 6.9 \quad 7.0 \quad 7.8 \quad 6.7 \quad 7.2 \quad 7.6 \quad 7.9$$

(i) Use these data to set up a 95% confidence interval for the mean length of time somebody sleeps after taking the pill.

The mean number of hours slept by a large control group is 6.6.
(ii) Carry out a test, at the 1% significance level, of the hypothesis that the new drug increases the number of hours a person sleeps.

SOLUTION

(i) For the given data,

$$n = 16, \quad v = 16 - 1 = 15, \quad \bar{x} = 7.094, \quad s = 1.276.$$

For a 95% confidence interval, with $v = 15$, $k = 2.131$ (from tables).

The confidence limits are given by

$$\bar{x} \pm k \frac{s}{\sqrt{n}} = 7.094 \pm 2.131 \times \frac{1.276}{\sqrt{16}}.$$

So the 95% confidence interval for μ is 6.41 to 7.77.

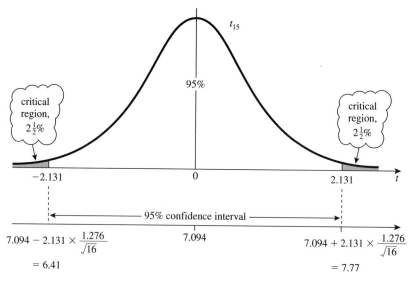

Figure 5.4

(ii) H_0: There is no change in the mean number of hours sleep. $\mu = 6.6$

H_1: There is an increase in the mean number of hours sleep. $\mu > 6.6$

One-tail test at the 1% significance level.

For this sample

$$n = 16, \quad v = 16 - 1 = 15, \quad \bar{x} = 7.094, \quad s = 1.276.$$

The critical value for t, for $v = 15$, at the 1% significance level, is found from tables to be 2.602.

$$t = \left(\frac{\bar{x} - \mu}{\frac{s}{\sqrt{n}}} \right) = \left(\frac{7.094 - 6.6}{\frac{1.276}{\sqrt{16}}} \right) = 1.55$$

This is to be compared with 2.602, the critical value, for the 1% significance level.

Since $1.55 < 2.602$, there is no reason at the 1% significance level to reject the null hypothesis that the mean number of hours sleep remains the same.

1 An aptitude test for entrance to university is designed to produce scores which may be modelled by the Normal distribution. In early testing 15 students from the appropriate age group are given the test. Their scores (out of 500) are as follows.

> 321　445　219　378　317　407　289　345
>
> 276　463　265　165　340　298　315

(i) Use these data to estimate the mean and standard deviation to be expected for students taking this test.

(ii) Construct a 95% confidence interval for the mean.

2 A fruit farmer has a large number of almond trees, all of the same variety and of the same age. One year he wishes to estimate the mean yield of his trees. He collects all the almonds from eight trees and records the following weights (in kg).

> 36　53　78　67　92　77　59　66

(i) Use these data to estimate the mean and standard deviation of the yields of all the farmer's trees.

(ii) Construct a 95% confidence interval for the mean yield.

(iii) What statistical assumption is required for your procedure to be valid?

(iv) How might you select a sample of eight trees from those growing in a large field?

3 A fair trading inspector visits a butcher who sells meat pies. The inspector investigates the meat content of 12 pies and records these figures (in grams).

> 234　256　171　234　251　251　243　216　251　232　250　253

(i) Use these figures to construct a 90% confidence interval for the mean mass of meat in one of the butcher's pies.

The pies are supposed to contain at least 250 g of meat each but there have been complaints that the butcher does not put enough meat in (which is why the inspector went to this shop). These data are used to carry out a suitable hypothesis test.

(ii) State the null and alternative hypotheses.

(iii) Carry out the test at the 5% significance level. State any assumptions you make and your conclusion.

The butcher says 'I don't know what all the fuss is about. Some are bound to be a bit over and some a bit under but you can count for yourself. Half the ones the inspector took are at least the right weight.'

(iv) Comment.

4 A forensic scientist is trying to decide whether a man accused of fraud could have written a particular letter. As part of the investigation she looks at the lengths of sentences used in the letter. She finds them to have the following numbers of words.

$$17 \quad 18 \quad 25 \quad 14 \quad 18 \quad 16 \quad 14 \quad 16 \quad 16 \quad 21 \quad 25 \quad 19$$

(i) Use these data to estimate the mean and standard deviation of the lengths of sentences used by the letter writer.

(ii) Construct a 90% confidence interval for the mean length of the letter writer's sentences.

(iii) What assumptions have you made to obtain your answer?

While the accused man is awaiting trial he writes a very large number of letters protesting his innocence. Many of these are passed on to the forensic scientist who is able to establish that overall the man uses a mean of 15.5 words per sentence. The scientist then uses the data from the original letter to carry out a suitable hypothesis test at the 5% significance level.

(iv) State the null and alternative hypotheses for the scientist's test.

(v) Carry out the test and state the conclusion.

(vi) Does this evidence support a prosecution?

5 A large company is investigating the number of incoming telephone calls at its exchange, in order to determine how many telephone lines it should have. During March one year the number of calls received each day was recorded and written down, across the page, as follows.

$$
\begin{array}{cccccccccc}
623 & 584 & 598 & 701 & 656 & 210 & 23 & 655 & 661 & 599 \\
634 & 681 & 197 & 25 & 592 & 643 & 642 & 698 & 659 & 201 \\
19 & 588 & 672 & 612 & 706 & 650 & 212 & 29 & 681 & 642 \\
677 & & & & & & & & &
\end{array}
$$

(i) What day of the week was 1 March?

(ii) Which of the data do you consider relevant to the company's research and why?

(iii) Construct a 95% confidence interval for the number of incoming calls per weekday.

(iv) Your calculation is criticised on the grounds that your data are discrete and so the underlying distribution cannot possibly be Normal. How would you respond to this criticism?

6 A tyre company is trying out a new tread pattern which it is hoped will result in the tyres giving greater distance. In a pilot experiment, 12 tyres are tested; the mileages ($\times 1000$ miles) at which they are condemned are as follows.

$$65 \quad 63 \quad 71 \quad 78 \quad 65 \quad 69 \quad 59 \quad 81 \quad 72 \quad 66 \quad 63 \quad 62$$

(i) Construct a 95% confidence interval for the mean distance that a tyre travels before being condemned.

(ii) What assumptions, statistical and practical, are required for your answer to part (i) to be valid?

Tyres with the company's usual tread pattern have been found to travel a mean distance of 62 000 miles before being condemned.

(iii) Carry out a test at the 0.5% significance level to determine whether the new tread gives a greater distance. State clearly your null and alternative hypotheses and your conclusion.

7   A fisherman claims that pollack are not as big as they used to be. 'They used to average three quarters of a kilogram each', he says. When challenged to prove his point he catches 20 pollack from the same shoal. Their masses (in kg) are as follows.

$$0.65 \quad 0.68 \quad 0.77 \quad 0.71 \quad 0.67 \quad 0.75 \quad 0.69 \quad 0.72 \quad 0.73 \quad 0.69$$
$$0.70 \quad 0.70 \quad 0.72 \quad 0.76 \quad 0.73 \quad 0.78 \quad 0.75 \quad 0.69 \quad 0.70 \quad 0.71$$

(i)   State the null and alternative hypotheses for this test.
(ii) Carry out the test at the 5% significance level and state the conclusion.
(iii) State any assumptions underlying your procedure and comment on their validity.

8   In the game of bridge a standard pack of 52 playing cards is dealt into four hands of 13 cards each. Players usually assess the value of their hands by counting 4 points for an ace, 3 for a King, 2 for a Queen, 1 for a Jack and nothing for any other card. The total points available from the four suits are $(4 + 3 + 2 + 1) \times 4 = 40$. So the mean number of points per hand is $\frac{40}{4} = 10$. Helene claims that she never gets good cards. One day she is challenged to prove this and agrees to keep a record of the number of points she gets on each hand next time she plays, with the following results.

$$5 \quad 16 \quad 7 \quad 1 \quad 11 \quad 2 \quad 8 \quad 9 \quad 14 \quad 12$$
$$21 \quad 10 \quad 0 \quad 7 \quad 12 \quad 7 \quad 6 \quad 8 \quad 13 \quad 4$$

(i)   What assumption underlies the use of the t test in this situation? To what extent do you think the assumption is justified?
(ii) State null and alternative hypotheses relating to Helene's claim.
(iii) Carry out the test at the 5% significance level and comment on the result.

(This question is set in memory of a lady called Helene who claimed that bridge hands had not been the same since the Second World War.)

9   A bus company is about to start a scheduled service between two towns some distance apart. Before deciding on an appropriate timetable they do ten trial runs to see how long the journey takes. The times, in minutes, are:

$$89 \quad 92 \quad 95 \quad 94 \quad 88 \quad 152 \quad 90 \quad 92 \quad 93 \quad 91$$

(i)   Construct a 95% confidence interval for the mean journey time, justifying any decision you make with regard to the data.

(ii) Explain why the company might actually be more interested in a one-sided confidence interval than in the two-sided one you have just calculated.

The company regards its main competition as the railway service, which takes 95 minutes, and claims that the bus journey time is less.

(iii) Use the sample data to test at the 5% significance level whether the company's claim is justified.

10 A history student wishes to estimate the life expectancy of people in Lincolnshire villages around 1750. She looks at the parish registers for five villages at that time and writes down the ages of the first ten people buried after the start of 1750. Those less than one year old were recorded as 0. The data were as follows.

2	6	72	0	0	18	45	91	6	2
0	12	56	4	25	1	1	5	0	7
8	65	12	63	2	76	70	0	1	0
9	15	3	49	54	0	2	71	6	8
6	0	67	55	2	0	1	54	1	5

(i) Use these data to estimate the mean life expectancy at that time.

(ii) Explain why it is not possible to use these data to construct a confidence interval for the mean life expectancy.

(iii) Is a confidence interval a useful measure in this situation anyway?

A friend tells the student that she could construct a confidence interval for the mean life expectancy of those who survive childhood (age $\geqslant 15$).

(iv) Construct a 95% confidence interval for the mean life expectancy of this group, and comment on whether you think your procedure is valid.

11 A large fishing-boat made a catch of 500 mackerel from a shoal. The total mass of the catch was 320 kg. The standard deviation of the mass of individual mackerel is known to be 0.06 kg.

Find a 99% confidence interval for the mean mass of a mackerel in the shoal.

An individual fisherman caught ten mackerel from the same shoal. These had masses (in kg) of

1.04 0.94 0.92 0.85 0.85 0.70 0.68 0.62 0.61 0.59

(i) From these data only, use your calculator to estimate the mean and standard deviation of the masses of mackerel in the shoal.

(ii) If the masses of mackerel are assumed to be Normally distributed, use your results from part (i) to find another 99% confidence interval for the mean mass of a mackerel in the shoal.

(iii) Give two statistical reasons why you would use the first limits you calculated in preference to the second limits.

12 A random sample of ten independent observations of a Normally distributed random variable X is taken from a population, and a test statistic, $t = 3.1$, is calculated. It is thought that the population mean μ is 110.0. Write down a suitable null hypothesis and a suitable alternative hypothesis for a two-tail significance test for μ. Use a t test to test your null hypothesis against your alternative hypothesis at the 1% significance level.

[Cambridge]

13 In a classroom experiment to estimate the mean height, μ cm, of seventeen-year-old boys, the heights, x cm, of ten such students were obtained. The data were summarised by

$$\Sigma x = 1727, \quad \Sigma x^2 = 298\,834.$$

(i) Find the mean and variance of the data, and use them to find the symmetrical 95% confidence interval of μ. State clearly but briefly the two important assumptions which you need to make.

An experiment is planned using the heights of 150 seventeen-year-old boys.
(ii) What effect will the use of a larger sample have on the width of the confidence interval for μ? Identify two distinct mathematical reasons for this effect.
(iii) To what extent are the assumptions made in part (i) still necessary with the larger sample size?

[MEI]

14 A rail commuter suspects that the train he travels to work by arrives late regularly. On five such journeys he noted the times, T minutes, by which the train was late. The data were summarised by

$$\Sigma t = 11.8, \quad \Sigma t^2 = 65.3.$$

(i) Find the mean and standard deviation of the data, and use them to find a and b, the lower and upper limits for the 90% confidence interval for μ, the mean time by which the train is late. State clearly two important assumptions you need to make.
(ii) The commuter interprets the result in part (i) as 'the probability that μ lies between a and b is 0.9'. Comment on this interpretation.
(iii) Use your result in part (i) to test whether the commuter's suspicions are justified. State the significance level at which the test is carried out.
(iv) The railway management notes the value of T on a further 40 occasions. State, with reasons, how you might expect its confidence interval for μ to differ from the one calculated in part (i).

[MEI]

15 When a darts player aims at the centre of the dart board the distance from the centre to the point where the dart lands is R, which is modelled as a continuous random variable. A suggested probability density function for R is as shown in the diagram.

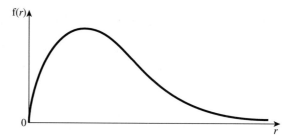

(i) Copy the diagram and show the position of the mode. Show also the approximate position of the mean in relation to the mode.

The mean value of R will vary for players of different ability. The famous darts player Willy Jackson aims 50 darts at the centre of the board. The distances from the centre are summarised as follows.

$$\Sigma r = 35.5, \quad \Sigma r^2 = 33.2$$

(ii) Construct a 90% confidence interval for the mean value of R. What assumption(s) have you made about the set of 50 throws?

(iii) Estimate the number of throws required if the 90% confidence interval for the mean of R for Willy Jackson is to be of width 0.1. Explain why your answer is only an estimate.

(iv) A second darts player records the results for 10 throws. Explain carefully why it would not be possible to obtain an accurate confidence interval for the mean value of R for this player.

[MEI]

16 A Youth Club has a large number of members (referred to as the *population* in the remainder of the question). In order to find the distribution of weekly allowances of the members, a random sample of ten is questioned.

(i) Describe a method of producing the random sample.

Such a random sample produced the following weekly allowances:

£5.20, £4.40, £3.00, £2.00, £3.30,

£7.50, £5.00, £6.50, £4.80, £5.70.

(ii) Estimate the population mean and variance.

(iii) Find a 95% confidence interval for the population mean. State any assumptions on which your method is based.

(iv) Explain how the width of the confidence interval may be reduced. Assuming the same variance as in part (ii) what must the sample size be to reduce the width to £2?

[MEI]

17 An experiment to determine the acceleration due to gravity, $g \, \mathrm{ms}^{-2}$, involves measuring the time, T seconds, taken by a pendulum of length 1 m to perform complete swings. T is regarded as a random variable.

30 measurements are made on T, and they are summarised by

$$\Sigma t = 59.8, \quad \Sigma t^2 = 119.7.$$

Construct a two-sided 98% confidence interval for μ, the mean value of T. Determine the corresponding range of values of g, using the formula

$$g = \frac{4\pi^2}{\mu^2}.$$

This result for g is not precise enough, so a longer series of measurements of T is made. Assuming that the sample mean and standard deviation remain about the same, how many measurements will be required in total to halve the width of the 98% confidence interval for μ? What will be the corresponding effect on the range of values for g? **[MEI]**

18 At a bottling plant, wine bottles are filled automatically by a machine. The bottles are meant to hold 75 cl. Under-filling leads to contravention of regulations and complaints from customers. Over-filling prevents the bottles being sealed securely.

The contents of 10 bottles are carefully measured and found to be as follows, in centilitres.

    75.6   76.2   74.3   74.8   75.3   76.3   75.9   74.2   75.6   76.7

(i) State appropriate null and alternative hypotheses for the usual t test for examining whether the bottles are being filled correctly.
(ii) State the conditions necessary for correct application of this test.
(iii) Carry out the test, using a 5% significance level.
(iv) Provide a two-sided 99% confidence interval for the true mean amount of wine delivered into the bottles. **[MEI]**

19 Sugar is automatically packed by a machine into bags of nominal weight 1000 g. Due to random fluctuations and the set-up of the machine, the weights of bags are in fact Normally distributed with mean 1020 g and standard deviation 25 g. Two bags are selected at random.
(i) Find the probability that the total weight of the two bags is less than 2000 g.
(ii) Find the probability that the weights of the two bags differ by less than 20 g.

Another machine is also in use for packing sugar into bags of nominal weight 1000 g. It is assumed that the distribution of the weights for this machine is also Normal. A random sample of nine bags packed by this machine is found to have the following weights (in grams).

    1012   996   984   1005   1008   994   1003   1017   1002

(iii) Test at the 5% level of significance whether it may be assumed that the mean weight for this machine is 1000 g. **[MEI]**

20 A trial is being made of a new diet for feeding pigs. Ten pigs are selected and their increases in weight (in kilograms) are measured, over a certain period using the new diet. The data are as follows.

15.2   13.8   14.6   15.8   13.1   14.9   17.2   15.1   14.9   15.2

The underlying population can be assumed to be Normally distributed.

(i) Using an established diet, the mean increase in weight of pigs over the period is known to be 14.0 kg. Test at the 5% level of significance whether the new diet is an improvement, stating carefully your null and alternative hypotheses and your conclusion.

(ii) Provide a 95% confidence interval for the mean increase in weight using the new diet.

(iii) Little information about the conduct of the trial is given in the opening paragraph of the question. Comment on *two* aspects of how the trial should have been conducted.

[MEI]

21 A tax inspector is carrying out an audit survey of firms located in a certain city. From the list of all N such firms, a random sample of size n is selected for detailed study.

(i) Define what is meant by a random sample.

(ii) Explain why a sample, even though random, might nevertheless be biased, explaining also the meaning of the word 'biased' in this context.

(iii) For a random sample of size $n = 14$, the values of a particular financial indicator are found to be

8.6 9.1 9.3 8.2 8.9 9.2 9.9 9.2 9.4 8.7 9.1 10.2 9.2 9.1.

Obtain a two-sided 99% confidence interval for the mean value of this indicator in the underlying population. State any required assumption and explain carefully the interpretation of the interval.

[MEI]

22 A commuter's train journey to work is scheduled to take 52 minutes. Having noticed that he is *always* late, even when the trains are running normally, he decided to keep records for a random sample of ten journeys. On two of these occasions, there were major signal failures leading to severe disruption and complete suspension of services. He therefore decided to eliminate these two occasions from his records. On the other eight occasions, his journey times in minutes were as follows.

65   61   62   60   59   62   61   57

(i) Carry out a two-sided 5% test of the hypothesis that his overall mean lateness is 10 minutes. State the required distributional assumption underlying your analysis.

(ii) Provide a 99% confidence interval for the mean journey time. Hence comment on the railway company's policy of offering refunds for journeys that are more than 15 minutes late.

(iii) Comment on the commuter's decision not to include the two occasions when there were major signal failures.

[MEI]

23 A notional allowance of 9 minutes has been given for the completion of a routine task on a production line. The operatives have complained that it appears usually to be taking slightly longer.

An inspector took a sample of 12 measurements of the time required to undertake this task. The results (in minutes) were as follows.

9.4   8.8   9.3   9.1   9.4   8.9   9.3   9.2   9.6   9.3   9.3   9.1

(i) Stating carefully your null and alternative hypotheses and the assumptions underlying your analysis, test at the 1% level of significance whether the task is indeed taking on average longer than 9 minutes.

(ii) Provide a two-sided 95% confidence interval for the mean time required to undertake the task.

[MEI]

THE AVONFORD STAR

Larks and Owls Investigation to be Televised

This year's *Avonford Star* investigation is to feature on local television. So, if you want to be a star, come to the Star's offices on Sunday morning and again in the evening. Volunteers will be given a specially devised set of alertness tests in the morning. The experiment will be repeated in the evening. The scientific question is 'Does your body clock slow down as the day goes on?'. Programme devisor Malini Ghosh believes the answer is yes. 'We are all naturally larks' she says.

Some people feel brighter in the morning; they are often called 'larks'. By contrast 'owls' feel more alert in the evening. The Avonford experiment is trying to find out whether people actually are more alert in the morning. Each volunteer is given a morning score and an evening score. (The higher the score, the more alert you are.)

Notice that the investigation is not about the mean score for the volunteers' performance, but the mean difference between their scores in the two different situations.

Twelve volunteers take part in the *Avonford Star* investigation. The results are shown overleaf.

Initials of subject	PH	GG	RS	TP	CF	GJ	ES	RP	CN	IH	DS	RB
Morning score	53	44	55	63	44	59	54	52	50	36	62	43
Evening score	51	37	59	48	39	48	57	40	45	33	63	51

These data are used in the next few pages.

Note

1 The volunteers in research projects are called *subjects* and 'morning' and 'evening' are the two *conditions* in which they were tested.

2 An experiment where one set of subjects is tested in each of two conditions is called a *paired design*, whereas if separate sets of subjects are tested in the two conditions this is an *unpaired design*. (Unpaired design is dealt with in *Statistics 4*.)

? When are you likely to be tested for alertness?
How would you devise an alertness test?

The paired sample *t* test

You are testing the hypotheses:

H_0: There is, on average, no difference between people's alertness in the morning and the evening.

H_1: People are less alert in the evening.

The form of the alternative hypothesis, which claims that people are less alert in the evening rather than just different, indicates that a one-tailed test is appropriate. This is used because the belief that motivated the investigation in the first place was the one-sided suggestion that people are naturally larks.

The Avonford data can be reduced to a set of values, d_1, d_2, ..., d_{12}, of the differences in the morning score and the evening score for each of the twelve volunteers.

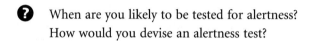

$$d_i = (\text{Morning score})_i - (\text{Evening score})_i : 1 \leqslant i \leqslant 12$$

Value of i	1	2	3	4	5	6	7	8	9	10	11	12
Initials of subject	PH	GG	RS	TP	CF	GJ	ES	RP	CN	IH	DS	RB
d_i	2	7	−4	15	5	11	−3	12	5	3	−1	−8

If these figures came from a population with a mean of zero, then you would expect to see approximately equal numbers and sizes of positive and negative differences in the sample. What you are trying to do is to decide whether the twelve differences listed above are, on the whole, so obviously positive that it is unlikely that they came from a population with a mean of zero.

A sensible measure of the average tendency in the sample for these differences to be positive is the mean of the sample differences, which takes the value $\overline{d} = 3.667$.

In line with the usual hypothesis testing principles, you need to discover whether such a result is reasonably likely to arise by chance from a sample of size twelve when the null hypothesis is true. To do this you need to know the sampling distribution of the means of samples of size 12.

It is helpful at this point to look at the more general case of samples of size n, and to bring in some appropriate notation. Call the random variable 'Difference between morning and evening scores' D and S^2 the unbiased estimator of its variance, based on a sample of size n.

Assume that D is Normally distributed. The null hypothesis is that the mean of D is zero and the sampling distribution of the statistic T, given by

$$T = \frac{\overline{D}}{\frac{S}{\sqrt{n}}}$$

has a t distribution with $n - 1$ degrees of freedom.

In this case $n = 12$, so the test statistic has 11 degrees of freedom and $s = 6.946$, so that the denominator of the test statistic, which is referred to as the standard error of the mean, is:

$$\frac{s}{\sqrt{n}} = 2.005$$

and the test statistic itself is:

$$t = \frac{\overline{d}}{\frac{s}{\sqrt{n}}} = \frac{3.667}{2.005} = 1.829.$$

The critical region, at the 5% significance level, for a one-tailed *t* test with 11 degrees of freedom, is found in the *t* tables under $n = 11$ and $p = 10\%$ (because the tables are constructed to give each tail a probability of $\frac{1}{2}p\%$). This gives a critical region of $t > 1.796$ which means that values of the test statistic larger than 1.796 would be unlikely (with probability less than 0.05) to arise by chance if the null hypothesis were true.

Since $1.829 > 1.796$, you reject the null hypothesis, and accept the alternative hypothesis that scores are lower in the evening.

Notice that you have done nothing different here from the *t* testing done earlier in this chapter. The new feature is that the variable used in the test statistic was obtained as the difference of the two variables which were actually measured in the sample. This means that the conclusions you drew were about the mean difference between the two measured variables. The test carried out here is called a *paired sample t test for the difference of two means*.

EXPERIMENTS

Test at least one of the hypotheses below by carrying out the experiment suggested. Each of them uses a paired sample *t* test.

1 People can hold their breath for longer after deep breathing exercises. The two conditions are as follows.

   (a) Take a deep breath and hold it for as long as possible.
   (b) Breathe in and out very deeply and slowly four times. On the fifth intake of breath, hold it for as long as possible.

2 People's reaction times are shorter first thing in the morning than late in the afternoon.

   You can use a 30 cm ruler as a reaction timer: hold the ruler vertically with the zero mark downwards, while the subject holds his thumb and forefinger 2 cm apart at the zero mark of the ruler. You drop the ruler without warning and your subject tries to catch it between thumb and forefinger. The distance, *d*, in millimetres, through which the ruler has fallen before it is caught can be used to measure the reaction time, *t*, in seconds, using the formula:

$$t = \frac{\sqrt{d}}{70}.$$

You could also use the reaction timer to test whether people's performance improves with practice: give each subject a preliminary test, ten practice drops and then a final test and record the difference between the first and last reaction times.

3   Presenting words in groups with related meanings makes them easier to recall than presenting them in alphabetical order.

You will need to produce lists of words (about 25 words each works well) some organised by meaning, others alphabetically.

For example:

peach	lion	table	flute	beer
pear	puma	chair	violin	cola
apple	zebra	bed	cello	wine
grape	badger	sofa	drum	cider
apricot	elk	stool	piano	water

is organised by meaning, whereas:

apple	cello	elk	pear	table
apricot	chair	flute	piano	violin
badger	cider	grape	puma	water
bed	cola	lion	sofa	wine
beer	drum	peach	stool	zebra

is organised alphabetically.

Each subject should be given a list of words to study, without writing anything, for one minute. At the end of this time, ask your subject to count out loud backwards, going down in threes from 587 (the point of this is to clear the short-term memory). After about 30 seconds, give each subject a sheet of paper and ask them to write down as many words as they can remember in one minute. Each subject needs to be tested twice, once with a list in alphabetical order, once with a list organised by meaning – but not a list with the same words on, of course. It is a good idea to have a number of different lists of each type, so that if some words are simply more memorable than others (what if one list had 'hippopotamus' on?), this will not spoil the effect you are looking for. It is also sensible to give half the subjects the alphabetical list first, and half the list organised by meaning first, in case there is a 'practice effect'.

Assumptions for the *t* test

There are two crucial assumptions in carrying out a *t* test.

1 That the sample is random.

2 That the variable is Normally distributed.

Was the Avonford sample random?

Strictly, this requires every possible sample to have an equal probability of being chosen. If you simply pick a group of volunteers, therefore, yours is probably not a random sample. However, this method is very close to the method often used by academic psychologists when choosing their samples. The hope in choosing a random sample is that the effects of all the irrelevant differences between members of the population which influence the variables you are testing will average out.

Many psychology experiments are done on samples of American university students: these are clearly not strictly random samples of the human population. However, the psychologists' argument is that the characteristics they are trying to measure are universal; that is, they are shared by everyone, independently of other characteristics such as age and level of education. This means that a random sample of American students will have the same properties as a random sample of the whole population. This argument is not accepted by everyone: some results verified on American students have later been found not to apply to groups of older, less well-educated or culturally different subjects.

Are the differences between morning and evening scores Normally distributed?

This is a plausible assumption, but not obviously correct. If you were doing this hypothesis test in earnest, you might want to make some prior check that Normality of the differences is an acceptable assumption: there are various tests which can be used and you will meet one of them in Chapter 7.

Notice that no claim is made about the distributions of morning and evening scores separately, but only about the distribution of differences. It is not necessary, for the *t* test to be used, that the morning and evening scores themselves are Normally distributed, nor even sufficient, since the scores in the two conditions are unlikely to be independent.

Testing for a non-zero value of the difference of two means

In the previous example the null hypothesis was that the mean value of the difference, D, was zero. Sometimes, as in the next example, you will need to test that it has some other value, denoted by k. In this case the statistic T is given by

$$T = \frac{\overline{D} - k}{\dfrac{S}{\sqrt{n}}}$$

and this has a t distribution with $n - 1$ degrees of freedom, provided that D is distributed Normally and that the null hypothesis is true.

EXAMPLE 5.2

In the population as a whole, the mean difference in heights of 17-year-old boys and girls is 4.3 cm. A scientist suspects that this difference would not be the same if she looked at boys and girls who were (non-identical) twins. Her hypotheses are:

H_0: The mean difference between 17-year-old twin boy and girl heights is 4.3 cm.
H_1: The mean difference between 17-year-old twin boy and girl heights is different from 4.3 cm.

She assumes that the difference between twin boy and girl heights is modelled by a Normal random variable. The data she has collected are shown in this table.

Should she accept the null hypothesis?

Family	A	B	C	D	E	F	G	H
Boy's height (cm)	176	157	170	166	162	175	157	171
Girl's height (cm)	156	162	163	168	159	174	170	165
Difference (cm)	20	−5	7	−2	3	1	−13	6

SOLUTION

The average difference is $\overline{d} = 2.125$ and the sample estimate of the population standard deviation is $s = 9.687$.

The test statistic is therefore $\dfrac{2.125 - 4.3}{\dfrac{9.687}{\sqrt{8}}} = -0.635$.

There are (size of sample $- 1$) $= (8 - 1) = 7$ degrees of freedom.

The critical region for a two-tailed test with seven degrees of freedom at the 5% significance level is $t > 2.365$ or $t < -2.365$, so that in this case, since $-2.365 < -0.635 < 2.365$, she accepts the null hypothesis that the mean difference between heights of twin boys and girls is 4.3 cm.

Confidence intervals for the difference of two means from a paired sample

The ideas developed in the last few pages can also be used in constructing confidence intervals for the difference in the means of paired data. This is shown in the next example.

EXAMPLE 5.3

In an experiment on group behaviour, twelve subjects were each asked to hold one arm out horizontally while supporting a 2 kg weight, under two conditions:
- while together in a group
- while alone with the experimenter.

The times, in seconds, for which they were able to support the weight under the two conditions were recorded as follows.

Subject	A	B	C	D	E	F	G	H	I	J	K	L
'Group' time	61	71	72	53	71	43	85	72	82	54	70	73
'Alone' time	43	72	81	35	56	39	63	66	38	60	74	52
Difference	18	−1	−9	18	15	4	22	6	44	−6	−4	21

Find a 90% confidence interval for the true difference between 'group' times and 'alone' times. You may assume that the differences are Normally distributed.

SOLUTION

The mean difference in the sample is $\bar{d} = 10.67$ and the standard deviation of these differences is $s = 15.24$.

Given the assumption that the differences are Normally distributed, you may use the t distribution. The degrees of freedom are given by $v = 12 - 1 = 11$; only the 12 differences are used in the calculation of the two statistics.

For $v = 11$, the two-tailed critical value from the t distribution at the 10% level of significance is 1.796.

The 90% symmetrical confidence interval for the mean difference between the 'group' and 'alone' times is

$$\bar{d} - 1.796 \times \frac{s}{\sqrt{12}} \quad \text{to} \quad \bar{d} + 1.796 \times \frac{s}{\sqrt{12}}$$

$$2.77 \quad \text{to} \quad 18.57.$$

In this exercise, you are expected to make a sensible choice of significance level for the hypothesis tests involved. Remember that the 5% level is conventional in scientific contexts.

1   Fourteen rats were timed as they ran through a maze. In one condition, the rats were hungry; in the other, they had just been fed.

   (i)   Use a paired *t* test to test the hypothesis that the rats run the maze more quickly when they are hungry. The data below give the rats' times in each condition.

Rat	A	B	C	D	E	F	G	H	I	J	K	L	M	N
Fed time (seconds)	30	31	25	23	50	26	14	27	31	39	38	39	44	30
Hungry time (seconds)	29	18	14	27	37	34	15	22	29	18	20	10	30	32

   (ii)   Do you think the assumptions for the paired *t* test are justified here?

   (iii)   Half the rats were made to run the maze first when hungry and half ran it first when fed. Why did the experimenter do this?

2   Twelve voters, who form part of a newspaper's public opinion panel, are asked to rate the Prime Minister's performance on a scale from one to ten, before and after the party conference.

   (i)   Test, using a paired *t* test, the hypothesis that the Prime Minister's rating has improved after the party conference. The panel's ratings are given in the table below.

Voter number	1	2	3	4	5	6	7	8	9	10	11	12
Rating before	4	7	8	3	4	5	2	1	2	5	3	5
Rating after	9	6	7	7	6	6	3	2	6	8	5	5

   (ii)   Assuming that these voters are a random sample of the electorate, do you think that the assumptions of the test are justified?

3   Two voters are asked on eight separate occasions to rate the Prime Minister's performance, on a scale from one to ten.

   (i)   Test, using a paired *t* test, the hypothesis that the voters' ratings of the Prime Minister do not differ, on average. The ratings are as follows.

Month	Feb	Mar	Apr	May	Jun	Jul	Sep	Oct
Rating of voter 1	4	4	5	7	9	10	8	10
Rating of voter 2	5	3	4	9	7	8	4	9

(ii) Explain clearly the difference between this question and the previous one. What is the random variable in each case? What is the population? What are the assumptions for this test to be valid? Are they different from the assumptions you needed to make in question 2?

4 Seventeen subjects were given a test of concentration: to go through a written passage crossing out every 'a' and ringing every 't'. They were timed on this task. Each was then given a placebo (a harmless pill containing no active ingredients) which they were told would enhance their concentration and hence their speed on the test; the test was then repeated (with a different written passage).

(i) Using a paired *t* test, test the hypothesis that the placebo has the effect of improving subjects' performance. The times for each subject are given in the table below.

Subject	A	B	C	D	E	F	G	H	I	J	K	L	M	N	O	P	Q
Original time (seconds)	54	27	55	51	53	56	77	62	18	18	46	61	43	59	34	20	72
Placebo time (seconds)	36	51	45	29	70	56	44	30	41	47	41	21	26	72	16	25	47

(ii) Do you consider that the assumptions appropriate to the *t* test are justified?

(iii) Criticise the experiment.

5 A new computerised job-matching system has been developed which finds suitably-skilled applicants to fit notified vacancies. It is hoped that this will reduce unemployment rates, and a trial of the system is conducted in seven areas.

(i) Using a paired *t* test, test the hypothesis that the new system reduces the rate of unemployment. The unemployment rates in each area just before the introduction of the system and after one month of its operation are recorded in the table below.

Area	1	2	3	4	5	6	7
Rate before new sytem (%)	10.3	3.6	17.8	5.1	4.6	11.2	7.7
Rate after new system (%)	9.3	4.1	15.2	5.0	3.3	10.3	8.1

(ii) Do you think that the assumptions for the *t* test would be justified here?

(iii) What do you think is wrong with this trial of the system?

6 Two timekeepers at an athletics track are being compared. They each time the nine sprints one afternoon.

(i) Using the paired t test, test the hypothesis that the two timers are equivalent, on average. The times they record are listed below.

Race	1	2	3	4	5	6	7	8	9
Timer 1	9.65	10.01	9.62	21.90	20.70	20.90	42.30	43.91	43.96
Timer 2	9.66	9.99	9.44	22.00	20.82	20.58	42.39	44.27	44.22

(ii) Are the assumptions appropriate to the t test justified in this case?

7 In a certain country, past research showed that in the average married couple, the man was 7 cm taller than his wife. A sociologist believes that, with changing roles, people are now choosing marriage partners nearer their own height. She has measured the heights of twelve couples. Her results are shown in the table below.

Couple	1	2	3	4	5	6	7	8	9	10	11	12
Man	188.2	174.2	192.4	163.4	183.2	171.4	180.6	173.5	166.8	171.9	175.5	163.2
Woman	178.4	165.1	191.9	156.3	178.7	163.0	180.4	170.2	164.2	166.2	176.9	158.8

(i) Test the hypothesis that men are on average less than 7 cm taller than their wives.

(ii) Explain clearly what assumptions you make in this case.

8 In 1979, the world price of crude oil rose by 60%. My macroeconomic model suggests that such a rise should result in an increase in the inflation rate of 2% between 1979 and 1980. The data I have available on inflation rates in these years are shown in the table below.

Country	Inflation rate 1979 (%)	Inflation rate 1980 (%)
Australia	9.1	10.2
Italy	14.8	21.2
Japan	3.7	7.7
Spain	15.6	15.6
UK	13.4	18.0
USA	11.3	13.5
Germany	4.1	5.5

(i) Test the hypothesis that the inflation rate rose by 2% between 1979 and 1980.

(ii) State carefully the assumptions you are making. What is a random sample in this context?

(iii) Do you think this is an adequate test of my model? Explain.

9 A fermentation process causes the growth of an enzyme. The amount of enzyme present in the mixture after a certain number of hours needs to be measured accurately. An inspector is comparing two procedures for doing this, there being a suspicion that the procedures are leading to different results. Eight samples are therefore taken and each is divided into two sub-samples of which one is randomly assigned for analysis by the first procedure and the other by the second. The data (in a convenient unit of concentration) are as follows.

Sample	Result from first procedure	Result from second procedure
1	214.6	211.8
2	226.2	224.7
3	219.6	219.8
4	208.4	205.2
5	215.1	212.6
6	220.8	218.0
7	218.4	219.2
8	212.3	209.7

It is understood that the underlying populations are satisfactorily modelled by Normal distributions.

(i)   Use an appropriate *t* test to examine these data, stating clearly the null and alternative hypotheses you are testing. Use a 1% significance level.

(ii) Provide a two-sided 95% confidence interval for the difference between the mean results of the procedures.

(iii) Explain why it is sensible to carry out the investigation by dividing samples into two sub-samples as described above, and why the sub-sample to be analysed by the first method should be assigned at random.

[MEI]

10 Nineteen pairs of brothers, where the elder was born two years before the younger, have their salaries at age 25 recorded (in thousands of pounds, to the nearest thousand pounds).

Salary of older brother	23	14	16	11	9	17	9	11	9	16
Salary of younger brother	7	9	16	25	12	8	6	8	8	10

Salary of older brother	35	8	7	9	11	10	7	8	8
Salary of younger brother	12	7	9	9	6	8	13	7	8

(i) Use these data to determine a 90% confidence interval for the mean amount by which the elder brother's salary exceeds the younger's at age 25.

(ii) What assumptions are you making in constructing your confidence interval?

1 For situations where the population mean, μ, and variance, σ^2 (or standard deviation, σ), are both unknown, sample data may be interpreted using the t distribution provided the distribution from which they are drawn is Normal.

Confidence intervals

2 Two-sided confidence intervals for μ are given by $\bar{x} - k\dfrac{s}{\sqrt{n}}$ to $\bar{x} + k\dfrac{s}{\sqrt{n}}$.

3 The degrees of freedom, v, are given by $v = n - 1$.

4 The value of k for any confidence level can be found using tables of critical values (or percentage points) for the t distribution.

Hypothesis testing

5 Sample data may be used to carry out a hypothesis test on the null hypothesis that the population mean has some particular value, μ.

The test statistic is $t = \left(\dfrac{\bar{x} - \mu}{\frac{s}{\sqrt{n}}} \right)$ and the t distribution is used.

6 If there is paired sample data (X, Y), this can be used to carry out a hypothesis test on the null hypothesis that $\mu_{X-Y} = \delta$.

The statistic is $t = \dfrac{\bar{d} - \delta}{\frac{s_d}{\sqrt{n}}}$ where $\bar{d}$ and s_d are the mean and standard deviation of the differences of each data pair. The t distribution is used providing the differences are distributed Normally.

7 The distribution of the mean, $\overline{x}$, of a sample

Population: mean μ, variance σ^2

Sample: $x_1, x_2, \ldots, x_n$

$$\overline{x} = \frac{(x_1 + x_2 + \ldots + x_n)}{n} \qquad s^2 = \frac{\sum (x_i - \overline{x})^2}{(n-1)}$$

Population variance	Underlying population	Sampling distribution
Known The variance is σ.	Any population.	The distribution is $N\left(\mu, \dfrac{\sigma^2}{n}\right)$ for all samples.
Unknown The variance is estimated by s^2.	Normal	The distribution is t for all samples; the mean is μ and the variance $\dfrac{s^2}{n}$ and there are $n-1$ degrees of freedom.

Large samples	Small samples
You may also use $N\left(\mu, \dfrac{s^2}{n}\right).$	You must use the t distribution.

	Large samples	Small samples
Not normal	You may use the distribution $N\left(\mu, \dfrac{s^2}{n}\right)$	Nothing useful can be done.

6 Non-parametric tests of location

Whenever a large sample of chaotic elements are taken in hand and marshalled in the order of their magnitude, an unsuspected and most beautiful form of regularity proves to have been latent all along.

Sir Francis Galton

THE AVONFORD STAR

Local M.P.'s popularity plummets

Following her controversial remarks about men fast becoming drones in our new society, local M.P. Glenda Sykes has seen her approval rating drop from 52% to a mere 29% in Avonford.

In the past a politician's popularity was measured by the size of the crowds he drew. These days it is more common for opinion pollsters to ask us questions like the one below.

'The Prime Minister is doing the best possible job, in the circumstances.'

Please choose one of the following responses.

agree strongly	agree	inclined to agree	have no opinion	inclined to disagree	disagree	disagree strongly

You will probably recognise this as the sort of question that is asked by opinion pollsters. However, surveys of people's attitudes are not just undertaken on political issues: market researchers for businesses, local authorities, psychologists and pressure groups, for instance, are all interested in what we think about a very wide variety of issues.

You are going to test the hypothesis:

The Prime Minister's performance is generally disapproved of.

The question above was asked of a group of twelve 17-year-olds and each reply recorded as a number from 1 to 7, where 1 indicates 'agree strongly', and 7 'disagree strongly'. This method of recording responses gives a *rating scale* of attitudes to the Prime Minister's performance. The data obtained are shown below.

$$3 \quad 6 \quad 7 \quad 4 \quad 3 \quad 4 \quad 7 \quad 3 \quad 5 \quad 6 \quad 5 \quad 6$$

What do these data indicate about the validity of the hypothesis in the population from which the sample was drawn?

You should recognise this question as similar to those you asked when conducting *t* tests. You want to know whether attitudes in the population as a whole are centred around the neutral response of '4' or show lower approval in general. That is, you want a *test of location* of the sample: one which decides what values are taken, on average, in the population. You could not use a *t* test here to decide whether the mean of the underlying distribution equals 4 because the response variable is clearly not Normally distributed: it only takes discrete values from 1 to 7 (and the sample size is small). This chapter looks at some tests of location which are valid even for small samples without the strict distributional assumptions required by the *t* test, and are therefore more widely applicable.

❸ The sign test

One very simple way of handling the sort of data you have here is to make the hypotheses:

H_0: People are equally likely to agree or disagree with the statement.

H_1: People are more likely to disagree than agree.

An opinion has been expressed by ten people (the two whose response is coded as '4' expressed no opinion); in carrying out the test, it is assumed that they constitute a random sample from the population. If the null hypothesis is true then each of these people will, independently, agree or disagree with the statement with probability $\frac{1}{2}$. The number agreeing, X, will therefore have a binomial distribution $B(10, \frac{1}{2})$.

To test the (one-tailed) hypothesis at the 5% level you are looking for the greatest value of x that makes $P(X \leqslant x) \leqslant 0.05$. Cumulative binomial probability tables for $n = 10$ show that this critical value is $x = 1$ and so the critical region for the test is $\{0, 1\}$ (see figure 6.1).

n	x p	0.050	0.100	0.150	1/6	0.200	0.250	0.300	1/3	0.350	0.400	0.450	0.500	0.55(
10	0	0.5987	0.3487	0.1969	0.1615	0.1074	0.0563	0.0282	0.0173	0.0135	0.0060	0.0025	0.0010	0.00(
	1	0.9139	0.7361	0.5443	0.4845	0.3758	0.2440	0.1493	0.1040	0.0860	0.0464	0.0233	0.0107	0.00
	2	0.9885	0.9298	0.8202	0.7752	0.6778	0.5256	0.3828	0.2991	0.2616	0.1673	0.0996	0.0547	0.02
	3	0.9990	0.9872	0.9500	0.9303	0.8791	0.7759	0.6496	0.5593	0.5138	0.3823	0.2660	0.1719	0.10
	4	0.9999	0.9984	0.9901	0.9845	0.9672	0.9219	0.8497	0.7869	0.7515	0.6331	0.5044	0.3770	0.26
	5	1.0000	0.9999	0.9986	0.9976	0.9936	0.9803	0.9527	0.9234	0.9051	0.8338	0.7384	0.6230	0.49
			0.9999	0.9997	0.9991	0.9965	0.9894	0.9802						

Figure 6.1 Extract from the cumulative binomial probability tables

In this example, three of those responding agree with the statement, so you accept the null hypothesis that people are equally likely to agree or disagree with the statement.

This is the sign test. It has the advantage of great simplicity, is useful in many circumstances and can be decisive. Because the calculation required is so quick to carry out, the sign test is often useful in an initial exploration of a set of data, and may indeed be all that is necessary.

However, there is information in the sample which is ignored in the sign test: nobody in the sample *strongly* agreed with the statement while, of the seven who disagreed, three did so strongly. The test described in the next section, while it is slightly more complicated, takes this extra information contained in the sample into account.

The Wilcoxon single sample test

Suppose that, despite your hypothesis, there is no tendency to approve or disapprove of the Prime Minister. Then it would seem plausible that in the population from which the data are drawn the response variable should be modelled as follows.

- It has a median value of 4: that is, half approve and half disapprove.

- It is symmetrically distributed about this median value: so, for example, you do not have half strongly approving and half slightly disapproving.

The strategy you adopt, therefore, is to test, on the assumption that responses are symmetrically distributed about the median response, the following hypotheses.

H_0: The median response is 4.

H_1: The median response is greater than 4.

Note the form of the alternative hypothesis which reflects the fact that the original question was one-tailed ('is the Prime Minister generally disapproved of?').

The Wilcoxon test, like Spearman's rank correlation test (see *Statistics 2*), is based on ranks. In the Wilcoxon case, however, you do not rank the actual data themselves, but their distances from the hypothesised median of the population, in this case 4.

For these data this gives the following results.

Rating, r	$r - 4$	$[r - 4]$	Rank
3	-1	1	3
6	2	2	7
7	3	3	9.5
3	-1	1	3
7	3	3	9.5
3	-1	1	3
5	1	1	3
6	2	2	7
5	1	1	3
6	3	2	7

Notes

1 The two people who gave a rating of 4 are omitted (they expressed no opinion).

2 The ratings are ranked according to their absolute – not their signed – differences from the median.

3 The rating with the smallest difference is given the lowest ranking and the rating with the largest difference has the highest ranking.

4 Where two or more ratings have the same difference, they are given the appropriate 'average rank'. For instance, the five ratings with differences of 1 should occupy the ranks 1, 2, 3, 4, 5 so they are all given the average rank of 3 and the two ratings with differences of 3 should occupy the ranks 9 and 10 so they are both given the average rank of 9.5.

Suppose that the assumption of symmetry is correct, and the null hypothesis that the median is 4 is true. Then you would expect a rating of 5 to come up as often as a rating of 3, a rating of 6 to come up as often as a rating of 2 and a rating of 7 to come up as often as a rating of 1. In other words, ratings at each distance from the supposed median of 4 should be equally likely to be above or below that median.

To test whether the data support this, the next step is to calculate the sum of the ranks of the ratings above 4 and below 4 and compare these with the total sum of the ranks. Here:

sum of ranks of ratings above $4 = 7 + 9.5 + 9.5 + 3 + 7 + 3 + 7 = 46$

sums of ranks of ratings below $4 = 3 + 3 + 3 = 9$

total sums of ranks $= 9 + 46 = 55$.

Note that because of the way in which the ratings were ranked, the total sum of ranks must be equal to the sum of the numbers from 1 to 10:

$$1 + 2 + \ldots + 10 = \frac{1}{2} 10 \times (10 + 1) = 55.$$

If the null hypothesis is true, you may expect the sum of the ranks of ratings above 4 to be approximately equal to the sum of the ranks of ratings below 4. This means that each would be about half of 55, i.e. 27.5. The fact that for these data the sum of ranks of ratings above 4 is considerably more than this, and the sum of ranks of ratings below 4 correspondingly less, implies either that more people disapproved than approved or that those who disapproved tended to disapprove more, so that the larger rank sum is associated with disapproval. Actually, both of these are true of the data.

In order to conduct an hypothesis test, you need to know the critical values of the test statistic. Tables of the critical values for the Wilcoxon test are available, and a section of one is shown in figure 6.2. Later in the chapter you will see how these tables are calculated.

1-tail	5%	$2\frac{1}{2}$%	1%	$\frac{1}{2}$%
2-tail	10%	5%	2%	1%
n				
2	–	–	–	–
3	–	–	–	–
4	–	–	–	–
5	0	–	–	–
6	2	0	–	–
7	3	2	0	–
8	5	3	1	0
9	8	5	3	1
10	10	8	5	3
11	13	10	7	5
12	17	13	9	7
13	21	17	12	9
14	25	21	15	12
15	30	25	19	15

Figure 6.2 Critical values for the Wilcoxon single sample and paired sample tests

The test you are conducting is one-tailed because you are trying to decide whether your data indicate disapproval; that is, whether the sum of ranks corresponding to approval is significantly smaller and, equivalently, the sum of ranks corresponding to disapproval significantly larger, than chance would suggest. The table is constructed to give the largest value of the rank sum that can be regarded as significantly smaller than chance would suggest, so it is the sum of ranks corresponding to approval (those ratings below 4) that provide the test statistic. Its value is 9 and so this is the number to be compared with the critical value.

Once the two subjects with no opinion are excluded, you have a sample size of 10, and for a one-tailed test at the 5% significance level the table gives a critical value of 10. This means that any value less than or equal to 10 for the sum of the ranks of the ratings below 4 lies in the critical region. In this example, the data give a test statistic $W = 9$, so you can reject the null hypothesis in favour of the alternative hypothesis that the median is greater than 4.

Formal procedure for the Wilcoxon single sample test

The work in the previous example may be stated more formally as follows.

The hypotheses to be tested are as follows.

H_0: The population median of a random variable is equal to a given value M.

H_1: **(a)** The population median $\neq M$

or **(b)** The population median $> M$

or **(c)** The population median $< M$.

Here **(a)** is a two-tailed test, and **(b)** and **(c)** are both one-tailed tests.

Assumption: That the random variable is symmetrically distributed about its median.

Data: The values $x_1, x_2, \ldots, x_n$ of the random variable form a sample of size n. If any of these is equal to M, remove it from the list and reduce n accordingly.

Calculation of the test statistic

1 Calculate the absolute differences between each sample value and the hypothesised median M, i.e.

$$|x_1 - M|, |x_2 - M|, \ldots, |x_n - M|.$$

2 Rank these values from 1 to n, giving the lowest rank to the smallest absolute difference. If two or more absolute differences are equal, each is given the rank which is the average of the ranking positions they occupy together.

3 Calculate the sum W_+ of the ranks of the sample values which are greater than M, and the sum W_- of the ranks of the sample values which are less than M.

4 Check that $W_+ + W_- = \frac{1}{2}n(n+1)$; this must work because the right-hand side is the formula for the sum of the numbers from 1 to n, i.e. the total of all the ranks.

5 The test statistic W is then found as follows:

- for the two-tailed alternative hypothesis **(a)**, take the test statistic W to be the smaller of W_- and W_+
- for the one-tailed alternative hypothesis **(b)**, take $W = W_-$
- for the one-tailed alternative hypothesis **(c)**, take $W = W_+$.

The significance of the test statistic

The null hypothesis is rejected if W is *less than or equal to* the appropriate critical value found in the tables which depends on the sample size, the chosen significance level and whether the test is one- or two-tailed.

Note

If the assumption of symmetry of the distribution about its median is true then this median is also the mean.

Rationale for the Wilcoxon test

As noted above, the sum of W_+ and W_- is determined by the sample size, so that the criterion for rejecting the null hypothesis is that the difference between W_+ and W_- is large enough. What makes this difference large?

This requires W_+ to contain *more* ranks, or *larger* ranks than W_- (or vice versa). This will occur if *most* of the sample or the *more extreme* values (those furthest from the hypothesised median) in the sample are above the median rather than below (or vice versa). The largest difference between W_+ and W_- will therefore occur if the sample contains a few values just below the hypothesised median and many values well above the hypothesised median (or vice versa). This is exactly the situation which would cast most doubt on the claim that the suggested median is the true one.

You can also see from this argument why the assumption of symmetry is important. The random variable X, for example, with the highly skewed distribution:

$$P(0) = 0.5, P(2) = P(4) = P(6) = P(8) = P(10) = 0.1$$

has median 1, but samples from this distribution will usually have about half their values just below the median (at 0), but the other half ranging over values substantially above the median (from 2 to 10). Thus large values of W_+ and correspondingly smaller values of W_- will be expected, and should not be taken to cast doubt on the null hypothesis median = 1.

EXAMPLE 6.1

A railway Customer Service Division knows from long experience that if passengers are asked to rate a railway company's buffet car service on a scale from 1 to 10 their responses are symmetrically distributed about a median of 4.5.

After an experimental trolley service is introduced on a particular route, passengers are asked to rate this service on a scale from 1 to 10. The ratings of a sample of 16 passengers were as follows.

$$
\begin{array}{cccccccc}
2 & 4 & 1 & 4 & 9 & 3 & 3 & 5 \\
6 & 2 & 1 & 2 & 5 & 6 & 2 & 4
\end{array}
$$

Is there evidence at the 5% level that passengers rate this service differently?

SOLUTION

You are conducting a test of the following hypotheses.

H_0: The ratings are symmetrically distributed about a median of 4.5.

H_1: The ratings are symmetrically distributed about a median different from 4.5.

When placed in order the ratings are as follows.

$$
\begin{array}{cccccccc}
1 & 1 & 2 & 2 & 2 & 2 & 3 & 3 \\
4 & 4 & 4 & 5 & 5 & 6 & 6 & 9
\end{array}
$$

The first step in calculating W_+ and W_- is to draw up a table giving the absolute differences of the ratings from the hypothesised median.

Rating, r	Frequency	$r - 4.5$	$|r - 4.5|$
1	2	-3.5	3.5
2	4	-2.5	2.5
3	2	-1.5	1.5
4	3	-0.5	0.5
5	2	0.5	0.5
6	2	1.5	1.5
9	1	4.5	4.5

The ranks are calculated from these data as follows.

The smallest absolute difference that you are ranking is 0.5. This corresponds to ratings of 4 and 5 and occurs with frequency $3 + 2 = 5$; so the ranks, 1, 2, 3, 4 and 5 are associated with 0.5. The average of these ranks is 3.

The next absolute difference being ranked is 1.5, which occurs with frequency $2 + 2 = 4$, so the ranks 6, 7, 8 and 9 are associated with 1.5. The average of these ranks is 7.5.

A complete list of ranks can now be drawn up by the same method and added to the table.

Rating, r	Frequency	r − 4.5	|r − 4.5|	Rank
1	2	−3.5	3.5	14.5
2	4	−2.5	2.5	11.5
3	2	−1.5	1.5	7.5
4	3	−0.5	0.5	3
5	2	0.5	0.5	3
6	2	1.5	1.5	7.5
9	1	4.5	4.5	16

The sum of the ranks for the ratings below the median of 4.5 is:

$$W_- = 14.5 \times 2 + 11.5 \times 4 + 7.5 \times 2 + 3 \times 3 = 99$$

and the sum of the ranks for the ratings above the median is:

$$W_+ = 3 \times 2 + 7.5 \times 2 + 16 \times 1 = 37.$$

Check: $W_+ + W_- = 99 + 37 = 136 = \dfrac{1}{2} \times 16 \times 17.$

This is a two-tailed test, so the test statistic, W, is taken to be the smaller of W_+ and W_- which in this case is $W_+ = 37$.

From the tables, the critical value for a two-tailed test on a sample of size 16, using the 5% significance level, is 29. But $37 > 29$ so there is no significant evidence that the rankings of the trolley service are different from those of the buffet car and you accept the null hypothesis.

Why Wilcoxon?

Both the Wilcoxon test and the t test are testing whether the distribution of a random variable in a population has a given value of a *location parameter*. A location parameter is any parameter which, when it varies, shifts the position of all the values taken by the random variable but not the shape of the distribution. For instance, in the family of Normal distributions, the mean is a location parameter but the variance is not; in the family of rectangular distributions, the mid-range is a location parameter but the range is not.

The value of the Wilcoxon test is that it does not make the rather strict distributional assumption of the t test – that the distribution of the random variable is Normal. It is therefore very useful when this assumption is not thought to be justified, and when the sample size is not large enough for the sample means nevertheless to be Normally distributed. In fact, although the

Wilcoxon test places a less severe restriction than the t test on the family of distributions which the underlying variable might possess, it is nonetheless of comparable power when compared to the t test under a wide range of conditions. This means that it is a sensible choice for testing location, even when a t test might also be justifiable.

❺ Calculating critical values

Imagine taking a sample of size six from a distribution which is symmetrical about a value M. Assume for simplicity that no two of the six sample values are equal. A sample value above M can therefore have any of the ranks from 1 to 6. This means that the set of sample values which are above M can correspond to any of the 64 possible subsets of the ranks from 1 to 6. These subsets are listed below, together with the rank sum W_+ which is given by each.

Set	W_+	Set	W_+	Set	W_+	Set	W_+
{}	0	{1}	1	{2}	2	{3}	3
{4}	4	{5}	5	{6}	6	{1,2}	3
{1,3}	4	{1,4}	5	{1,5}	6	{1,6}	7
{2,3}	5	{2,4}	6	{2,5}	7	{2,6}	8
{3,4}	7	{3,5}	8	{3,6}	9	{4,5}	9
{4,6}	10	{5,6}	11	{1,2,3}	6	{1,2,4}	7
{1,2,5}	8	{1,2,6}	9	{1,3,4}	8	{1,3,5}	9
{1,3,6}	10	{1,4,5}	10	{1,4,6}	11	{1,5,6}	12
{2,3,4}	9	{2,3,5}	10	{2,3,6}	11	{2,4,5}	11
{2,4,6}	12	{2,5,6}	13	{3,4,5}	12	{3,4,6}	13
{3,5,6}	14	{4,5,6}	15	{1,2,3,4}	10	{1,2,3,5}	11
{1,2,3,6}	12	{1,2,4,5}	12	{1,2,4,6}	13	{1,2,5,6}	14
{1,3,4,5}	13	{1,3,4,6}	14	{1,3,5,6}	15	{1,4,5,6}	16
{2,3,4,5}	14	{2,3,4,6}	15	{2,3,5,6}	16	{2,4,5,6}	17
{3,4,5,6}	18	{1,2,3,4,5}	15	{1,2,3,4,6}	16	{1,2,3,5,6}	17
{1,2,4,5,6}	18	{1,3,4,5,6}	19	{2,3,4,5,6}	20	{1,2,3,4,5,6}	21

What are the probabilities of each possible sum W_+? The symmetry of the distribution implies that each possible rank from 1 to 6 is equally likely to arise from a sample value above or below M and so the 64 subsets above are all equally likely.

This means you can calculate, for instance:

$$P(W_+ = 5) = \frac{\text{number of subsets where } W_+ = 5}{\text{total number of subsets}} = \frac{3}{64}$$

The complete distribution of the values of W_+ found in this way is:

Value	0	1	2	3	4	5	6	7	8	9	10	11	12	13	14	15	16	17	18	19	20	21
Probability ×64	1	1	1	2	2	3	4	4	4	5	5	5	5	4	4	4	3	2	2	1	1	1

The cumulative probabilities can also easily be found from the table: the first few, correct to three decimal places, are:

$$P(W_+ \leqslant 0) = \frac{1}{64} = 0.016$$

$$P(W_+ \leqslant 1) = \frac{1}{64} + \frac{1}{64} = \frac{2}{64} = 0.031$$

$$P(W_+ \leqslant 2) = \frac{1}{64} + \frac{1}{64} + \frac{1}{64} = \frac{3}{64} = 0.047$$

$$P(W_+ \leqslant 3) = \frac{1}{64} + \frac{1}{64} + \frac{1}{64} + \frac{2}{64} = \frac{5}{64} = 0.078$$

These cumulative probabilities enable you to find the critical values you require. For instance, note that $P(W_+ \leqslant 2) \leqslant 0.05$, but that $P(W_+ \leqslant 3) > 0.05$. This means that the one-tailed critical value at the 5% level is 2.

ACTIVITY

Check the critical values given in the tables for $n = 6$.

You may have noticed that not all the work in this section was necessary. You only actually used the information shown below from the first two lines of the complete list of rank sums.

Set	W_+	Set	W_+	Set	W_+	Set	W_+
{}	0	{1}	1	{2}	2	{3}	3
						{1,2}	3

ACTIVITY

Find the critical values for the $n = 7$ case, only writing down the rank sums that are necessary.

℮ Normal approximation

The tables only give critical values where the sample size, n, is at most 50. For larger sample sizes you use the fact that, under the null hypothesis, the test statistic, W, is approximately Normally distributed with mean $\dfrac{n(n+1)}{4}$ and variance $\dfrac{n(n+1)(2n+1)}{24}$.

EXAMPLE 6.2

Determine the 1% one-tailed (2% two-tailed) critical value for a sample of size 84.

SOLUTION

You want to find the integer w so that:

$$P(W \leqslant w) \leqslant 0.01$$

where W has mean $\dfrac{84 \times 85}{4} = 1785$ and variance $\dfrac{84 \times 85 \times 169}{24} = 50\,277.5$.

Note that W is a discrete variable, so that you must make a continuity correction:

$$P(W \leqslant w) \approx P(\text{Normal approximation to } W < w + 0.5).$$ Thus you require:

$$\Phi\left(\frac{w + 0.5 - 1785}{\sqrt{50\,277.5}}\right) \leqslant 0.01$$

so:
$$w \leqslant 1784.5 + \sqrt{50\,277.5}\,\Phi^{-1}(0.01)$$
$$= 1784.5 - \sqrt{50\,277.5}\,\Phi^{-1}(0.99)$$
$$= 1784.5 - \sqrt{50\,277.5} \times 2.326$$
$$= 1262.95$$

This means that values of W less than or equal to 1262 are in the critical region: 1262 is the critical value.

EXERCISE 6A

1 An ancient human settlement site in the Harz mountains has been explored by archaeologists over a long period. They have established by a radio-carbon method that the ages of bones found at the site are approximately uniformly distributed between 3250 and 3100 years. A new potassium-argon method of dating has now been developed and eleven samples of bone randomly selected from finds at the site are dated by this new method. The ages, in years, determined by the new method are as listed below.

3115	3234	3247	3198	3177	3226
3124	3204	3166	3194	3220	

Is there evidence at the 5% level that the potassium-argon method is producing different dates, on average, for bones from the site?

2   A local education authority sets a reasoning test to all eleven-year-olds in the borough. The scores of the whole borough on this test have been symmetrically distributed around a median of 24 out of 40 over many years.

One year a primary school's 33 leavers have the following scores out of 40.

21	11	34	32	19	23	26	35	21	35	40
13	15	28	31	26	21	16	24	22	29	36
38	37	27	22	20	18	32	37	29	28	33

Is there evidence at the 5% level to support the headteacher's claim that her leavers score better on the reasoning test than average?

When must this claim have been made if the hypothesis test is to be valid?

3   An investigator stopped a sample of 72 city workers and checked the time shown by their watches against an accurate timer. The number of minutes fast $(+)$ or slow $(-)$ is recorded for each watch, and the data are shown.

$+2$	0	$+4$	0	-1	-7	$+1$	$+2$	$+2$
-1	-3	$+2$	-4	-1	0	$+3$	$+2$	$+3$
$+1$	-1	$+8$	$+4$	-2	-4	$+5$	$+1$	-2
-3	$+2$	0	$+2$	$+4$	$+2$	0	$+3$	-1
-2	-4	$+1$	$+3$	$+6$	$+2$	0	-6	0
-1	-2	$+1$	$+2$	$+2$	-3	$+2$	0	$+2$
-1	$+2$	$+2$	-5	-1	0	$+5$	$+2$	$+3$
$+1$	-2	$+9$	$+4$	-2	-3	$+4$	$+1$	-2

Is there evidence at the 5% level that city workers tend to keep their watches running fast?

4   Becotide inhalers for asthmatics are supposed to deliver 50 mg of the active ingredient per puff. In a test in a government laboratory, 17 puffs from randomly selected inhalers in a batch were tested and the amount of active ingredient that was delivered was determined. The results, in milligrams, are given below.

| 43 | 47 | 52 | 51 | 44 | 50 | 51 | 41 | 48 |
| 46 | 52 | 50 | 47 | 45 | 49 | 46 | 42 | |

Is there evidence at the 2% level that the inhalers are not delivering the correct amount of active ingredient per puff?

5 When a consignment of grain arrives at Rotterdam docks the percentage of moisture in 11 samples is measured. It is claimed that when the ship left Ontario, the percentage of moisture in the grain was 2.353% on average. The percentages found in the samples were as follows

| 5.294 | 0.824 | 3.353 | 1.706 | 3.765 | 3.235 |
| 8.235 | 0.760 | 3.412 | 6.471 | 3.471 | |

(i) Test at the 5% level whether the median percentage of moisture in the grain is greater than 2.353, using the Wilcoxon single sample test. What assumptions are you making about the distribution of the percentage of moisture in the grain?

(ii) Test at the 5% level whether the mean percentage of moisture in the grain is greater than 2.353, using the t test. What assumption are you making about the distribution of the percentage of moisture in the grain?

(iii) Compare your two conclusions and comment.

e Question 6 and part of question 7 relate to enrichment material.

6 Check the claim in the tables that the critical value for the Wilcoxon single
e sample test, at the 5% level, for a sample of size nine is 8.

Hint: There are $2^9 = 512$ different sets of ranks that, under the null hypothesis, are equally likely to make up W_+ but it is only necessary to write down those with the smallest rank sums – the sets giving rank sums up to and including 9 are sufficient to verify the result.

7 An estate agent claims that the median price of detached houses in a certain area is £115 000. An advertising standards officer takes a random sample of ten such houses that have recently been sold and finds that their prices (in £) are

| 138 000 | 110 000 | 117 500 | 130 000 | 121 900 |
| 106 000 | 165 000 | 134 000 | 129 500 | 125 000. |

(i) Suggest why a Normal distribution might not be a suitable model for the underlying population of prices.

(ii) Calculate the value of the Wilcoxon single sample test statistic for examining the estate agent's claim.

(iii) Taking the alternative hypothesis to be that the median price is not £115 000, use the appropriate table in the Students' Handbook to state the critical region for a test at

(a) the 5% level of significance

(b) the 1% level of significance.

(iv) What is your conclusion in respect of the estate agent's claim?

(v) Find the level of significance of the data as given by the Normal
e approximation

$$N\left(\frac{n(n+1)}{4}, \frac{n(n+1)(2n+1)}{24}\right)$$

to the distribution of the test statistic if the null hypothesis is true.
Comment on the accuracy of the approximation in the light of your
answers to part (iii).

[MEI]

The Wilcoxon paired sample test

A few years ago, some people believed that Maths and English GCSE exams were
of different levels of difficulty and it was claimed that, in the country as a whole,
candidates were getting, on average, at least one-and-a-half grades higher in
English than in Maths. A group of eleven students who took their GCSE exams
at that time gained the following results in Maths and English.

Student	1	2	3	4	5	6	7	8	9	10	11
Maths grade	A	D	F	F	C	G	U	F	D	B	E
English grade	B	C	C	A	D	E	G	B	C	E	E

Are those claiming a difference of as much as one-and-a-half grades justified?

For each student, you can calculate how many grades better their English result
was than their Maths result.

Student	1	2	3	4	5	6	7	8	9	10	11
Grades better in English	−1	1	3	5	−1	2	1	4	1	−3	0

The hypotheses are:

H_0: The median number of grades better in English is 1.5.

H_1: The median number of grades better in English is less than 1.5.

The Wilcoxon single sample test described above can now be used. The number
of grades better in English is the value, g, of the random variable, G, which you
are assuming is symmetrically distributed about its hypothesised median.

Student	g	g − 1.5	[g − 1.5]	Rank
1	−1	−2.5	2.5	8
2	1	−0.5	0.5	2.5
3	3	1.5	1.5	5.5
4	5	3.5	3.5	10
5	−1	−2.5	2.5	8
6	2	0.5	0.5	2.5
7	1	−0.5	0.5	2.5
8	4	2.5	2.5	8
9	1	−0.5	0.5	2.5
10	−3	−4.5	4.5	11
11	0	−1.5	1.5	5.5

So that : $W_+ = 5.5 + 10 + 2.5 + 8 = 26$

$W_- = 8 + 2.5 + 8 + 2.5 + 2.5 + 11 + 5.5 = 40.$

Check: $W_+ + W_- = 26 + 40 = 66 = \dfrac{1}{2} \times 11 \times 12$ as required.

The test statistic is $W = W_+ = 26$.

From the tables, if you use the 5% significance level, the critical value for a sample size of 11 is 13. Since $13 < 26$ you accept the null hypothesis: you have no good evidence to suggest that the claim is incorrect.

In general, when the values of a random variable have been measured on a sample in two different conditions, you may want to test the hypothesis that the medians differ by some given amount between the two conditions.

In this situation the Wilcoxon paired sample test procedure is as follows.

1 Find the differences between the values in the two conditions.

2 Use the Wilcoxon single sample test with the hypothesis that these differences have the suggested median.

The distributional assumption is then that, in the population, the differences between the values of the random variables in the two conditions are symmetrically distributed about the median difference.

Perhaps the most natural context in which this test is used is when you are trying to detect a shift in a location parameter of the distribution of a random variable between two conditions.

It is worth noticing that the Wilcoxon paired sample test and the Wilcoxon single sample test are related in the same way as the paired sample t test and the single sample t test.

EXAMPLE 6.3

Seven randomly selected economists were asked on two occasions to predict what the annual growth rate of GDP would be in December 1995. Their predictions, made in June 1994 and December 1994 were as listed below.

Economist	1	2	3	4	5	6	7
June 1994 prediction (%)	2.2	3.7	2.1	2.3	3.4	2.5	2.1
December 1994 prediction (%)	2.8	3.8	2.6	3.1	3.0	2.6	2.7

Is there evidence at the 5% level that economists have become more optimistic between June and December about the future growth rate?

SOLUTION

The increases in the predictions between June and December 1994 are as shown.

Economist	1	2	3	4	5	6	7
Increase in prediction (%)	0.6	0.1	0.5	0.8	−0.4	0.1	0.6

The hypotheses under test are:

H_0: The median increase in prediction is zero.

H_1: The median increase in prediction is positive.

So it is the absolute increases in prediction themselves that you need to rank.

Economist	1	2	3	4	5	6	7
Increase in prediction (%)	0.6	0.1	0.5	0.8	−0.4	0.1	0.6
Absolute increase in prediction (%)	0.6	0.1	0.5	0.8	0.4	0.1	0.6
Rank	5.5	1.5	4	7	3	1.5	5.5

Hence:

$$W_+ = 5.5 + 1.5 + 4 + 7 + 1.5 + 5.5 = 25$$

$$W_- = 3$$

Check: $W_+ + W_- = 25 + 3 = 28 = \dfrac{1}{2} \times 7 \times 8.$

The test statistic is therefore: $W = W_- = 3$.

From the tables the critical value at the 5% level for a sample of size 7 is 3 and $3 \leqslant 3$, so that the test statistic lies in the critical region and you reject the null hypothesis in favour of the alternative that economists have become more optimistic.

1 The amount of lead in airborne dust (in parts per million) at 23 sampling spots around London was measured before and after government measures to encourage the use of lead-free petrol were introduced. Does the data below give evidence at the 2.5% level that the government measures have reduced the average amount of lead in the air?

Amount of lead	
Before	**After**
43	47
11	8
133	102
57	51
28	34
91	72
48	41
90	99
205	196
37	37
81	15
111	104
23	56
29	17
78	59
170	138
53	62
61	56
14	13
40	27
167	158
80	97
19	8

2 The speed with which 13 subjects react to a stimulus is timed in hundredths of a second. They then play a computer game for 20 minutes and their reaction times are re-measured. Is there evidence at the 5% level that playing the computer game has reduced their reaction times?

Subject	Reaction time	
	before game	after game
A	231	201
B	337	346
C	168	183
D	243	215
E	197	188
F	205	181
G	265	291
H	170	175
I	302	281
J	250	242
K	316	306
L	252	211
M	226	198

3 A construction company operating at many sites uses a computer model to assess the depth of bedrock at each site. Trial borings are also made at some sites to help check the model. Neither the model nor the trial borings can be expected to give completely accurate answers, but it is important that they do not consistently differ from each other.

For a random sample of six sites, the depths (in metres) given by the model and by the trial borings are as follows.

Site	A	B	C	D	E	F
Result from model	9.2	6.5	4.8	8.7	9.6	12.5
Result from trial boring	9.9	6.3	5.1	8.1	9.5	13.0

Investigate the situation using the Wilcoxon paired sample test and a 5% significance level.

[MEI]

4 A psychologist is studying the possible effect of hypnosis on dieting and weight loss. Nine people (who may be considered as a random sample from the population under study) volunteer to take part in an experiment. Their weights are measured. Then, under hypnosis, they are told that they will seldom feel hungry and will eat less than usual. After a month, their weights are measured again. The results (in kilograms) are as follows.

Person	Initial weight	Weight after one month
A	83.7	81.5
B	83.9	80.0
C	68.2	68.8
D	74.9	74.1
E	81.0	82.6
F	72.8	69.2
G	61.3	63.4
H	77.9	74.7
I	69.6	66.2

(i) Use an appropriate t test to examine whether, overall, the mean weight has been reduced over the month, at the 5% level of significance.

(ii) Provide an alternative analysis using an appropriate Wilcoxon test, again at the 5% level of significance.

(iii) What distributional assumption is needed in part (i) but not in part (ii)? By considering the data, comment briefly and informally on whether this assumption appears to hold. (You may wish to use a simple diagram.)

[MEI]

e *Parts of the next two questions relate to enrichment material. They are marked with the* **e** *icon.*

5 A paired comparison situation is being investigated in which underlying Normality cannot be assumed. The Wilcoxon paired sample test is therefore to be used to test the null hypothesis H_0 that the location parameters of the two underlying populations are equal against the alternative hypothesis H_1 that they are not equal.

The observations in the sample from one population are denoted by $x_1, x_2, \ldots, x_n$. The corresponding observations in the other sample are denoted by $y_1, y_2, \ldots, y_n$. The respective differences are denoted by z_i where $z_i = x_i - y_i$ for $i = 1, 2, \ldots, n$. The absolute values of the z_i are ranked (it may be assumed that no two $|z_i|$ are exactly equal). The quantity T is the sum of these ranks for those z_i that are positive.

(i) Find the value of T and carry out the test, at the 5% level of significance, for the following data.

x_i	6.8	7.2	5.5	9.4	8.8	8.2	7.7	6.6
y_i	8.4	8.5	6.9	9.1	9.6	7.6	9.7	8.5

(ii) Show that, if H_0 is true, the expected value of T is
e
$$\tfrac{1}{4} n(n+1).$$

(iii) Find the *actual* level of significance for the data in part (i) as given by
e the Normal approximation
$$N(\tfrac{1}{4} n(n+1), \tfrac{1}{24} n(n+1)(2n+1))$$

to the distribution of T under H_0.

6 A highly skilled typist is comparing the abilities of two word-processing systems for the typing of complicated mathematical expressions. Although both systems provide special facilities, they both have some difficulties in dealing with such expressions. The typist has taken several mathematical articles that have been professionally typeset and has typed each one using both word-processors. For each article, she has counted the number of such expressions with which, in her opinion, there has been unusual difficulty. The results are as follows.

Article	A	B	C	D	E	F	G	H	I	J
Word-processor I	2	15	21	6	1	3	10	14	7	7
Word-processor II	1	20	29	2	11	5	3	25	20	22

Underlying Normality cannot be assumed for these counts. An appropriate Wilcoxon procedure is therefore to be used to test whether the two word-processors have, on the whole, the same ability in coping with such expressions.

(i) Carry out the test at the 10% level of significance, using the appropriate table in the Students' Handbook.

(ii) Find the actual level of significance of the data as given by the Normal
e approximation to the distribution of the Wilcoxon statistic under the null hypothesis.

You are reminded that the parameters of this Normal approximation are
$$\mu = \frac{n(n+1)}{4} \quad \text{and} \quad \sigma^2 = \frac{n(n+1)(2n+1)}{24}.$$

[MEI]

The Wilcoxon single sample test

1 This is used for testing the null hypothesis that the population median of a random variable is equal to a given value M, under the assumption that the variable is symmetrically distributed about its median.

2 Given a sample, remove any element equal to M. Let n be the size of the reduced sample.

3 To calculate the test statistic:
   - Find the absolute differences between each sample value and M.
   - Rank these values giving the lowest rank to the smallest difference.
   - W_+ and W_- are the sums of ranks of sample values respectively greater or less than M.
   - Take the test statistic W to be the smaller of W_- and W_+ for a two-tailed test, or make the appropriate choice for a one-tailed test.

4 The null hypothesis is rejected if W is less than or equal to the appropriate critical value.

The Wilcoxon paired sample test

5 For paired data the differences of each pair are found first. The null hypothesis is that the difference of the population medians is equal to a given value, M, under the assumption that the differences are symmetrically distributed about their median. The test procedure is then as in points 2 to 4 above.

7

The χ^2 (chi-squared) distribution

The fact that the criterion which we happen to use has a fine ancestry of statistical theorems does not justify its use. Such justification must come from empirical evidence that it works.

W. A. Shewhart

THE AVONFORD STAR
The die that Roald rolled

Those of you who watched the big match last night will have missed Jane McNulty's fascinating documentary 'Mind Over Matter?' In her usual incisive and questioning style Ms McNulty explored the extraordinary world of Roald Drysdale.

Those of us who live in Avonford have long known of Roald and his equally extraordinary mother Blanche. Roald's claims to be able to influence the world around him by mind alone are just as remarkable as Uri Geller's spoon bending.

I was fascinated by his demonstration of his influence over a die being thrown. 'You must realise that objects we take to be inanimate do in fact have a spirit,' he explained. 'Take this die. At the moment its spirit is willing it to produce a certain result. I can't change that, but by concentrating my Thought Field on the die, I can enhance its spirit and help it to produce the outcome that it is seeking.'

The power of the mind – Roald Drysdale claims to have psychic influence

That evening the die's spirit was clearly willing it to show 1, as you can see from these remarkable results from 120 throws.

Score	6	5	4	3	2	1
Frequency	12	16	15	23	24	30

Do these figures provide evidence that Roald had influenced the die, or is this just the level of variation you would expect to occur naturally? Clearly a formal statistical test is required.

If Roald's claim had been that he could make a particular number, say 6, turn up more often than the other numbers, you could use a binomial test.

However, all he said was that he could 'enhance the spirit of the die' by making some number come up more than the others. So all six outcomes are involved and a different test is needed.

The expected distribution of the results, based on the null hypothesis that the die is not biased, is easily obtained. The probability of each outcome is $\frac{1}{6}$ and so the expectation for each number is $120 \times \frac{1}{6} = 20$.

Outcome	1	2	3	4	5	6
Expected frequency, f_e	20	20	20	20	20	20

You would not, however, expect exactly this result from 120 throws. Indeed you would be very suspicious if somebody claimed to have obtained it, and might well disbelieve it. You expect random variation to produce small differences in the frequencies. The question is whether the quite large differences in Roald's case can be explained in this way or not.

When this is written in the formal language of statistical tests, it becomes:

H_0: $p = \frac{1}{6}$ for each outcome.

H_1: $p \neq \frac{1}{6}$ for each outcome.

The expected frequencies are denoted by f_e and the observed frequencies by f_o. To measure how far the observed data are from the expected, you clearly need to consider the difference between the observed frequencies, f_o, and the expected, f_e. The measure which is used as a test statistic for this is denoted by X^2 and given by:

$$X^2 = \sum_{\text{All classes}} \frac{(f_o - f_e)^2}{f_e}.$$

You have already met this statistic when carrying out tests involving contingency tables in Chapter 3 of *Statistics 2*. In this case the calculation of X^2 is as follows.

Outcome	6	5	4	3	2	1
Observed frequency, f_o	12	16	15	23	24	30
Expected frequency, f_e	20	20	20	20	20	20
Difference, $f_o - f_e$	−8	−4	−5	3	4	10
$(f_o - f_e)^2$	64	16	25	9	16	100
$(f_o - f_e)^2/f_e$	3.2	0.8	1.25	0.45	0.8	5

$$X^2 = 3.2 + 0.8 + 1.25 + 0.45 + 0.8 + 5 = 11.5$$

The test statistic X^2 has the χ^2 (chi-squared) distribution. Critical values for this distribution are given in tables but, before you can use them, you have to think about two more points.

What is to be the significance level of the test?

This should really have been set before any data were collected. Because many people will be sceptical about Roald's claim, it would seem advisable to make the test rather strict, and so the 1% significance level is chosen.

How many degrees of freedom are involved?

You will recall from reading about the χ^2 distribution at the end of Chapter 2 that the shape of the curve depends on the number of free variables involved, the degrees of freedom, v.

In this case there are six classes (corresponding to scores on the die of 1, 2, 3, 4, 5 and 6) but since the total number of throws is fixed (120) the frequency in the last class can be worked out if you know those of the first five classes.

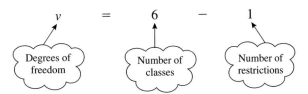

$$v \quad = \quad 6 \quad - \quad 1$$

Degrees of freedom / Number of classes / Number of restrictions

Looking in the tables for the 1% significance level and $v = 5$ gives a critical value of 15.09; see figure 7.1.

Since $11.5 < 15.09$, H_0 is accepted.

There is no reason at this significance level to believe that any number on the die was any more likely to come up than any other. Roald's powers are not proved.

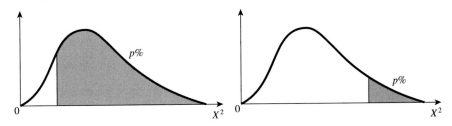

$p\%$	99	97.5	95	90		10	5.0	2.5	1.0	0.5
$v = 1$	.0001	.0010	.0039	.0158		2.706	3.841	5.024	6.635	7.879
2	.0201	.0506	0.103	0.211		4.605	5.991	7.378	9.210	10.60
3	0.115	0.216	0.352	0.584		6.251	7.815	9.348	11.34	12.84
4	0.297	0.484	0.711	1.064		7.779	9.488	11.14	13.28	14.86
5	0.554	0.831	1.145	1.610		9.236	11.07	12.83	15.09	16.75
6	0.872	1.237	1.635	2.204		10.64	12.59	14.45	16.81	18.55
7	1.239	1.690	2.167	2.833		12.02	14.07	16.01	18.48	20.28
8	1.646	2.180	2.733	3.490		13.36	15.51	17.53	20.09	21.95
9	2.088	2.700	3.325	4.168		14.68	16.92	19.02	21.67	23.59

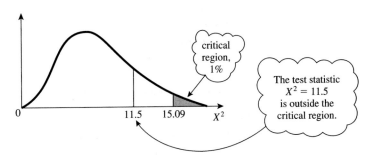

critical region, 1%

The test statistic $X^2 = 11.5$ is outside the critical region.

Figure 7.1

This is a one-tail test with only the right-hand tail under consideration. The interpretation of the left-hand tail (where the agreement seems to be too good) is discussed later in the chapter.

Properties of the test statistic X^2

$$X^2 = \sum_{\text{All classes}} \frac{(f_o - f_e)^2}{f_e}$$

- It is clear that as the difference between the expected values and the observed values increases then so will the value of this test statistic. Squaring the top gives due weight to any particularly large differences. It also means that all values are positive.
- Dividing $(f_e - f_o)^2$ by f_e has the effect of standardising that element, allowing for the fact that, the larger the expected frequency within a class, the larger will be the difference between the observed and the expected.

The χ^2 distribution with v degrees of freedom is that of

$$Z_1^2 + Z_2^2 + \ldots + Z_v^2$$

where $Z_1, Z_2, \ldots, Z_v$ are v independent standardised Normal variables.

The detailed mathematics of how the expression

$$\sum_{\text{All classes}} \frac{(f_o - f_e)^2}{f_e}$$

fulfils this requirement is, however, beyond the scope of this book.

Notation

- An alternative notation which is often used is to call the expected frequency in the ith class E_i and the observed frequency in the ith class O_i

  In this notation, $X^2 = \sum_i \frac{(E_i - O_i)^2}{E_i}$.
- The usual convention in statistics is to use a Greek letter for a parent population parameter and the corresponding Roman letter for the equivalent sample statistic.

Parent population parameters (Greek letters)	Values of sample statistics (Roman letters)
μ	m
σ	s
ρ	r

Unfortunately, when it comes to χ^2, there is no Roman equivalent to the Greek letter χ since it translates into CH. Since X looks rather like χ a sample statistic from a χ^2 population is denoted by X^2. (In the same way Christmas is abbreviated to χmas but written Xmas.)

Using the χ^2 test

The χ^2 test is commonly used to see if a proposed model fits observed data.

 Why is it the model that should fit the data and not the other way round?

Minimum expected frequencies

The expected frequency of any class must be at least five. If a class has an expected frequency of less than five, then it must be grouped together with one or more other classes until their combined expected frequency is at least five. In that case the number of classes is reduced accordingly when working out the degrees of freedom.

Degrees of freedom

The degrees of freedom for the test are given by:

degrees of freedom = number of classes − number of restrictions

In the case of Roald's die, there was one restriction, namely that the total of the frequencies had to be 120, the total number of throws. In some situations there are more restrictions than that, as you will see in the following examples.

When a particular distribution is fitted to the data, it may be necessary to estimate one or more parameters of the distribution. This, together with the restriction on the total, will reduce the number of degrees of freedom:

$$v = \text{number of classes} - \text{number of estimated parameters} - 1$$

EXAMPLE 7.1

Poisson distribution
The number of telephone calls made to a counselling service is thought to be modelled by the Poisson distribution. Data are collected on the number of calls received during one-hour periods as shown in the table. Use these data to test at the 5% significance level whether a Poisson model is appropriate.

No. of calls per hour	0	1	2	3	4	5	6	Total
Frequency	6	13	26	14	7	4	0	70

SOLUTION

H_0: The number of calls can be modelled by the Poisson distribution.

H_1: The number of calls cannot be modelled by the Poisson distribution.

Nothing is known about the form of the Poisson distribution, so the data must be used to estimate the Poisson parameter λ.

From the data, the mean number of calls per hour is

$$\frac{0 \times 6 + 1 \times 13 + 2 \times 26 + 3 \times 14 + 4 \times 7 + 5 \times 4}{70} = \frac{155}{70} = 2.214.$$

The Poisson distribution with parameter $\lambda = 2.214$ is as follows.

x	$P(X = x)$	$70 \times P(X = x)$	Expected frequency
0	$e^{-2.214}$	70×0.1093	7.6
1	$P(X = 0) \times \frac{2.214}{1}$	70×0.2419	16.9
2	$P(X = 1) \times \frac{2.214}{2}$	70×0.2678	18.7
3	$P(X = 2) \times \frac{2.214}{3}$	70×0.1976	13.8
4	$P(X = 3) \times \frac{2.214}{4}$	70×0.1094	7.7
5	$P(X = 4) \times \frac{2.214}{5}$	70×0.0484	3.4
$\geqslant 6$	$1 - P(X < 6)$	70×0.0256	1.8

The expected frequencies for the last two classes are both less than 5 but if they are put together to give an expected value of 5.2, the problem is overcome.

Note

The expected frequencies are not rounded to the nearest whole number. To do so would invalidate the test. Expected frequencies do not need to be integers.

The expected frequency for the last class was worked out as $1 - P(X < 6)$ and not as $P(X = 6)$, which would have cut off the right-hand tail of the distribution. The classes need to cover all *possible* outcomes, not just those that occurred in your survey.

The table for calculating the test statistic is shown below.

No. of calls, X	0	1	2	3	4	5+	Total
Observed frequency, f_o	6	13	26	14	7	4	70
Expected frequency, f_e	7.6	16.9	18.7	13.8	7.7	5.2	70
$(f_o - f_e)$	−1.6	−3.9	7.3	0.2	−0.7	−1.2	0.1
$(f_o - f_e)^2/f_e$	0.336	0.900	2.849	0.002	0.064	0.277	4.428

$$X^2 = 0.336 + 0.900 + 2.849 + 0.002 + 0.064 + 0.277 = 4.428$$

The degrees of freedom are

$$v = \text{number of classes} - \text{number of estimated parameters} - 1$$

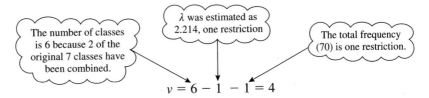

The number of classes is 6 because 2 of the original 7 classes have been combined.

λ was estimated as 2.214, one restriction

The total frequency (70) is one restriction.

$$v = 6 - 1 - 1 = 4$$

From the tables, the critical value for a significance level of 5% and 4 degrees of freedom is 9.488.

The calculated test statistic, $X^2 = 4.428$.

Since $4.428 < 9.488$, H_0 is accepted.

The data are consistent with a Poisson distribution for the number of calls.

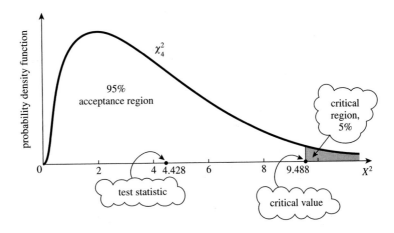

Figure 7.2

Note

The mode of χ^2_4 occurs at 2. The mode of χ^2_{10} occurs at 8. In general, the mode of χ^2_k occurs at $k - 2$.

EXAMPLE 7.2

Binomial distribution

An egg packaging firm has introduced a new box for its eggs. Each box holds six eggs. Unfortunately it finds that the new box tends to mark the eggs. Data on the number of eggs marked in 100 boxes are collected.

No. of marked eggs	0	1	2	3	4	5	6	Total
No. of boxes, f_o	3	3	27	29	10	7	21	100

It is thought that the distribution may be modelled by the binomial distribution. Carry out a test on the data at the 0.5% significance level to determine whether the data can be modelled by the binomial distribution.

SOLUTION

H_0: The number of marked eggs can be modelled by the binomial distribution.

H_1: The number of marked eggs cannot be modelled by the binomial distribution.

The binomial distribution has two parameters, n and p. The parameter n is clearly 6, but p is not known and so must be estimated from the data.

From the data, the mean number of marked eggs per box is

$$\frac{0 \times 3 + 1 \times 3 + 2 \times 27 + 3 \times 29 + 4 \times 10 + 5 \times 7 + 6 \times 21}{100} = 3.45.$$

Since the population mean is np you may estimate p by putting

$$6p = 3.45$$

$$\text{estimated } p = 0.575 \quad \text{and estimated} \quad q = 1 - p = 0.425.$$

These parameters are now used to calculate the expected frequencies of 0, 1, 2, ..., 6 marked eggs per box in 100 boxes.

x	$P(X = x)$		Expected frequency, f_e $100 \times P(X = x)$
0	0.425^6	0.0059	0.59
1	$6 \times 0.575^1 \times 0.425^5$	0.0478	4.78
2	$15 \times 0.575^2 \times 0.425^4$	0.1618	16.18
3	$20 \times 0.575^3 \times 0.425^3$	0.2919	29.19
4	$15 \times 0.575^4 \times 0.425^2$	0.2962	29.62
5	$6 \times 0.575^5 \times 0.425^1$	0.1603	16.03
6	0.575^6	0.0361	3.61

In this case there are three classes with an expected frequency of less than 5. The class for $x = 0$ is combined with the class for $x = 1$, bringing the expected frequency just over 5, and the class for $x = 6$ is combined with that for $x = 5$.

No. of marked eggs, x	0, 1	2	3	4	5, 6	Total
Observed frequency, f_o	6	27	29	10	28	100
Expected frequency, f_e	5.37	16.18	29.19	29.62	19.64	100
$(f_o - f_e)$	0.68	10.82	−0.19	−19.62	8.36	
$(f_o - f_e)^2/f_e$	0.07	7.24	−0.00	13.00	3.56	

The test statistic, $X^2 = 0.07 + 7.24 + 0.00 + 13.00 + 3.56 = 23.87$

The degrees of freedom,

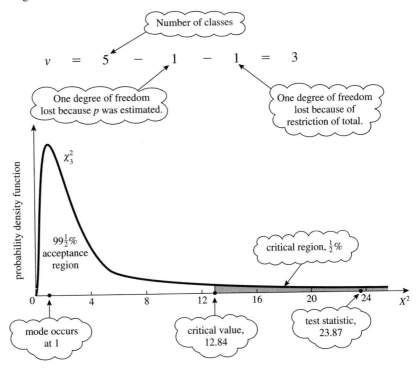

Figure 7.3

From the tables, for the 0.5% significance level and $v = 3$, the critical value of χ^2 is 12.84.

Since $23.87 > 12.84$, H_0 is rejected.

The data indicate that the binomial distribution is not an appropriate model for the number of marked eggs. If you look at the distribution of the data you can easily see why, since it is bimodal (figure 7.4).

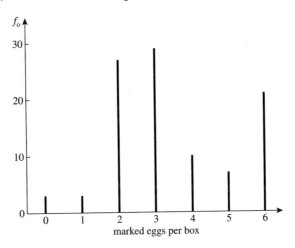

Figure 7.4

EXAMPLE 7.3

Given proportions

It is generally believed that a particular genetic defect is carried by 10% of people. A new and simple test becomes available to determine whether somebody is a carrier of this defect, using a blood specimen. As part of a research project, 100 hospitals are asked to carry out this test anonymously on the next 30 blood samples they take. The results are as follows.

Number of positive tests	0	1	2	3	4	5	6	7+
Frequency, f_o		11	29	26	20	9	3	1	1

Do these figures support the model that 10% of people carry this defect, independently of any other condition, at the 5% significance level?

SOLUTION

H_0: The model that 10% of people carry this defect is appropriate.

H_1: The model that 10% of people carry this defect is not appropriate.

The expected frequencies may be estimated using the binomial distribution B(30, 0.1).

Number of positive tests	0	1	2	3	4	5	6	7+
Expected frequency, f_e	4.24	14.13	22.77	23.61	17.71	10.23	4.74	2.58

The calculation then proceeds as follows.

No. of positive tests	0, 1	2	3	4	5	6+	Total
Observed frequency, f_o	40	26	20	9	3	2	100
Expected frequency, f_e	18.37	22.77	23.61	17.71	10.23	7.32	100.01
$(f_o - f_e)$	21.63	3.23	−3.61	−8.71	−7.23	−5.32	
$(f_o - f_e)^2/f_e$	25.47	0.46	0.55	4.28	5.11	3.87	

The test statistic $X^2 = 25.47 + 0.46 + 0.55 + 4.28 + 5.11 + 3.87$
$$= 39.74$$

The degrees of freedom,

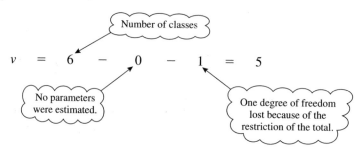

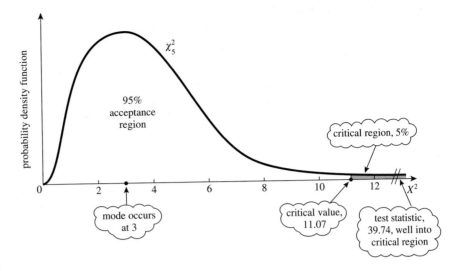

Figure 7.5

From the tables, for 5% significance level and $v = 5$, the critical value of χ^2 is 12.84.

Since $39.74 > 11.07$, H_0 is rejected.

The data indicate that the binomial distribution with $p = 0.1$ is not an appropriate model.

Notes

1 Although this example is like the previous one in that both used the binomial distribution as a model, the procedure is different. In this case the given model included the information $p = 0.1$ and so you did not have to estimate the parameter p. Consequently a degree of freedom was not lost from doing so.

The model B(30, 0.1) specified the probability for each of the classes. This is an example of a 'given' proportions model.

2 The value of X^2 was very large in comparison with the critical value. What went wrong with the model?

You will find that if you use the data to estimate p, it does not work out to be 0.1 but a little under 0.07. Fewer people are carriers of the defect than was believed to be the case. If you work through the example again with the model $p = 0.07$, you will find that the fit is good enough for you to start looking at the left-hand tail of the distribution.

The left-hand tail

The χ^2 test is conducted as a one-tail test, looking to see if the test statistic gives a value to the right of the critical value, as in the previous examples.

However, examination of the left-hand tail also gives information. In any modelling situation you would expect there to be some variability. Even when using the binomial to model a clear binomial situation, like the number of heads obtained in throwing a coin a large number of times, you would be very surprised if the observed and expected frequencies were identical. The left-hand tail may lead you to wonder whether the fit is too good to be credible. The following is a very famous example of the Poisson distribution.

Death from horse kicks

For a period of 20 years in the 19th century data were collected of the annual number of deaths caused by horse kicks per army corps in the Prussian army.

No. of deaths	0	1	2	3	4
No. of corps, f_o	109	65	22	3	1

These data give a mean of 0.61. The variance of 0.6079 is almost the same, suggesting that the Poisson model may be appropriate.

The distribution Poisson (0.61) gives these figures.

No. of deaths	0	1	2	3	4 or more
No. of corps, f_e	108.7	66.3	20.2	4.1	0.7

This looks so close that there seems little point in using a test to see if the data will fit the distribution. However, proceeding to the test, and remembering to combine classes to give expected values of at least 5, the null and alternative hypotheses are as follows.

H_0: Deaths from horse kick can be modelled by a Poisson distribution.

H_1: Deaths from horse kick cannot be modelled by a Poisson distribution.

No. of deaths	0	1	2 or more
Observed frequency, f_o	109	65	26
Expected frequency, f_e	108.7	66.3	25
$(f_o - f_e)$	0.3	−1.3	1
$(f_o - f_e)^2 / f_e$	0.001	0.025	0.040

The test statistic $X^2 = 0.001 + 0.025 + 0.040$

$$= 0.066$$

The degrees of freedom are given by

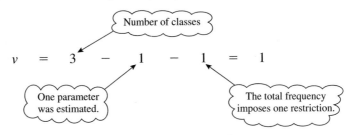

$$\nu = 3 - 1 - 1 = 1$$

Number of classes

One parameter was estimated.

The total frequency imposes one restriction.

The critical value of χ^2 for 1 degree of freedom at the 5% significance level is 3.841.

As $0.066 < 3.841$ it is clear that the null hypothesis, that the Poisson distribution is an appropriate model, should be accepted.

? Looking at the expected values of the Poisson distribution in comparison with the observed values suggests that the fit is very good indeed. Is it perhaps suspiciously good? Might the data have been fixed?

The tables relating to the left-hand tail of the χ^2 distribution give critical values for this situation. For example the value for 95% significance level for $\nu = 1$ is 0.0039. This means if the null hypothesis is true you would expect a value for X^2 less than 0.0039 from no more than 5% of samples.

In this case, the test statistic is $X^2 = 0.066$. This is greater than the 95% critical value, and so you can conclude that a fit as good as this will occur with more than 1 sample in 20. That may well help allay your suspicions.

If your test statistic does lie within the left-hand critical region, you should check the data to ensure that the figures are genuine and that all the procedures have been carried out properly. There are three situations you should particularly watch out for.

• The model was constructed to fit a set of data. It is then being tested by seeing how well it fits the same data. Once the model is determined, new data should be used to test it.

• Some of the data have been omitted in order to produce a better fit.

• The data are not genuine.

Although looking at the left-hand tail of the χ^2 distribution may make you suspicious of the quality of the data, it does not provide a formal hypothesis test that the data are not genuine. Thus the term *critical region* is not really appropriate to this tail; *warning region* would be better.

Note

The χ^2 test is a distribution-free test; that means that there are no modelling assumptions associated with the test itself. This has the advantage that the test can be widely used, but on the other hand it is not a very sensitive test. The test for rank correlation is another example of a distribution-free test: one can test for rank correlation without knowing anything about the underlying bivariate distribution, but one frequently finds there is no significant evidence of correlation.

EXERCISE 7A

All the questions in this exercise require you to carry out a hypothesis test. The answer to each question must contain a clear statement of your null and alternative hypotheses and the conclusion drawn from the test.

1 Part of a large simulation study requires the provision of many simulated observations that can be taken as coming from the Poisson distribution with parameter 2. There is a suspicion that this part of the simulation is not working properly.

200 of the simulated observations are recorded in the form of a frequency table as follows.

Simulated observations	0	1	2	3	4	$\geqslant 5$
Frequency	20	40	52	49	27	12

Carry out a χ^2 test, at the 5% level of significance, to examine whether the required Poisson distribution can be assumed for the simulated observations.

[MEI, *part*]

2 A typist makes mistakes from time to time in a 200-page book. The number of pages with different numbers of mistakes are as follows.

Mistakes	0	1	2	3	4	5
Pages	18	62	84	30	5	1

(i) Test at the 5% significance level whether the Poisson distribution is an appropriate model for these data.
(ii) What factors would make it other than a Poisson distribution?

3 A biologist crosses two pure varieties of plant, one with pink flowers, the other white. The pink is dominant so that the flowers of the second generation should be in the ratio

$$\text{pink}:\text{white} = 3:1.$$

He plants the seeds in batches of 5 in 32 trays and counts the numbers of plants with pink and with white flowers in each tray.

White flowers	0	1	2	3	4	5
Frequency	9	12	7	2	1	1

(i) What distribution would you expect for the number of plants with white flowers?

(ii) Use these figures to test at the 2.5% significance level whether the distribution is that which you expected.

4 As part of a survey, a railway company took a sample of 80 people, each of whom had recently travelled three times on a particular route, and asked them on how many of these three occasions they were generally satisfied with their journeys. The results were as follows.

Number of occasions generally satisfied	0	1	2	3
Number of people	4	20	44	12

The company is considering fitting a binomial model to these data, with p taken as the probability of being generally satisfied on a journey.

(i) Estimate the value of p.

(ii) Use a suitable statistical procedure and 10% significance level to assess the goodness of fit of a binomial model.

(iii) What assumption is required about the sample? Discuss briefly whether this assumption is likely to hold.

[MEI]

5 The manager of a large supermarket has recently moved from one store to another. At the previous store, it was known from surveys that 42% of the customers lived within 5 miles of the store, 35% lived between 5 and 10 miles from the store and the remaining 23% lived more than 10 miles from the store. The manager wishes to test whether the same proportions apply at the new store.

One Saturday morning, the first 100 customers to enter the store after 11.00 am were asked how far from the store they lived. The results, grouped into the same categories as for the previous store, were as follows.

Distance (miles)	0–5	5–10	more than 10
Number of customers	34	48	18

(i) Assuming that this is a random sample of all the customers at the store, test at the 5% level of significance whether the proportions at the manager's new store may be taken as the same as those at the previous store. Discuss your conclusions briefly.

(ii) Discuss whether this is likely to be a random sample.

[MEI]

6 A man accuses a casino of having two loaded dice. He throws them 360 times with the following outcomes for their sum at each throw.

Total	2	3	4	5	6	7	8	9	10	11	12
Freq.	5	15	30	35	45	61	53	45	31	24	16

Does he have grounds for his accusation at the 5% significance level?

7 An examination board is testing a multiple-choice question. They get 100 students to try the question and their answers are as follows.

Choice	A	B	C	D	E
Frequency	32	18	10	28	12

Are there grounds, at the 10% significance level, for the view that the question was so hard that the students guessed the answers at random?

8 A student on a geography field trip has collected data on the size of rocks found on a scree slope. The student counts the number of large rocks (that is, heavier than a stated weight) found in a 2 m square at the top, middle and bottom of the slope.

	Top	Middle	Bottom
Number of large rocks	5	10	18

(i) Test at the 5% significance level whether these data are consistent with the hypothesis that the size of rocks is distributed evenly on the scree slope.

(ii) What does your test tell the student about the theory that large rocks will migrate to the bottom of the slope?

9 A regular gambler at a casino thinks that the roulette wheel is biased. The wheel has 37 equal sectors, each of which is given a number between 0 and 36. The number 0 is coloured green and the other numbers are equally divided between red and black. You can bet on which colour sector the ball will settle in when the wheel stops turning. At the suggestion of the management, the gambler records the number of times each of these three colours occurs during an evening's gambling. The results are as follows.

	Green	Red	Black	Total
Frequency	28	325	387	740

Carry out a test at the 1% significance level to see if the gambler is justified in his allegation that the wheel is biased.

10 A university student working in a small seaside hotel in the summer holidays looks at the records for the previous holiday season of 30 weeks. She records the number of days in each week on which the hotel had to turn away visitors because it was full. The data she collects are as follows.

Number of days visitors turned away	0	1	2	3	4	5+	Total
Number of weeks	11	13	4	1	1	0	30

(i) Calculate the mean and variance of the data.
(ii) The student thinks that these data can be modelled by the binomial distribution. Carry out a test at the 5% significance level to see if the binomial distribution is a suitable model.
(iii) What other distribution might be used to model these data? Give your reasons.

11 Morag is writing a book. Every so often she uses the spell check facility in her word processing software, and for interest records the number of mistakes she has made on each page. In the first 20 pages the results were as follows.

No. of mistakes/page	0	1	2	3	4+	Total
Frequency	9	6	4	1	0	20

(i) Explain why it is not possible to use the χ^2 test on these data to decide whether the occurrence of spelling mistakes may be modelled by the Poisson distribution.

In the next 30 pages Morag's figures are as follows.

No. of mistakes/page	0	1	2	3	4+	Total
Frequency	14	7	7	0	2	30

(ii) Use the combined figures, covering the first 50 pages, to test whether the occurrence of Morag's spelling mistakes may be modelled by the Poisson distribution. Use the 5% significance level.

(iii) If the distribution really is Poisson, what does this tell you about the incidence of spelling mistakes? Do you think this is realistic?

12 In a survey of five towns the population of the town and the number of petrol-filling stations were recorded as follows.

Town	Population (to nearest 10 000)	Number of filling stations
A	4	22
B	3	16
C	7	35
D	6	27
E	12	60
Totals	32	160

(i) An assistant researcher, who wanted to find out whether the petrol stations were evenly distributed between the towns, performed a χ^2 test on the number of filling stations, with a null hypothesis that there was no difference in the number of filling stations in each town. She found that her X^2 value was 36.69. Without repeating her calculation, state with reasons what her conclusion was.

(ii) The senior researcher decided to use the hypothesis that the number of filling stations was directly proportional to the size of the town's population. Show that, on this basis, the expected number of garages for town A would be 20, and test the hypothesis at the 10% significance level stating your conclusions clearly.

[MEI]

13 A local council has records of the number of children and the number of households in its area. It is therefore known that the average number of children per household is 1.40. It is suggested that the number of children per household can be modelled by the Poisson distribution with parameter 1.40. In order to test this, a random sample of 1000 households is taken, giving the following data.

Number of children	0	1	2	3	4	5+
Number of households	273	361	263	78	21	4

(i) Find the corresponding expected frequencies obtained from the Poisson distribution with parameter 1.40.

7

Exercise 7A

(ii) Carry out a χ^2 test, at the 5% level of significance, to determine whether or not the proposed model should be accepted. State clearly the null and alternative hypotheses being tested and the conclusion which is reached.

[MEI]

14 (i) A random sample of supermarkets were sent a questionnaire on which they were asked to report the number of cases of shoplifting they had dealt with in each month of the previous year. The totals for each month were as follows.

J	F	M	A	M	J	J	A	S	O	N	D
16	12	10	17	6	18	16	17	10	22	14	16

Carry out a χ^2 test at an appropriate level of significance to determine whether or not shoplifting is more likely to occur in some months than others. (You may take all months to be of the same length.) Make clear your null and alternative hypotheses, the level of significance you are using, and your conclusion.

You may, if you wish, use the fact that, when all the values of f_e are equal, the usual χ^2 test statistic may be written as

$$\frac{1}{f_e}\sum f_o^2 - \sum f_o$$

(ii) Prove the result given at the end of part (i). [MEI]

15 In a survey 200 motorists, chosen at random, were asked how many attempts they took at the driving test until they passed. The results are summarised by the following frequency distribution.

Number of attempts	1	2	3	4	5	6	7	8+
Number of motorists	71	47	35	20	15	9	3	0

(i) Calculate the sample mean $\bar{x}$.

A statistician suggests that the number of attempts required to pass the driving test can be modelled by the random variable X defined as follows:

$$P(X = r) = p(1 - p)^{r-1} \quad \text{for} \quad r = 1, 2, 3, \ldots$$

where p represents the probability of a motorist passing any particular test. You are given that, for this model, $E(X) = \dfrac{1}{p}$, so p can be estimated by $\dfrac{1}{\bar{x}}$.

(ii) Calculate the expected frequencies according to the statistician's model.
(iii) Carry out an appropriate test, at the 5% level, to determine whether the model is a good one or not. State your hypotheses and conclusions carefully, and justify the number of degrees of freedom used.

[MEI]

175

16 Properties where people live are placed in one of eight bands for council tax assessment. Band A represents the lowest-value properties (up to £40 000) and band H represents the highest-value properties (over £320 000).

It is desired to investigate whether the distribution of properties within the eight bands in the city of Trumpton matches the national distribution.

A random sample of 500 properties in Trumpton is taken. The percentage of properties in each band nationally and the number of properties in each band in the sample are as follows.

Band	Percentage of properties nationally	Number of properties in sample
A	14.2%	53
B	22.6%	105
C	20.8%	111
D	14.3%	80
E	11.4%	63
F	9.8%	49
G	5.9%	36
H	1.0%	3
Total	100.0%	500

(i) Find the expected frequency within each band in Trumpton based on the national proportions.

(ii) Carry out an appropriate hypothesis test, at the 10% significance level. State your hypotheses and conclusions carefully.

(iii) If a random sample of 1000 properties had been taken and there had been precisely *twice* as many properties in each band, what effect would this have on your conclusions in part (ii)?

[MEI]

Testing whether data come from a given Normal distribution

It is a common assumption in statistics that a set of data arises from a Normal distribution, for instance when conducting a t test. How can you test, from the information in a sample, whether this assumption is justified? One method, using the χ^2 test, is shown in the example below.

EXAMPLE 7.4

When an intelligence test was standardised, scores on the test were distributed Normally with mean 100 and standard deviation 15. Twenty years later, it is thought that the distribution of scores may have changed.

The intelligence scores of a random sample of 40 people were measured and are given below.

92	106	91	112	106	113	125	108
103	127	110	112	120	97	115	90
119	87	114	90	88	117	119	108
103	94	104	116	97	112	103	97
86	82	114	120	115	94	110	106

Use these data to test whether the distribution is indeed still Normal.

SOLUTION

The hypotheses are:

H_0: Q has the distribution $N(100, 15^2)$

H_1: Q does not have the distribution $N(100, 15^2)$

where Q is the random variable giving an individual's test score.

One possible way of grouping these data is as follows.

Range of IQ scores	Observed frequency, f_o
−86.5	2
86.5–95.5	8
95.5–104.5	10
104.5–113.5	8
113.5–	12

You can now calculate the frequencies you would expect in these intervals under the assumption that the null hypothesis is true.

You know that Q is a random variable for which the distribution is $N(100, 15^2)$ under the null hypothesis, so that:

$$P(86.5 < Q < 95.5) = P\left(\frac{86.5 - 100}{15} < Z < \frac{95.5 - 100}{15}\right)$$
$$= P(-0.9 < Z < -0.3)$$
$$= \Phi(0.9) - \Phi(0.3)$$
$$= 0.8159 - 0.6179$$
$$= 0.1980$$

and so the expected frequency for the interval 86.5–95.5 is $0.1980 \times 40 = 7.920$.

The other expected frequencies can be found by similar calculations (and the symmetry of the intervals about the hypothesised mean), resulting in the table of observed and expected frequencies below.

Range of IQ scores	Observed frequency, f_o	Expected frequency, f_e
–86.5	2	7.362
86.5–95.5	8	7.920
95.5–104.5	10	9.433
104.5–113.5	8	7.920
113.5–	12	7.362

The statistic

$$X^2 = \sum_{\text{All classes}} \frac{(f_o - f_e)^2}{f_e}$$

has an approximately χ^2 distribution under the null hypothesis. Its degrees of freedom are given by

$$v = \text{number of classes} - 1,$$

where one degree of freedom is lost because the totals of expected and observed frequencies are equal.

Here:

$$X^2 = \frac{(2 - 7.362)^2}{7.362} + \frac{(8 - 7.920)^2}{7.920} + \frac{(10 - 9.433)^2}{9.433} + \frac{(8 - 7.920)^2}{7.920} + \frac{(12 - 7.362)^2}{7.362}$$
$$= 6.863$$

and $v = 5 - 1 = 4$

Observe that the expected frequencies for each cell are greater than 5, as required for the χ^2 distribution to be a good approximation, so that you can use the χ^2 tables to determine the critical value: for four degrees of freedom at the 5% level this is 9.488. Since $6.863 < 9.488$, you can accept the null hypothesis that the sample is drawn from an underlying $N(100, 15^2)$ distribution.

Note

It is very important to be clear exactly what the acceptance of the null hypothesis means: that it is not particularly implausible that the data seen could have arisen from random sampling of the stated Normal distribution. In no sense have you confirmed that the underlying distribution does have this form, merely that it is not unreasonable to assume that it does. The same data used in a *t* test to test the null hypothesis $\mu = 100$ on the *assumption* that the sample is drawn from a Normal distribution with mean μ leads to rejection of the null hypothesis at the 1% level.

Testing for Normality without a known mean and variance

When testing for Normality of the underlying distribution, in preparation for conducting a *t* test for instance, you are merely asking whether it is appropriate to assume that the underlying distribution is Normal in shape; not whether it has a specific mean and variance.

EXAMPLE 7.5

An experiment is conducted to determine whether people's estimates of one minute have a mean duration of one minute. Data is to be collected by asking a sample of people to say 'Start' and 'Stop' at times they estimate to be one minute apart. The actual time apart, in seconds, is recorded by the experimenter. A *t* test is to be conducted of the hypothesis that the mean actual time apart is 60 seconds. Before this is done, a preliminary sample is taken.

The estimates (in seconds) obtained when this preliminary sample was taken are listed below.

55	40	50	53	57	61	38	29	43	52
37	57	55	56	57	48	59	40	54	53
63	58	56	48	55	58	57	56	59	55
50	60	58	51	42	47	62	57	49	43
51	42	39	56	53	53	58	51	50	55
40	38	41	55	45	61	53	53	41	53

Use these data to decide whether the assumption of Normality is reasonable.

SOLUTION

The hypotheses to be tested are:

H_0: Estimates are Normally distributed.

H_1: Estimates are not Normally distributed.

With these data, start by calculating the sample mean and the usual sample estimate of the population standard deviation.

$$\bar{x} = 51.1 \text{ and } s = \sqrt{\frac{\sum (x - \bar{x})^2}{n - 1}} = 7.564$$

Now use these estimated parameters to calculate the expected frequencies; that is, test the fit of the data to the Normal distribution N(51.1, 7.564²).

The data must now be grouped. One possible grouping is shown below.

Estimates (seconds)	Observed frequency, f_o
–41.5	10
41.5–45.5	5
45.5–49.5	4
49.5–53.5	14
53.5–57.5	16
57.5–	11

The expected frequencies for these groups can be calculated as set out below.

Class	Upper class boundary	Standardised value z	$P(Z < z)$	Probability for class	Expected frequency, f_e
–41.5	41.5	–1.2692	0.1022	0.1022	6.132
41.5–45.5	45.5	–0.7404	0.2295	0.1273	7.638
45.5–49.5	49.5	–0.2115	0.4162	0.1867	11.202
49.5–53.5	53.5	0.31729	0.6244	0.2082	12.492
53.5–57.5	57.5	0.84611	0.8012	0.1768	10.608
57.5–	∞	∞	1	0.1988	11.928

The statistic is

$$X^2 = \sum_{\text{All groups}} \frac{(f_o - f_e)^2}{f_e}$$

$$= \frac{(10 - 6.132)^2}{6.132} + \frac{(5 - 7.638)^2}{7.638} + \frac{(4 - 11.202)^2}{11.202} + \frac{(14 - 12.492)^2}{12.492}$$

$$+ \frac{(16 - 10.608)^2}{10.608} + \frac{(11 - 11.928)^2}{11.928}$$

$$= 2.440 + 0.911 + 4.630 + 0.182 + 2.741 + 0.072 = 10.976$$

To calculate the degrees of freedom, recall that you have used the data to estimate two parameters (the mean and the standard deviation) for the distribution. This means that both the observed and expected frequencies must give the same total frequency, the same sample mean and the same sample estimate of the standard deviation. These three restrictions on the possible frequencies in each class reduce the degrees of freedom by three from the number of classes.

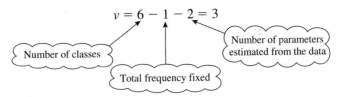

$$v = 6 - 1 - 2 = 3$$

Number of classes

Total frequency fixed

Number of parameters estimated from the data

With three degrees of freedom, the critical value at the 5% level for the χ^2 distribution is 7.815.

Since $10.976 > 7.815$, you reject the null hypothesis that the data were drawn from a Normally distributed population, and conclude that it would not be appropriate to use a t test for assessing the hypothesis $\mu = 60$.

❓ Explain why, despite this result, you could use a Normal test.

As before, from the values of $\dfrac{(f_o - f_e)^2}{f_e}$ for each cell calculated above you can see which differences between observed and expected frequencies are important, in the sense of making a large contribution to the X^2 statistic. The observed frequency of 10 in the first cell is itself substantially higher than the expected frequency of 6.132, but this excess of low estimates also brings down the estimate of the mean to the lower end of the main peak of the distribution. Hence the class above that containing the estimated mean has a significantly higher observed than expected frequency and the class below that containing the estimated mean a significantly lower observed than expected frequency.

Notes

1   When testing for an underlying Normal distribution as a prelude to conducting a t test it is important that different samples are used for the preliminary test of the distributional assumption and the actual test: this is because the sampling distribution of the t statistic in the two cases:
    (i)   the population is Normally distributed and a sample is taken at random
    (ii) the population is Normally distributed and a sample is taken at random except for the restriction that it 'passes' the χ^2 test for Normality,
    are not the same.

2   There is a certain amount of arbitrariness in the grouping of data which precedes the 'goodness-of-fit' test: you want to ensure that there are enough classes to discriminate between different distributions, but that each is wide enough to have an expected frequency of at least 5. There is no need to choose constant class widths, and in fact it would be wise to have narrower classes where the expected distribution has the greatest density. Picking class widths so that the expected frequencies are all about 8–12 is a reasonable rule of thumb.

Testing goodness of fit with other continuous distributions

You can also use the χ^2 test for the goodness of fit of a set of data to other continuous underlying distributions, not just the Normal, as the example below illustrates.

EXAMPLE 7.6

It is suggested that the time intervals between arrivals of passengers at a bus stop can be modelled by an exponential distribution, provided that buses appear sufficiently frequently and unpredictably for passengers simply to turn up independently at random.

The time intervals between 36 successive arrivals at a bus stop were measured (in seconds) and are recorded below.

60	43	25	25	31	37	23	23	14
13	36	3	63	50	33	18	60	52
6	38	41	33	52	28	36	30	42
16	10	55	161	21	1	3	14	13

Use these data to investigate the suggestion.

SOLUTION

The hypotheses to be tested are as follows.

H_0: The time intervals between passenger arrivals are exponentially distributed.

H_1: The time intervals between passenger arrivals are not exponentially distributed.

A grouped frequency distribution for the sample looks like this.

Time interval (nearest second)	0–9	10–19	20–29	30–39	40–49	50–59	60–69	70–79
Observed frequency, f_o	4	7	6	8	3	4	3	1

To calculate the expected frequencies, you need to use the density function for the exponential distribution. This is given by:

$$f(t) = \lambda e^{-\lambda t}$$

The mean of these data is 33.58.

The mean of the distribution is $\dfrac{1}{\lambda}$ so you can estimate λ from the sample mean as $\dfrac{1}{\bar{t}} = 0.029\,78$.

The probability that an exponentially distributed variable lies between a and b is:

$$\int_a^b \lambda e^{-\lambda t}\,dt = \left[-e^{-\lambda t}\right]_a^b = e^{-\lambda a} - e^{-\lambda b}$$

so the expected frequencies can be calculated, for example, for the class interval 20–29 (i.e. with class boundaries 19.5 and 29.5) as:

$$36 \times \left(e^{-0.02978 \times 19.5} - e^{-0.02978 \times 29.5}\right) = 36 \times 0.144\,10 = 5.1874.$$

The complete set of expected frequencies is as follows.

Time interval (nearest second)	Probability	Expected frequency, f_e
0–9	0.246 39	8.8700
10–19	0.194 07	6.9867
20–29	0.144 10	5.1874
30–39	0.106 99	3.8515
40–49	0.079 44	2.8597
50–59	0.058 98	2.1232
60–69	0.043 79	1.5764
70–	0.126 25	4.5451

Note that the expected frequency is calculated for the entire interval 70–∞, not just the interval 70–79 in which the maximum of the actual data lies. In conducting a χ^2 test, it is essential that the intervals for which the expected frequency are calculated cover the whole range of the theoretical distribution, not just the range of the actual data. An alternative way of doing this would have been to add an extra interval 80–∞, with observed frequency 0. However, in this example, the expected frequency would have been considerably less than 5, so the figures used to calculate the final X^2 statistic would have been the same. These expected frequencies are not all greater than 5, so the class boundaries need to be redrawn. One way of doing this is as follows.

Time interval (nearest second)	Observed frequency, f_o	Expected frequency, f_e
0–9	4	8.8700
10–19	7	6.9867
20–29	6	5.1874
30–49	11	6.7112
50–	8	8.2447

The statistic is

$$X^2 = \sum_{\text{All groups}} \frac{(f_o - f_e)^2}{f_e}$$

$$= \frac{(4 - 8.8700)^2}{8.8700} + \frac{(7 - 6.9867)^2}{6.9867} + \frac{(6 - 5.1874)^2}{5.1874} + \frac{(11 - 6.7112)^2}{6.7112}$$

$$+ \frac{(8 - 8.2447)^2}{8.2447}$$

$$= 5.549$$

and the degrees of freedom are:

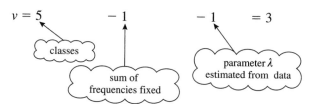

The critical value at the 5% level for 3 degrees of freedom is 7.815.

Since $5.549 < 7.815$ you accept the null hypothesis that the underlying distribution from which the data are drawn is exponential.

INVESTIGATION

Generate data from a rectangular distribution on $[0, 1]$, using a calculator or computer. With sample size n, test whether the data you have generated could be taken as arising from the Normal distribution

$$N\left(\frac{1}{2}, \frac{1}{12}\right)$$

(which has the same mean and variance as the uniform (rectangular) distribution on $[0, 1]$).

How large does n have to be before the null hypothesis is reliably rejected?

What does this tell you about how powerful the χ^2 test is?

Repeat for other pairs of distributions.

1 Engineers at a factory are investigating models for the life-length of a particular component.

Data on 100 of these life-lengths are collected and recorded in a frequency table as follows.

Life-length	0–0.2	0.2–0.4	0.4–0.6	0.6–0.8
Frequency	49	25	14	12

Investigation is now to be made of a model representing a uniform rate of decline of life-length over the time interval (0, 0.8), and a test is therefore required of whether the frequencies in the above cells may be taken as being in the proportions $7:5:3:1$.

Show that, if this is true, the expected frequency in the first cell is 43.75, and find the three other expected frequencies.

Carry out the test, using a 5% level of significance.

[MEI]

2 The height, in centimetres, gained by a conifer in its first year after planting is denoted by the random variable X. The value of X is measured for a random sample of 86 conifers and the results obtained are summarised in the table.

X	< 35	35–45	45–55	55–65	> 65
Observed frequency	10	18	28	18	12

(i) Assuming that the random variable X is modelled by a $N(50, 15^2)$ distribution, calculate the expected frequencies for each of the five classes.

(ii) Carry out a χ^2 goodness-of-fit analysis to test, at the 5% significance level, the hypothesis that X can be modelled as in part (i).

[Cambridge]

3 A city bus route runs through very congested streets and it is not practical to expect buses to keep to a timetable. The bus manager is endeavouring to investigate the running of these buses by modelling the times X (in minutes) between successive arrivals at a monitoring point as a continuous random variable having probability density function

$$f(x) = \begin{cases} \lambda e^{-\lambda x} & x > 0 \\ 0 & \text{elsewhere.} \end{cases}$$

where $\lambda > 0$.

(i) Obtain the mean of X.

(ii) Deduce that a plausible estimate of λ is $(\bar{x})^{-1}$ where $\bar{x}$ denotes the mean of a random sample of observations from X.

Data are available showing the intervals between one hundred successive arrivals at the monitoring point. These data, assumed to be a random sample, are summarised as follows.

Time between successive arrivals (minutes)	0–3	3–10	> 10
Frequency in this category	46	42	12
Average time (minutes) between arrivals in this category	1	5	12

(iii) Show that the estimate of λ obtained as in part (ii) is 0.25.

(iv) Use a χ^2 test to examine the fit of the model to the data, using a 5% significance level.

4 The electrical resistances of 120 inductor coils are measured, with results (in ohms) as shown below.

Range of resistances (ohms)	Frequency
160–	2
170–	5
180–	6
190–	3
200–	0
210–	11
220–	19
230–	27
240–	15
250–	17
260–	8
270–	3
280–	0
290–	3
300–310	1

Test the hypothesis that the population of inductors, from which this sample was drawn, have resistances which are Normally distributed.

5　The random variable X has the uniform (rectangular) distribution on (a, b) so that its probability density function is

$$f(x) = \begin{cases} \dfrac{1}{b-a} & \text{for } a \leqslant x \leqslant b, \\ 0 & \text{otherwise.} \end{cases}$$

(i)　Show that the mean of X is $\frac{1}{2}(a + b)$. Use integration to obtain the variance of X.

(ii)　The mean of a random sample of size n from this uniform (rectangular) distribution is $\overline{X}$. Write down the mean and variance of $\overline{X}$. Verify that these are 0 and 1 respectively in the case $a = -6$, $b = 6$, $n = 12$.

(iii)　A computer generates 12 observations taken at random from the uniform (rectangular) distribution on $(-6, 6)$ and calculates their mean; this is repeated 100 times. The distribution of the 100 sample means is grouped into four classes as follows.

Sample mean	Observed frequency
less than −0.674	26
between −0.674 and 0	21
between 0 and 0.674	27
greater than 0.674	26

Use a χ^2 test to examine the hypothesis that the sample means are equally likely to fall into any of these four classes.

(iv)　The numbers −0.674, 0, 0.674 used in part (iii) are the quartiles of the $N(0, 1)$ distribution. Comment on the implications of your result in part (iii) in respect of the Central Limit Theorem.

[MEI]

6　The time intervals (in minutes) between 25 successive buses arriving at the stop whose passenger arrivals were investigated in Example 7.6 were recorded as shown below.

10.7	0.4	6.8	1.4	2.0
8.8	3.1	1.8	1.0	5.5
11.5	8.4	1.0	1.1	5.7
0.4	11.7	5.0	2.8	2.2
4.5	3.1	4.4	6.3	5.5

(i)　Test whether these data can be taken as arising from an exponential distribution.

(ii)　Why would you expect an exponential model to be less appropriate for the inter-arrival times of buses than passengers?

7 Fifty-five people are asked to estimate a one-metre length, by marking off their estimate on a blank straight edge. The actual length marked off is then recorded.

The results are given below, in centimetres.

112	109	89	110	116	99	109	120	132
80	95	101	107	142	110	111	76	89
100	103	132	117	121	112	110	126	105
98	108	80	87	97	116	126	104	110
128	103	88	118	72	77	87	117	126
114	115	118	120	98	117	81	91	107
115								

Use these data to carry out a χ^2 test for goodness of fit to the distribution $N(100, \sigma^2)$, where σ^2 is to be estimated from the data.

8 A random sample of 60 independent observations is under investigation. It is desired to examine whether a reasonable model for the underlying population is the continuous random variable X whose probability density function is

$$f(x) = \lambda e^{-\lambda x} \quad x \geqslant 0$$

where λ is a parameter ($\lambda > 0$).

(i) Show that $P(a \leqslant X < b) = e^{-\lambda a} - e^{-\lambda b}$ where $b > a > 0$.

(ii) Using the fact that $E(X) = \dfrac{1}{\lambda}$, explain why a reasonable estimate of λ is $\dfrac{1}{\bar{x}}$ where $\bar{x}$ is the mean of a random sample of observations of X.

(iii) The random sample of 60 observations under investigation is recorded as the following frequency distribution.

Range	$0 \leqslant x < 5$	$5 \leqslant x < 10$	$10 \leqslant x < 15$	$15 \leqslant x < 20$
Frequency	14	16	16	14

Use the value of $\bar{x}$ given by this frequency distribution to obtain the value $\frac{1}{10}$ for the estimate of λ.

(iv) Using $\frac{1}{10}$ as an estimate of λ, set up the appropriate table of estimated expected frequencies.

(v) Use a χ^2 test at the 5% level of significance to show that the model X appears not to fit the data well.

(vi) Discuss briefly the principal differences between the model X and the data.

9 A market researcher is supposed to stop every second passer-by and ask a question. The researcher records the time at which each person is stopped as well as the response to the question. The researcher's supervisor suspects that the researcher is not carrying out instructions and decides to test whether the times between questions fit the appropriate distribution, which, if passers-by arrive independently and at random at a constant uniform rate, is given by a gamma distribution, with density function:

$$f(t) = \lambda^2 t e^{-\lambda t}$$

with parameter λ.

The supervisor's data for the times between 80 successive questions are listed below.

7.8	10.4	3.9	4.7	5.5	2.3	13.6	8.2
21.4	5.3	15.8	5.7	18.1	7.8	11.5	8.5
3.3	6.3	9.5	9.9	9.3	5.3	2.3	9.0
10.1	14.0	13.0	8.0	8.9	13.5	6.7	3.3
9.3	13.2	7.3	1.9	0.8	10.4	4.7	15.2
3.4	16.5	6.7	6.9	5.0	5.7	22.2	7.0
4.9	8.4	4.4	7.2	8.2	4.2	12.5	16.0
8.3	9.1	3.3	1.1	7.3	9.3	5.7	10.0
14.5	4.7	2.8	2.9	6.3	9.1	3.7	23.4
10.3	9.0	10.5	5.5	4.8	10.0	15.2	7.1

(i) Show that the mean of the gamma distribution is $\dfrac{2}{\lambda}$ and hence use the sample mean to estimate an appropriate value for λ.

(ii) Use this value of λ to test whether the data are fitted by the gamma distribution.

(iii) If the researcher was stopping every third passer-by, the appropriate gamma distribution would have the density function:

$$f(t) = \frac{\lambda^3 t^2}{2} e^{-\lambda t}$$

$\left(\text{The mean of this distribution is } \dfrac{3}{\lambda}. \right)$

Are the data fitted by this distribution?

(iv) Comment.

10 The adult Heath Blue butterflies of Northern France have wing-tip to wing-tip widths which are Normally distributed with mean width 31.2 mm and standard deviation 2.8 mm. The butterfly is extinct in Britain and, as part of a plan to re-introduce it from France, a lepidopterist wants to know whether the British population of the past is identical with the current French population. She has a sample of adult British butterflies from a museum, and proposes to test whether their wing-tip to wing-tip widths are well modelled by the same Normal distribution as the current French population.

The wing-tip to wing-tip widths of the museum sample are given in the frequency table below.

Width class (mm)	Frequency
25–	1
26–	2
27–	0
28–	0
29–	4
30–	1
31–	8
32–	4
33–	6
34–	3
35–	1
36–	4
37–	2
38–	2
39–40	1

Carry out the lepidopterist's test.

11 The daily number of hours of sunshine at a weather station during spring is thought to be modelled by the density function:

$$f(t) = \begin{cases} k(12 - t)(4t^2 - 33t + 90) & 0 \leqslant t \leqslant 12 \\ 0 & \text{otherwise.} \end{cases}$$

(i) Sketch the density function and explain the relevance of its shape to the variable being modelled.

(ii) Show that k must have the value $\dfrac{1}{3888}$.

(iii) The data below show the number of hours of sunshine recorded on randomly chosen spring days at the station. Use these data to test whether the model is appropriate.

t values (hours)	Frequency
$0 \leqslant t < 1$	5
$1 \leqslant t < 2$	10
$2 \leqslant t < 3$	4
$3 \leqslant t < 4$	3
$4 \leqslant t < 5$	2
$5 \leqslant t < 6$	1
$6 \leqslant t < 7$	0
$7 \leqslant t < 8$	4
$8 \leqslant t < 9$	8
$9 \leqslant t < 10$	2
$10 \leqslant t < 11$	4
$11 \leqslant t < 12$	2

(iv) Explain why, if the data were recorded on 45 consecutive days during one spring, one of the assumptions of your hypothesis test would be invalid.

12 The continuous random variable X has probability density function

$$f(x) = \begin{cases} \alpha(\alpha + 1)x^{\alpha-1}(1 - x) & 0 \leqslant x \leqslant 1 \\ 0 & \text{elsewhere} \end{cases}$$

where α is a parameter.

(i) Show that $\mu = \dfrac{\alpha}{\alpha + 2}$ where μ is the mean of X.

(ii) Show that $\alpha = \dfrac{2\mu}{1 - \mu}$, from which you may assume that a reasonable

estimate of α is $\alpha = \dfrac{2\bar{x}}{1 - \bar{x}}$ where $\bar{x}$ is the mean of a random sample of

observations from X.

(iii) A random sample of 100 observations is to be tested to see whether the random variable X is a reasonable model for the underlying population. The data are given as the following grouped frequency distribution.

Range	$0 \leqslant x < 0.2$	$0.2 \leqslant x < 0.6$	$0.6 \leqslant x \leqslant 1.0$
Frequency	16	56	28

Use the value of $\bar{x}$ as given by this frequency distribution to obtain the value 1.73 for α.

(iv) Using this value of α show that the estimated expected frequency in the range $0 \leqslant x < 0.2$ for 100 random observations from X is 14.7.

(v) Given that the corresponding frequencies for $0.2 \leqslant x < 0.6$ and $0.6 \leqslant x \leqslant 1.0$ are 55.2 and 30.1, respectively, use a χ^2 test to examine at the 5% level of significance the goodness of fit of X to the data.

13 It is thought that the lifetime of a miniaturised pump component has a distribution given by the density function:

$$f(t) = \frac{\pi}{2\mu^2} t e^{-\left(\frac{\pi t^2}{4\mu^2}\right)} \qquad (0 \leqslant t < \infty)$$

where μ is the mean lifetime of the component.

(i) Use the following data, which give lifetimes (in hours) of 30 randomly-selected components, to test the hypothesis that the lifetimes might have this distribution, estimating the value of μ by the sample mean.

181	135	142	184	102	82
80	187	160	149	63	77
118	130	74	75	100	140
163	214	146	112	92	179
150	150	107	112	169	133

(ii) Test instead whether the data could be taken as arising from a Normal distribution.

The steps in using the χ^2 test are as follows.

1 **Select your model**

This means deciding which distribution is to be used to model the situation. For a discrete situation it may be a standard distribution such as the binomial distribution or it may just be some known probabilities. For a continuous case it may be a standard distribution such as the Normal distribution or it may be given by a particular probability density function.

2 **Set up null and alternative hypotheses and choose the significance level**

Since the χ^2 test is one-tailed, the null hypothesis will be that the data are drawn from the model population, the alternative hypothesis that they are not. Choose a significance level appropriate to the situation.

3 **Collect data**

For discrete data, record the observed frequency for each possible outcome. For continuous data, group the outcomes into classes and record the observed frequencies in each class. In either situation the observed frequencies are denoted by f_o.

Add or extend classes as necessary so that the classes cover the whole range of the theoretical distribution.

4 **Calculate the expected frequencies**

Calculate the expected frequency in each class by using the distribution specified in the null hypothesis to find the expected probabilities and then multiplying by the total observed frequency. The expected frequencies are denoted by f_e. These should not be rounded.

5 **Check the size of the classes**

Ensure that the expected frequency in each class is greater than about 5. If not, amalgamate adjacent classes in the tails until this is the case.

6 **Calculate the test statistic**

This is given by $X^2 = \sum_i \dfrac{(f_o - f_e)^2}{f_e}$.

7 **Work out the degrees of freedom**

Find the degrees of freedom, v, for the test using the formula

v = number of classes − number of estimated parameters − 1

where the number of classes is counted *after* any necessary combining has been done.

8 Find the critical value and carry out the test

Read the critical value from the χ^2 tables for the appropriate degrees of freedom and the required significance level.

If $X^2 <$ critical value then accept H_0.

If $X^2 >$ critical value then reject H_0.

9 Draw conclusions from the test

State what the test tells you about the model.

Answers

Chapter 1

❓ (Page 3)

It is reasonable to regard the height of a wave as random. No two waves are exactly the same and in a storm some are much bigger than others.

Exercise 1A (Page 9)

1 (i) $k = \frac{2}{35}$

(ii)

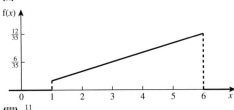

(iii) $\frac{11}{35}$

(iv) $\frac{1}{7}$

2 (i) $k = \frac{1}{12}$

(ii)

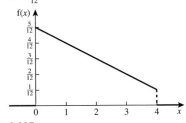

(iii) 0.207

3 (i) $a = \frac{4}{81}$

(ii)

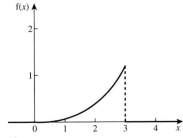

(iii) $\frac{16}{81}$

4 (i) $k = \frac{1}{4}$

(ii)

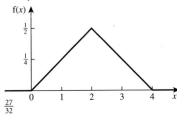

(iii) $\frac{27}{32}$

5 (i) $c = \frac{1}{8}$

(ii)

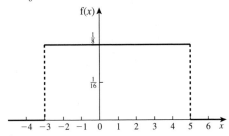

(iii) $\frac{1}{4}$

(iv) $\frac{3}{8}$

6 (i) $k = 0.048$

(ii)

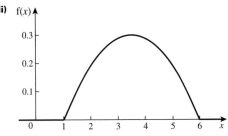

(iii) 0.248

7 (i) $a = \frac{5}{12}$

(ii)

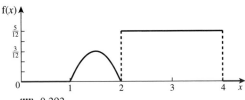

(iii) 0.292

(iv) $\frac{7}{12}$

8 (i) $k = \frac{2}{9}$

(ii) 0.067

9 (i) $k = \frac{1}{100}$

(ii)

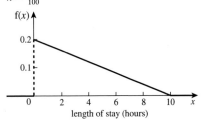

(iii) 19, 17, 28, 36

(iv) Yes

(v) Further information needed about the group 4–10 hours. It is possible that many of these stay all day are so are part of a different distribution.

10 (i)

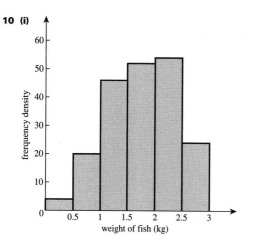

weight of fish (kg)

Negative skew

(ii) $f_1(w)$

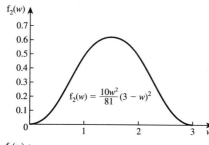

$$f_1(w) = \frac{2w}{9}(3 - w)$$

$f_2(w)$

$$f_2(w) = \frac{10w^2}{81}(3 - w)^2$$

$f_3(w)$

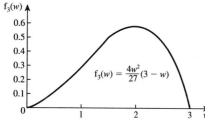

$$f_3(w) = \frac{4w^2}{27}(3 - w)$$

$f_4(w)$

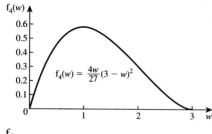

$$f_4(w) = \frac{4w}{27}(3 - w)^2$$

f_3

(iii) 1.62, 9.49, 20.14, 28.01, 27.55, 13.19
(iv) Model seems good.

11 (i) $a = 100$ **(ii)** 0.045   **(iii)** 0.36
12 0.803, 0.456

13 (i) 0, 0.1, 0.21, 0.12, 0.05, 0.02, 0
  (ii) 0.1, 0.31, 0.33, 0.17, 0.07, 0.02
  (iii) $k = \frac{1}{1728}$
  (iv) 0.132, 0.275, 0.280, 0.201, 0.095, 0.016
  (v) Model quite good. Both positively skewed.

❓ (Page 16)

(b) and (d)

❓ (Page 20)

68%. The Normal distribution has a greater proportion of values near the mean, as can be seen from its shape.

Exercise 1B (Page 23)

1 (i) 2.67
  (ii) 0.89
  (iii) 2.828
2 (i) 2   **(ii)** 2   **(iii)** 1.76
3 (i) 0.6
  (ii) 0.04
4 (i)

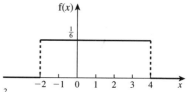

  (ii) $\frac{2}{3}$
  (iii) 1
  (iv) $\frac{1}{3}$
5 (i) 1.5
  (ii) 0.45
  (iii) 1.5
  (iv) 1.5
  (v) $f(x)$

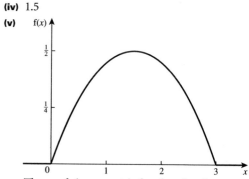

The graph is symmetrical and peaks when $x = 1.5$ thus E(X) = mode of X = median value of $X = 1.5$.
6 (i) $f(x) = \frac{1}{7}$ for $-2 \leqslant x \leqslant 5$
  (ii) 1.5
  (iii) 4.08
  (iv) $\frac{5}{7}$

7 **(ii)** 1.083, 0.326

    (iii) 0.5625

8 **(i)** $f(x) = \frac{1}{3}$ for $4 \leqslant x \leqslant 7$

    (ii) 5.5

    (iii) $\frac{3}{4}$

    (iv) 0.233

9 **(i)** $f(x) = \frac{1}{10}$ for $10 \leqslant x \leqslant 20$

    (ii) 15, 8.33

    (iii) **(a)** 57.7%

        (b) 100%

10 **(i)**

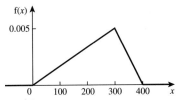

    (iii) $233\frac{1}{3}$ hours

    (iv) 7222.2

    (v) 0.083

11 **(i)** $k = 1.2 \times 10^{-8}$

    (ii)

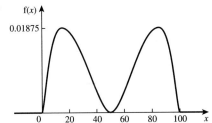

    (iii) The distribution is the sum of two smaller
    distributions, one of moderate candidates and
    the other of able ones.

    (iv) Yes if the step size is small compared to the
    standard deviation.

12 **(ii)** 8.88, 2.88; 0.724

    (iii) $m^3 - 9m^2 + 39m - 450 = 0$

13 **(i)** $a = k$

    (ii) $\frac{1}{k}$

    (iii) $\frac{1}{k^2}$

    (iv) $\frac{\ln 2}{k}$

    (v) For example, the lifetime in hours of an electric
    light bulb.

14 **(i)** 200

    (ii) 0.082

    (iii) 0.139

    (iv) $k = 7.31$

15 **(i)** $a = 1.443$

    (ii)

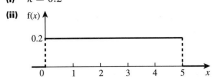

(iii) 1.443, 0.083

(iv) 41.5%

(v) 1.414

16 **(i)**

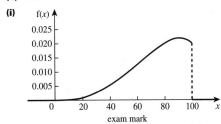

The model suggests that these candidates were
generally of high ability as a large proportion
of them scored a high mark.

(iii) 12.5%

(iv) No; 91

Exercise 1C (Page 30)

1 0.8, 0.16, £8

2 **(i)** $k = 0.2$

    (ii)

    (iii) 2.5

    (iv) 7

3 **(i)** 0.8

    (ii) 0.6̇

    (iii) 0.026̇

4 **(i)** 1.5

    (ii) 2.7

    (iii) 0.45

    (iv) 13.9

    (v) 0.45; both are the variance of Y.

5 **(i)** 0.6

    (ii) -3.4

    (iii) 0.2

    (iv) 0.64

6 **(i)** $3\frac{2}{3}$

    (ii) $66\frac{1}{6}$

    (iii) $14\frac{5}{6}$, $66\frac{1}{6}$

7 **(i)** $f(x) = \frac{1}{6}$ for $2 \leqslant x \leqslant 8$

    (ii) $a = \frac{x^2\sqrt{3}}{4}$

    (iii) 0.352

    (iv) 12.12, 57.6

8 $k = \frac{3}{32}$, 2; $\frac{5}{32}$

9 **(i)** $f(t) = 0.1$ for $0 \leqslant t \leqslant 10$
                $= 0$ otherwise
           mean $= 5$, variance $= 8\frac{1}{3}$

(ii)

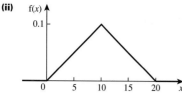

(iii) $E(X) = 10$, $Var(X) = 16\frac{2}{3}$

(iv) 0.18; because $T_1 \geqslant 7$ and $T_2 \geqslant 7$ is not the only way for $X \geqslant 14$. The latter inequality also includes other possibilities, such as waiting 9 minutes in the morning and 6 minutes in the evening.

10 (i) $E(X) = 3.2$

(ii) p.d.f.

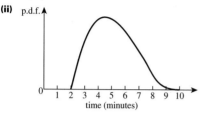

The model implies that all of the doctor's appointments last between 2 and 10 minutes, the mean time being 5.2 minutes and the variance of the distribution being 2.56 minutes².

11 (i) **(a)** 100, 11.55

(b) 1013.3, 231.2

(ii) **(a)** $f(u) = \frac{1}{400}u - \frac{1}{5}$, $80 \leqslant u \leqslant 100$

$f(u) = \frac{3}{10} - \frac{1}{400}u$, $100 \leqslant u \leqslant 120$

(b) 100, 66.7

(c) 1007, 26 729

12 (i) 100 days

(ii) 0.026

(iii) 300 days

(iv) £75 000 + £5000 = £80 000

(v) £8333

❓ (Page 36)

The model's predictions agree closely with the actual data. However, the value of the model lies in how well it will predict the pattern for future years. With a large entry the pattern should be reasonably consistent from year to year. This model is not very good from $1\frac{1}{2}$ to 2 hours, when more people finish than it predicts.

Exercise 1D (Page 47)

1 (i) 2.5

(ii) $F(x) = 0$ for $x < 0$

$= \dfrac{x}{5}$ for $0 \leqslant x \leqslant 5$

$= 1$ for $x > 5$

(iii) 0.4

2 (i) $k = \frac{2}{39}$

(ii)

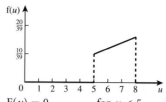

(iii) $F(u) = 0$ for $u < 5$

$= \dfrac{u^2}{39} - \dfrac{25}{39}$ for $5 \leqslant u \leqslant 8$

$= 1$ for $u > 8$

(iv)

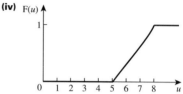

3 (i) $c = \frac{1}{21}$

(ii) $F(x) = 0$ for $x < 1$

$= \dfrac{x^3}{63} - \dfrac{1}{63}$ for $1 \leqslant x \leqslant 4$

$= 1$ for $x > 4$

(iii) 3.19

(iv) 4

4 (i) $F(x) = 0$ for $x < 0$

$= 1 - \dfrac{1}{(1+x)^3}$ for $x \geqslant 0$

(ii) $x = 1$

5 (i) $\frac{1}{4}$

(ii) 0.134

(iii) $f(x) = 2 - 2x$ for $0 \leqslant x \leqslant 1$

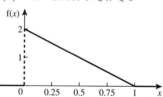

6 $E(X) = \frac{3}{4}$, $Var(X) = \frac{19}{80}$

$F(x) = 0$ for $x < 0$

$= \dfrac{3x}{4} - \dfrac{x^3}{16}$ for $0 \leqslant x \leqslant 2$

$= 1$ for $x > 2$

7 $\frac{3}{5}$, 0.683

8 (ii) $F(t) = 0$ for $t < 0$

$= \dfrac{t^3}{432} - \dfrac{t^4}{6912}$ for $0 \leqslant t \leqslant 12$

$= 1$ for $t > 12$

(iv) 0.132

9 (i) 2.93

(ii) $F(x) = 1 - \dfrac{(x-10)^2}{100}$ for $0 \leqslant x \leqslant 10$

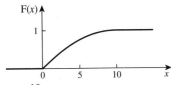

(iii) $f(x) = \dfrac{10-x}{50}$ for $0 \leqslant x \leqslant 10$

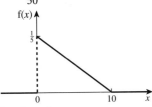

10 $F(x) = \dfrac{k}{2} - \dfrac{k \cos 2x}{2}$; 0.146

11 (i) $\frac{1}{3}$ **(iii)** 4.39 **(iv)** 12.5

12 (i) (a) 0.3935

(b) 0.2231

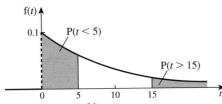

(ii) $F(t) = 1 - e^{-0.1t}$; median = 6.93

(iii) 0.183

13 (ii) $1 - \dfrac{1}{m} = 0.4$, $m = 1.67$

(iii) 0.495

(iv) $f(x) = \dfrac{1.25}{x^2}$ for $1 \leqslant x \leqslant 5$

$= 0$ otherwise

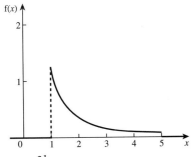

(v) $m = \dfrac{2b}{b+1}$, which is always less than 2

14 (i) $M = 3.568$; 5.335

(ii) $f(x) = \dfrac{324}{x^5}$ $3 \leqslant x$

$= 0$ otherwise

(iii) $\frac{81}{256}$

15 $F(x) = \int f(x) \, dx$ and so $F'(x) = f(x)$.

Uniform distribution with mean value $\dfrac{a}{2}$.

$F(x) = 1 - \dfrac{(a-x)^2}{a^2}$ for $0 \leqslant x \leqslant a$

Mean of sum of smaller parts $= a$

16 (i) (a) Validates p.d.f. form of Z.

(b) Demonstrates that $E(Z) = 0$.

(ii) (a) $E(Y) = 1$

(b) $\text{Var}(Y) = 2$

17 (i) $\{y : y \geqslant 0\}$

(ii) If $Y \leqslant y$ then either $0 \leqslant Z \leqslant \sqrt{y}$

or $-\sqrt{y} \leqslant Z \leqslant 0$

$\therefore P(Y \leqslant y)$

$= P(0 \leqslant Z \leqslant \sqrt{y}) + P(-\sqrt{y} \leqslant Z \leqslant 0)$

$= 2P(0 \leqslant Z \leqslant \sqrt{y})$

since Z is an even function.

Chapter 2

Exercise 2A (Page 57)

1 (i) (a) $E(X) = 3.1$

(b) $\text{Var}(X) = 1.29$

2 (i) (a) $E(X) = 0.7$

(b) $\text{Var}(X) = 0.61$

4 (i) $E(2X) = 6$

(ii) $\text{Var}(3X) = 6.75$

5 (i) 10.9, 3.09

(ii) 18.4, 111.24

6 (i) 2

(ii) 1

(iii) 9

7 (i) (a) 2.79

(b) 8.97

(c) 20.94

8

$\overline{N}$	2	3	4	5	6	7	8
Probability	$\frac{1}{16}$	$\frac{2}{16}$	$\frac{3}{16}$	$\frac{4}{16}$	$\frac{3}{16}$	$\frac{2}{16}$	$\frac{1}{16}$

5, 2.5

Exercise 2B (Page 63)

1 (i) 4, 0.875

(ii) 1.5, 0.167

(iii)

Main course	Dessert	Price
Fish and chips	Ice cream	£4
Fish and chips	Apple pie	£4.50
Fish and chips	Sponge pudding	£5
Bacon and eggs	Ice cream	£4.50
Bacon and eggs	Apple pie	£5
Bacon and eggs	Sponge pudding	£5.50
Pizza	Ice cream	£5

Pizza	Apple pie	£5.50
Pizza	Sponge pudding	£6
Steak and chips	Ice cream	£6.50
Steak and chips	Apple pie	£7
Steak and chips	Sponge pudding	£7.50

(iv) Mean of $T = 5.5$, variance $= 1.042$

2 (i) N(90, 25)

(ii) N(10, 25)

(iii) N(−10, 25)

3 0.196

4 (i) 0.0228

(ii) 56.45 minutes

(iii) 0.362

5 (i) 230 g, 10.2 g

(ii) 0.1587

(iii) 0.0787

6 (i) N(70, 25)

(ii) N(−10, 25)

7 5.92%

8 (i) 0.266

(ii) No, people do not choose their spouses at random: the height of a husband and wife may not be independent.

9 0.151

10 (i) 0

(ii) 0.0037

❓ (Page 68)

With folded paper it is not possible for pieces of paper that are thicker to be offset by others that are thinner, and vice versa.

Exercise 2C (Page 68)

1 N(120, 24)

Assume times are independent and no time is spent on changeovers between vehicles.

2 0.0745

3 0.1377

4 0.1946

5 (i) N(34, 30)

(ii) N(−4, 30)

(iii) N(24, 29)

6 (i) 0.316

(ii) 0.316

7 (i) N(100, 26)

(ii) N(295, 353)

(iii) N(200, 122)

(iv) N(−65, 377)

8 (i) 0.0827

(ii) 0.3103

(iii) 0.5

9 (i) 0.0827

(ii) 0.1446

(iii) 0.5

(iv) The situations in 8(i) and 9(i) are the same. 8(ii) considers $3X + 5Y$ whereas 9(ii) considers $X_1 + X_2 + X_3 + Y_1 + \ldots + Y_5$, so the probabilities are different.

8(iii) and 9(iii) have the same probabilities because $\dfrac{0}{\sigma} = 0$, so the variance does not affect the answer.

10 (i) N(7400, 28 900)

(ii) N(1200, 27 700)

(iii) N($600a + 1000b$, $400a^2 + 900b^2$)

11 (i) 311.6 kg

(ii) Assume that the composition of each crew is selected randomly so that the weights of each of the four individual oarsmen are independent of each other. This assumption may not be reasonable since there may be some light-weight and some heavy-weight crews; also men's and women's crews. If this is so it will cast doubt on the answer to part (i).

12 (i) 0.4546

(ii) 93.49 l

13 (i) 0.0202

(ii) 0.0856

(iii) 0.3338, 0.4082

14 0.9026

Assume weights of participants are independent since told teams were chosen at random.

15 (i) 0.0188

(ii) 0.1394

16 (i) 0.0367

(ii) 0.8144

(iii) 108, 1.4

17 (i) N(80, 8)

(ii) N($40n$, $4n$)

(iii) 0.0207

(iv) 0.0456

Choice of limits is ±2 standard deviations from the mean and so will include 95% of piles that contain 25 pamphlets.

18 (i) 0.037

(ii) 0.238

Assume that no time is lost during baton changeovers and that the runners' times are independent, i.e. that no runners are influenced by the performance of their team mates or competitors. The model does not seem entirely realistic in this.

19 (i) N(2000, 1250)

(ii) 1942

(iii) 0.7373

20 (i) 14%

(ii) 0.6

(iii) 15 m

(iv) 0.3043

21 (i) $S \sim N(600, 105.8)$; 0.0724

(ii) 0.839

(iii) 0.161

(iv) $\mu = 30.54\,\text{g}$

22 (i) 0.127

(ii) $N(75m + 65f, 36m + 25f)$

(a) 0.0016

(b) 0

(iii) 0.1002

23 (i) 0.4258

Assume customers arrive randomly, singly and independently.

(ii) $N(372, 372)$; 0.8675

(iii) $N(30, 714)$; 0.13

24 (i) 0.7333

(ii) 0.0668

(iii) 8.032 minutes

(iv) 0.8681

25 (i) 0.3341

(ii) 0.1469

(iii) 394.38 mm

(iv) 0.9595

(v) 0.1478

26 (i) 0.1056

(ii) 0.2660

(iii) £45.57

(iv) £45.75

Chapter 3

❓ (Page 83)

1 The population is made up of the M.P.'s constituents. The sample is a part of that population of constituents. Without information relating to how the constituents' views were elicited, the views obtained seem to be biased towards those constituents who bother to write to their M.P.

2 The population is made up of Manchester households. We are not told how the sample is chosen. Even if a random sample of households were chosen the views obtained are still likely to be biased as the interview timing excludes the possibility of obtaining views of most of those residents in employment.

3 The population is made up of black residents in Chicago.

The sample is made up of black people (and possibly some white people as the areas are 'predominantly black') from a number of areas in Chicago.

The survey may be biased in two ways:

(i) the areas may not be representative of all residential areas and therefore of all black people living in Chicago and

(ii) given that police officers are carrying out the survey they are unlikely to obtain negative views.

❓ (Page 84)

1 Each student is equally likely to be chosen but samples including two or more students from the same class are not permissible so not all samples are equally likely.

2 Yes

Exercise 3A (Page 86)

1 (i) Systematic sampling

(ii) (a) Simple random sampling

(b) $\frac{1}{25}$

(iii) (a) Cluster sampling

(b) No. The streets are chosen at random and then 15 houses are chosen at random. However, not every sample of size 15 (throughout the town) can be chosen.

(iv) (a) Quota sampling

(b) No

(c) The sample is small. It is questionable how reliable such information would be.

2 (i) (a) Years 1 and 2: 7 students from each; Years 3 and 4: 5 students from each; Year 5: 6 students.

(b) $\frac{1}{20}$

(ii) (a) 28 light vans, 2 company cars and 1 large-load vehicle.

(b) Randomly choose the appropriate number of vehicles from each type. This is stratified sampling.

(iii) (a) $\frac{1}{8}$

(b) 0–5: 5; 6–12: 10; 13–21: 13 or 14; 22–35: 25 or 26; 36–50: 22 or 23; 51+: 3 or 4.

3 (i) Cluster sampling. Choose representative streets or areas and sample from these streets or areas.

(ii) Stratified sample. Identify routes of interest and randomly sample trains from each route.

(iii) Stratified sample. Choose representative areas in the town and randomly sample from each area as appropriate.

(iv) Stratified sample as in part (iii).

(v) Depends on method of data collection. If survey is, say, via a postal enquiry, then a random sample may be selected from a register of addresses.

(vi) Cluster sampling. Routes and times are chosen and a traffic sampling station is established to randomly stop vehicles to test tyres.

(vii) Cluster sampling. Areas are chosen and households are then randomly chosen.

(viii) Cluster sampling. A period (or periods) is chosen to sample and speeds are surveyed.

(ix) Cluster sampling. Meeting places for 18-year-olds are identified: night clubs, pubs, etc. and samples of 18-year-olds are surveyed, probably via a method to maintain privacy. This might be a questionnaire to ascertain required information.

(x) Random sampling. The school student list is used as a sampling frame to establish a random sample within the school.

4 (i) Systematic sampling. Easy to set up but may be difficult to track down the student once they have been identified.

(ii) Stratified sampling. Will reflect all opinions, but only as defined by the surveyor. Easy to carry out. That is, it should be easy to access the desired sample, students as they enter the college premises.

(iii) The sample will be biased. Easy to survey. Those using the canteen will be surveyed.

(iv) Cluster sampling. Assumes first and second year students are representative of the whole college. (If there are only first and second year students this will be true. The sampling procedure is then stratified.) Similar to (i), that is, once students have been chosen from the lists they have to be located to seek their views.

5 (i) All production lines are identified. If it is judged they are equivalent then one (or more) can be chosen to produce a sample. This is cluster sampling. From this (or these) production line(s) a day (or days) is chosen to be the time when a sample is taken. A reasonable number of strip lights is chosen and then tested to destruction, that is, tested until they are exhausted.
An estimate is found from the mean life of the sample chosen.

(ii) The map of the forest is covered with a grid. Each grid square is numbered. A sample is chosen by randomly selecting the squares. The tree (or trees) in each of the chosen squares is sampled.

(iii) (a) A sample of 100 chips to be taken from each production line each working day (assuming a five day week).

(b) Stratified.

(iv) Depending on the number of staff, one could carry out a census of all staff or, if more appropriate, a stratified sample based on part-time staff, full-time staff, etc.

(v) Identify different courses in your school/college. Access students from each of the courses, choosing them at random in order to elicit their views. This is a stratified sample.

6 (i) Cluster sampling involves dividing the population into suitable sub-groups, selecting one or some of these sub-groups for study and then sampling within the selected sub-group(s).

(ii) Voting patterns in the selected clusters hopefully reflect the voting patterns of the nation, easier to do this rather than other sampling methods and in particular it would be virtually impossible to take a random sample.

(iii) There will be no sampling frame, which is necessary for a simple random sample. There may also be individuals who refuse to answer or do not tell the truth. Other factors include the time of day when the sample is taken and the effect of postal voting.

7 (i) Choose a random number in the range 1 to 20, say r, then choose the rth, $(r + 20)$th, $(r + 40)$th, ..., $(r + 980)$th student from the sampling frame.

(ii) Stratified sampling: the number of students in each year group in the sample is proportional to the number of students in each year group in the population. (i.e. 9 from Years 7 and 8, 10 from Years 9 and 11 and 12 from Year 10).

8 (i) The sample could well be biased, since the yoghurts chosen in the particular hour might not be representative of the flavour of those produced throughout the shift. Also, instead of selecting from the whole population (the whole shift) you are only selecting from part of it; the quality may vary throughout the shift.

(ii) Stratified or systematic sampling where the 50 yoghurts are taken throughout the shift and the number of each flavour taken is proportional to the production ratios (i.e. 15 Black Cherry, 10 each Peach, Raspberry and Strawberry, 5 Rhubarb).

Chapter 4

❓ (Page 91)

It tells you that μ is about 101.2 but it does not tell you what 'about' means, how close to 101.2 it is reasonable to expect μ to be.

❓ (Page 97)

You would expect 90 out of the 100 to enclose 3.5.

Exercise 4A (Page 99)

1 (i) 5.205   **(ii)** 5.117, 5.293

2 (i) 47.7

   (ii) 34.7 to 60.7

   (iii) 27.3 to 68.1

3 (i) 0.9456   **(ii)** £7790–£8810

4 (i) (a) 0.1685

      (b) 0.0207

   (ii) 163.8–166.6   **(iii)** 385

5 78.4, 40.64;

  76.44, 80.36;

  The 95% confidence limits have been constructed from the sample data in such a way that 95% of similar-sized random samples will lead to an interval which will contain the true parent mean of the distribution.

  0.2372

6 (i) 6.83, 3.04

   (ii) 6.58, 7.08

7 (i) 5.71 to 7.49

   (ii) It is more likely that the short manuscript was written in the early form of the language.

8 25.3, 3.6; 24.9, 25.8 (taking the last interval to be 38–40)

9

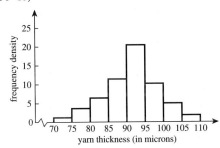

  91.32, 7.41; 0.43; 90.5, 92.2

10 (i) Players' scores cannot be Normally distributed because symmetry would require negative scores.

   (ii) 11.79, 13.64

   (iii) It would reduce the width of the confidence interval but the interval would be centred in the same place.

   (iv) Approximately 102 500

11 (i) 0.004 67

   (ii) 1.1128 to 1.352

   You must assume the data are from a random sample and that 0.004 67 is an acceptable value for σ^2.

   (iii) μ is not a random variable so cannot have a probability attached to it.

The correct interpretation is that 90% of all such intervals that could arise in repeated sampling will contain the population mean.

   (iv) It is not reasonable to suppose that the target is being met as 1.136 is not in the interval.

12 (i) 7.4, 4.05

   (ii) 7.64, 64.758

   This suggests that the mean is about right but that the variance is much too small.

   (iii) 6.316 to 8.964

   (iv) The confidence interval is only approximate because the distribution cannot be assumed to be Normal and because σ^2 is not known. The approximation is good because the sample is large enough to suggest that both the Central Limit Theorem would apply, so that $\overline{X}$ can be assumed to be approximately Normal, and that s^2 could be used as an approximation for σ^2 without serious loss of accuracy.

13 (i) 3.768, 0.4268

   (ii) 3.644 to 3.892

   (iii) 90% of all such intervals that could arise in repeated sampling will contain the population mean.

   (iv) N(0, 1)

   (v) The sample is large enough to suggest that v could be used as a good approximation for σ^2 without serious loss of accuracy.

14 (i) 1.838 mm

   (ii) 1.630 to 1.910

   (iii) The coach's suspicions seem to be confirmed as 4 mm is not in the confidence interval.

15 0.484 to 1.016

  Assume that the sample standard deviation is an acceptable approximation for σ.

  The aim has not been achieved as the interval contains values below 0.5.

16 0.223 to 1.403

  Assumptions: the Central Limit Theorem applies and s^2 is a good approximation for σ^2.

  The confidence interval suggests that reaction times are slower after a meal.

Chapter 5

Exercise 5A (Page 113)

1 (i) 322.9, 79.54

   (ii) 278.8–366.9

2 (i) 66, 17.15

   (ii) 51.7–80.3

   (iii) The distribution of the yield of all the fruit farmer's trees is Normal.

(iv) Number all the trees with different consecutive integers. Copy these integers on to separate pieces of paper; put these in a hat and pick out eight at random. The numbers chosen will identify the trees to be picked for the sample.

3 (i) 224.5–249.2

(ii) $H_0: \mu = 250\,g$, $H_1: \mu < 250\,g$

(iii) Assume the distribution is Normal;
$t = -1.914$, significant

(iv) The butcher's comment means that the other half were all underweight. This is much too big a proportion to be underweight. Furthermore, the underweight pies were often very much underweight.

4 (i) 18.25, 3.72

(ii) 16.32–20.18

(iii) The distribution of lengths of sentences written by the accused man is Normal and the text represented by the sample sentences is representative of the general lengths of sentences he writes.

(iv) $H_0: \mu = 15.5$, $H_1: \mu \neq 15.5$

(v) $t = 2.56$, significant

(vi) No

5 (i) Monday

(ii) The 23 weekdays

(iii) 629.7–661.9

(iv) True, this distribution is not a Normal one, but it may still be accurately modelled by one. $s = 37.24$ so the step size is small compared with the standard deviation. It is very common in statistics to make a Normal approximation to a discrete distribution and the results are usually very reliable.

6 (i) 63.6–72.0

(ii) Statistical: the distribution of tyre condemnation mileages is Normal and the 12 tyres tested in the sample are representative of the distribution.
Practical: the tyres are tested under genuine working conditions.

(iii) $H_0: \mu = 62\,000$, $H_1: \mu > 62\,000$;
$t = 3.047$, not significant

7 (i) $H_0: \mu = 750\,g$, $H_1: \mu < 750\,g$

(ii) $t = -4.57$, significant

(iii) The distribution of weights in the shoal is Normal; this may be reasonable.
The sample is random; this is certainly not the case since all the pollack came from one shoal. The masses are independent; this may not be true when all the fish are taken from one shoal and so are likely to be of the same age.

8 (i) The distribution of total points in a hand is Normal. This assumption is not fully justified because the distribution is not symmetrical about the mean; it is positively skewed. For example, you cannot have a hand with fewer than 0 points in it but you can get a hand with more than 20 points in it.

(ii) $H_0: \mu = 10$, $H_1: \mu < 10$

(iii) $t = -1.16$, not significant

9 (i) 89.8–93.3 (outlier excluded because something like an accident or a breakdown had clearly caused an atypical delay).

(ii) A one-sided confidence interval would result in the bus company claiming a shorter journey completion time than in the corresponding two-sided case. Also the confidence interval established in part (i) highlights the fact that the bus is very unlikely to complete the journey in less than 89.8 minutes. A one-sided confidence interval would not expose the company to such a lower-limit journey time.

(iii) $t = -4.498$, significant (if outlier excluded)

10 (i) 21

(ii) The distribution is not Normal.

(iii) No because the confidence interval obtained would be too wide to be meaningful.

(iv) 45.0–66.3; The procedure will be valid provided that the distribution of life expectancies for this group is Normal.

11 0.633–0.647

(i) 0.78, 0.160

(ii) 0.616–0.944

(iii) Large sample; no need for underlying Normality

12 $H_0: \mu = 110$, $H_1: \mu \neq 110$; accept H_0

13 (i) 172.7, 64.57; 166.95–178.45
The distribution of 17-year-old boys' heights is Normal and the sample used in the experiment is random.

(ii) A larger sample will reduce the width of the confidence interval for μ because (1) the standard deviation of the sample means is $\dfrac{\sigma}{\sqrt{n}}$ and so, as n increases, this will decrease and (2) the value of k in $\dfrac{k\sigma}{\sqrt{n}}$ is less.

(iii) Normality is no longer required; randomness is still needed.

14 (i) Mean = 2.36, standard deviation = 2.74;
$a = -0.558$, $b = 5.278$
Assumptions: journey times are a random sample; distribution of T is Normal.

(ii) Commuter's interpretation is wrong. It should be '90% of such confidence intervals should contain the true mean'.

(iii) Accept H_0 that $\mu = 0$, i.e. refute commuter's suspicions at 5% level.

(iv) Confidence interval is likely to be narrower because of lower percentage-point for t value and lower standard error since sample size is large.

15 (i)

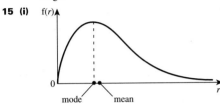

(ii) $0.616 < \mu < 0.804$

It is assumed that (1) the throws are independent, (2) that the sample size is large enough for the estimate of σ^2 to be reliable enough to regard σ^2 as known and (3) that the sample size is large enough for the Central Limit Theorem to indicate that $\overline{x}$ is Normally distributed.

(iii) 177. The standard deviation of the parent distribution is unknown and the distribution of R is not Normal.

(iv) The population is not Normal and the sample is small, therefore, neither the t distribution nor the Central Limit Theorem can be used.

16 (i) The method must ensure each club member has an equal chance of being chosen. Could put names in a hat and select at random or use the random number generator on a calculator.

(ii) Mean $= 4.74$, $s^2 = 2.74$

(iii) $3.56 < \mu < 5.92$.
Background population is Normal.

(iv) By increasing sample size; 13

17 1.934–2.052, 9.373–10.551; 120, halved

18 (i) $H_0: \mu = 75$, $H_1: \mu \neq 75$

(ii) The population must be Normally distributed and the sample must be random.

(iii) $t = 1.836$, not significant

(iv) 74.623–76.357

19 (i) 0.1290

(ii) 0.4284

(iii) $t = 0.7026$, not significant

20 (i) $H_0: \mu = 14.0$, $H_1: \mu > 14.0$;
$t = 2.895$, significant

(ii) 14.197–15.763

(iii) The sample should be random, pigs should be similar (e.g. in initial weight), pigs should be kept under controlled conditions (e.g. in respect of exercise).

21 (i) A random sample is one selected in such a way that all possible samples of the given size are equally likely.

(ii) All samples are possible so a sample of 'unusual' firms might be chosen. 'Biased' here means not representative of the population.

(iii) 8.748–9.552
The population is Normally distributed. 99% of all such intervals that could arise in repeated sampling will contain the population mean.

22 (i) $t = -1.350$, not significant.
The population is Normally distributed.

(ii) 57.960–63.790
15 minutes late corresponds to a journey time of 67 minutes which is well above the interval suggesting that refunds will hardly ever be made even if the trains are regularly quite late.

(iii) One possibility is that it would be reasonable to exclude them as they do not reflect usual daily conditions but doing so will mean that the sample is no longer random.

23 (i) $H_0: \mu = 9$, $H_1: \mu > 9$; $t = 3.51$, significant
Assume the population is Normally distributed and the sample is random.

(ii) 9.084–9.366

Exercise 5B (Page 129)

1 (i) $t = 2.805$, $v = 13$, 1-tailed
Reject H_0 at 1% level or above: rats run more quickly when hungry

(ii) Did the experimenter take a random sample of the relevant population of rats?
It seems plausible that the differences in the rats' times in the two conditions might be Normally distributed.

(iii) So that the effect of having learnt to run the maze on the second trial affects each condition in the same way.

2 (i) $t = 2.805$, $v = 13$, 1-tailed
Reject H_0 at 1% level or above: rating has improved

(ii) No: the distribution of differences is discrete so not Normal.

3 (i) $t = 1.528$, $v = 7$, 2-tailed

Accept H_0 at 10% level or below: no difference in ratings

(ii) In question 2, the population is voters, the random variable whose mean is hypothesised to be zero is the change in voters' ratings; in question 3 the population is dates Feb to Oct and the random variable the difference in ratings of the two voters. In both cases, the random variable is assumed to be Normally distributed in the population and the data constitute a random sample – in question 2 of voters, in question 3 of dates Feb to Oct.

4 (i) $t = 1.924$, $v = 16$, 1-tailed

Reject H_0 at 5% level or above: performance improves

(ii) Assumptions: random sample of population – you cannot tell how the subjects were selected; Normally distributed differences in time between conditions – seems reasonable.

(iii) The placebo test was done after the original test, there may be a learning effect improving the second attempt at the test.

5 (i) $t = 1.736$, $v = 6$, 1-tailed

Accept H_0 at 10% level or below: equivalent

(ii) Assumptions: random sample of areas – could well have been; Normally distributed differences in unemployment rates – not unreasonable.

(iii) There may have been a change in economic conditions over the period of the test causing the unemployment rate to fall or rise nationally.

6 (i) $t = 0.6738$, $v = 8$, 2-tailed

Accept H_0 at 10% level or below: equivalent

(ii) Assumptions: random sample of races – apparently not since all the sprints on just one afternoon are taken; Normally distributed differences in timings – not unreasonable.

7 (i) $t = 2.35$, $v = 11$, 1-tailed

Reject H_0 at $1\frac{1}{2}$% level and above: less

(ii) Assumptions: random sample of pairs; Normally distributed differences between male and female heights.

8 (i) $t = 0.953$, $v = 6$, 2-tailed

Accept H_0 even at 10% level: 2% rise

(ii) Assumptions: random sample of economic conditions with crude oil price rising by 60% – you can obviously choose a random sample of countries, but only at one particular date, and this is not really the same thing; Normally distributed changes in inflation rate.

(iii) No: the test is only of the model's prediction for this one event in the economic

circumstances of the time – for instance, a second rise might find governments having a better idea how to respond to such a shock.

9 (i) H_0: The procedures give the same results ($d = 0$), H_1: The procedures give different results ($d \neq 0$)

$t = 3.374$, $v = 7$, 2-tailed

Reject H_0.

(ii) 0.538–3.062

(iii) Division into sub-samples allows for possible variation between samples (e.g. due to being taken from different parts of the mixture). Random assignment reduces the risk of being misled due to possibly unsuspected sources of bias.

10 (i) −0.623–5.887

(ii) Random sample of brothers born two years apart; differences in salaries Normally distributed.

11 5.950–21.280

Chapter 6

Activity (Page 145)

With $n = 6$, the total number of possible orders $= 2^6 = 64$.

$P(W_+ = 0) = P(\{\}) = \frac{1}{64} = 0.0156 < 2\frac{1}{2}\%$

$P(W_+ \leqslant 1) = P(\{\},\{1\}) = \frac{2}{64} = 0.0312 > 2\frac{1}{2}\%$

$P(W_+ \leqslant 2) = P(\{\},\{1\},\{2\}) = \frac{3}{64} = 0.0469 < 5\%$

$P(W_+ \leqslant 3) = P(\{\},\{1\},\{2\},\{3\},\{1,2\}) = \frac{5}{64}$
$= 0.0781 > 5\%$

So the $2\frac{1}{2}$% 1-tailed or the 5% 2-tailed critical value is 0.

And the 5% 1-tailed or the 10% 2-tailed critical value is 2.

Activity (Page 145)

With $n = 7$, the total number of possible orders $= 2^7 = 128$.

$P(W_+ = 0) = P(\{\}) = \frac{1}{128} = 0.0078$

$P(W_+ \leqslant 1) = P(\{\},\{1\}) = \frac{2}{128} = 0.0156$

$P(W_+ \leqslant 2) = P(\{\},\{1\},\{2\}) = \frac{3}{128} = 0.0234$

$P(W_+ \leqslant 3) = P(\{\},\{1\},\{2\},\{3\},\{1,2\}) = \frac{5}{128} = 0.0391$

$P(W_+ \leqslant 4) = P(\{\},\{1\},\{2\},\{3\},\{1,2\},\{4\},\{1,3\}\})$
$= \frac{7}{128} = 0.0547$

So the 1% 1-tailed or the 2% 2-tailed critical value is 0.

The $2\frac{1}{2}$% 1-tailed or the 5% 2-tailed critical value is 2.

And the 5% 1-tailed or the 10% 2-tailed critical value is 3.

Exercise 6A (Page 146)

1 $W = 19.5$, critical value $= 10$
Accept H_0: no difference

2 $W = 166$, critical value $= 175$
Reject H_0: score better
She must have made the claim before she saw that year's scores were better than the borough average.

3 $W = 757$, critical value $= 767$ (Normal approximation)
Reject H_0: watches fast

4 $W = 15$, critical value $= 19$
Reject H_0: not correct

5 (i) $W = 16$, critical value $= 13$
Accept H_0: not greater
The percentage of moisture in samples of grain is symmetrically distributed about its median level.

(ii) $t = 1.933$, critical value $= 1.812$
Reject H_0: greater
The percentage of moisture in samples of grain is Normally distributed.

(iii) The half of the data which is between the upper and lower quartiles is closely grouped around 3.4, there are long upper and lower quartile tails and the data is positively skewed. It is this odd sample distribution which produces a significant t statistic and an insignificant Wilcoxon statistic. It could be an erratic sample (only 11 items) or, if it is representative of the population, both Normal distribution and symmetry look unreasonable as assumptions.

6 There are 25 sets of ranks with sums less than or equal to 8 and $\dfrac{25}{512} = 0.0488 < 0.05$, but 33 sets of ranks with sums less than or equal to 9 and $\dfrac{33}{512} = 0.0645 > 0.05$.

7 (i) The distribution is likely to be skewed.

(ii) $T = 6$

(iii) (a) $T \leqslant 8$

(b) $T \leqslant 3$

(iv) There is some but not strong evidence against the claim.

(v) $p = 0.0324$; good agreement

Exercise 6B (Page 152)

1 $W = 66.5$, critical value $= 65$
Accept H_0: no change

2 $W = 19.5$, critical value $= 21$
Reject H_0: improved

3 $T = 8$, critical value $= 0$
Accept H_0

4 (i) $t = 1.808$, $v = 5$, critical value $= 1.860$
Accept H_0

(ii) $T = 8$, critical value $= 8$
Reject H_0

(iii) In part (i) you must assume that the differences are Normally distributed. The sample is very small but it does not look Normal (for example from a plot on a number line).

5 (i) $T = 3$, critical value $= 3$
Reject H_0

(iii) 4.24%

6 (i) $T = 9$, critical value $= 10$
Reject H_0: word processors differ

(ii) $p = 0.0666$

Chapter 7

❓ (Page 161)

The data are real. Any model is just your theory.

❓ (Page 169)

The fit looks suspiciously good but see text that follows.

Exercise 7A (Page 170)

Note: in some of the questions in this exercise you have to combine different classes. There may be some variation in the value of X^2 according to the way you have done this.

1 H_0: The distribution of the observations can be modelled by the Poisson (2) distribution.
H_1: The distribution of the observations cannot be modelled by the Poisson (2) distribution.
$X^2 = 14.899$, $v = 5$, significant

2 (i) $\bar{x} = 1.725$
H_0: The number of mistakes on a page can be modelled by the Poisson distribution.
H_1: The number of mistakes on a page cannot be modelled by the Poisson distribution.
$X^2 = 36.3$, $v = 3$, significant

(ii) The mean rate may not be constant, for example, she may make more mistakes when she is tired. The mistakes might not be independent if, for example, some sections are about things she cannot spell.

3 (i) Binomial, $B(5, \frac{1}{4})$

(ii) H_0: The number of white flowers in each tray can be modelled by a binomial distribution, $B(5, \frac{1}{4})$.
H_1: The number of white flowers in each tray cannot be modelled by this distribution.
$X^2 = 0.343$, $v = 2$, not significant

4 (i) 0.6

(ii) H_0: The distribution of the number of times travellers were satisfied with their journeys has a binomial distribution.

H_1: The distribution of the number of times travellers were satisfied with their journeys does not have a binomial distribution.

$X^2 = 4.84$, $v = 2$, significant

(iii) The sample must be random. This is unlikely to be the case if only those who have made exactly three journeys are sampled.

5 (i) H_0: The distribution of the distances customers travel to the store is the same as at the manager's previous store.

H_1: The distribution of the distances customers travel to the store is not the same as at the manager's previous store.

$X^2 = 7.44$, $v = 2$, significant

There are more customers in the 5–10 miles category and fewer in the other two.

(ii) It is unlikely as all the customers were sampled at a similar time on a particular day.

6 H_0: The two dice used in the casino are fair.

H_1: The two dice used in the casino are not fair.

$X^2 = 10.1$, $v = 11$, not significant

7 H_0: The students guessed the answers at random.

H_1: The students did not guess the answers at random.

$X^2 = 18.8$, $v = 4$, significant

8 (i) H_0: The size of rocks is distributed evenly on the scree slope.

H_1: The size of rocks is not distributed evenly on the scree slope.

$X^2 = 7.82$, $v = 2$, significant

(ii) The test shows that rocks of different sizes are not evenly distributed. Another, different test will be needed to determine whether the larger rocks are nearer the bottom of the slope.

9 H_0: The roulette wheel is fair.

H_1: The roulette wheel is biased.

$X^2 = 8.63$, $v = 2$, not significant

10 (i) Mean $= 0.933$, variance $= 0.929$

(ii) $p = 0.1333$

H_0: These data can be modelled by the binomial distribution.

H_1: These data cannot be modelled by the binomial distribution.

$X^2 = 0.28$, $v = 1$, not significant

(iii) Poisson, because of general spread of data in table and because mean $\approx$ variance.

11 (i) Several observed frequencies are too small. In order to have $f_e \geqslant 5$ in each class there would

be only two classes. There are two constraints and so no degrees of freedom, therefore the χ^2 test cannot be used.

(ii) $\bar{x} = 0.92$

H_0: The occurrence of Morag's spelling mistakes may be modelled by the Poisson distribution.

H_1: The occurrence of Morag's spelling mistakes may not be modelled by the Poisson distribution.

$X^2 = 2.46$, $v = 1$, not significant

(iii) Spelling mistakes occur singly, randomly and independently. This could be realistic.

12 (i) Reject H_0 because the test statistic is much larger than the critical value, 9.488, at the 5% significance level when $v = 4$.

(ii) $X^2 = 0.57$, $v = 4$, not significant

13 (i)

No. of children	0	1	2	3	4	5+
f_e		246.6	345.2	241.7	112.8	39.5	14.2

(ii) H_0: Number of children per household can be modelled by the Poisson (1.40) distribution.

H_1: Number of children per household cannot be modelled by the Poisson (1.40) distribution.

$X^2 = 32.17$, $v = 5$, significant

14 (i) H_0: Shoplifting is equally likely to occur in all months.

H_1: Shoplifting is more likely to occur in some months than others.

$X^2 = 14.28$, $v = 11$, not significant at 5% level.

(ii) $$X^2 = \sum \frac{(f_o - f_e)^2}{f_e} = \sum \frac{f_o^2 - 2f_o f_e + f_e^2}{f_e}$$

$$= \frac{1}{f_e}\Sigma f_o^2 - 2\Sigma f_o + \Sigma f_e$$

$$= \frac{1}{f_e}\Sigma f_o^2 - \Sigma f_o \quad \text{because} \quad \Sigma f_o = \Sigma f_e$$

15 (i) 2.5

(ii)

x	1	2	3	4	5	6	7	8+
f_e	80.0	48.0	28.8	17.3	10.4	6.2	3.7	5.6

(iii) H_0: Number of attempts follows model suggested.

H_1: Number of attempts does not follow model suggested.

Conclusion: $10.36 < 11.07$ so accept H_0

Degrees of freedom $= 8 - 3 = 5$

i.e. number of classes $- 1$ for total $- 1$ for using sample mean and -1 for combining last two classes.

16 (i)

	A	B	C	D	E	F	G	H
f_e	71	113	104	71.5	57	49	29.5	5
f_o	53	105	111	80	63	49	36	3

(ii) H_0: Distribution of properties in Trumpton reflects the national distribution.

H_1: Distribution of properties in Trumpton does not reflect the national distribution.

Conclusion: $v = 5$, $9.475 < 12.02$ so accept H_0

(iii) There is now enough evidence to reject H_0.

❷ (Page 181)

You can use the Central Limit Theorem as the sample size of 60 is not small.

Exercise 7B (Page 185)

1 The other three expected frequencies are 31.25, 18.75 and 6.25.

$X^2 = 8.373$, $v = 3$, significant

2 (i) f_e: 13.65 18.14 22.43 18.14 13.65

(ii) 2.56; accept model as in part (i).

3 (i) $\dfrac{1}{\lambda}$

(iii) $\bar{x} = 4$

(iv) $v = 1$, $X^2 = 2.845$

Accept H_0 at the 5% level: the model is appropriate.

4 $\bar{x} = 233.6$, $s = 27.45$

With 7 cells: $v = 4$, $X^2 = 11.42$ (depends on cell boundaries)

So H_0 (that the population is Normally distributed) is rejected at the 5% level and above.

5 (i) Variance $= \dfrac{(b-a)^2}{12}$

(ii) Mean $= \dfrac{a+b}{2}$, variance $= \dfrac{(b-a)^2}{12n}$

(iii) $X^2 = 0.88$, $v = 3$, not significant

Accept H_0, that means equally likely to be in each of the four classes.

(iv) The observed numbers very nearly match those expected from $N(0, 1)$ so it appears that the distribution of $\overline{X}$ is very close to $N(0, 1)$ and the Central Limit Theorem applies well even though n is only 12.

6 (i) Estimate of $\lambda = 4.604$

With 4 cells: $v = 2$, $X^2 = 0.375$ (depends on cell boundaries)

So accept H_0 (c.v. $= 4.605$ even at 10% level): an exponential model is appropriate.

(ii) Bus arrival times are unlikely to be independent because, for example, they run to a timetable, they are affected in the same way by traffic conditions.

7 $s = 39.5$

With 7 cells: $v = 5$, $X^2 = 58.48$ (depends on cell boundaries)

So reject H_0 (c.v. $= 16.75$ even at 0.5% level): $N(100, \sigma^2)$ is not appropriate.

8 (iii) $\bar{x} = 10$

(iv) $0 \leqslant x < 5$: 23.61; $5 \leqslant x < 10$: 14.32; $10 \leqslant x < 15$: 8.68; $15 \leqslant x < \infty$: 13.39

(v) $X^2 = 10.31$, $v = 2$, c.v. 5.991

(vi) The data appear uniformly distributed, not as the model predicts; there are no data in the region 20 to ∞.

9 Sample mean $= 8.485$

(i) Estimate λ as 0.2357

(ii) With 8 cells: $v = 6$, $X^2 = 7.696$ (depends on cell boundaries)

So accept H_0 (c.v. $= 10.64$ even at 10% level): the distribution is appropriate.

(iii) Estimate λ as 0.3536

With 8 cells: $v = 6$, $X^2 = 2.810$ (depends on cell boundaries)

So accept H_0: the distribution is appropriate.

(iv) The χ^2 test does not appear to be very powerful in discriminating between similarly shaped distributions.

10 With classes -29, 29–31, 31–32, 32–34, 34–

$v = 4$, $X^2 = 14.74$ (depends on cell boundaries)

So reject H_0 at the 1% level and above: the British population is different.

11 (i)

Most days tend to be either fairly sunny or overcast.

(iii) With 6 cells: $v = 5$, $X^2 = 10.29$ (depends on cell boundaries)

So accept H_0 at the 5% level and below: the model is appropriate.

(iv) The weather on consecutive days will not be independent.

12 (iii) $\bar{x} = 0.464$

(iv) $100 \displaystyle\int_0^{0.2} f(x)\,dx = 14.7$

(v) $v = 1$, $X^2 = 0.2731$

Accept H_0 at the 5% level: the model is appropriate.

13 $\bar{x} = 130.2$, $s = 39.89$

(i) With 5 cells: $v = 3$, $X^2 = 12.457$ (depends on cell boundaries)

So reject H_0 at the 1% level and above: the given model is not appropriate.

(ii) With 5 cells: $v = 2$, $X^2 = 1.024$ (depends on cell boundaries)

So accept H_0 (c.v. $= 4.605$ even at 10% level): a Normal model is appropriate.

Index